STERLING ETHOS
New York

An Imprint of Sterling Publishing Co., Inc.
1166 Avenue of the Americas
New York, NY 10036

This Sterling Ethos edition published in 2019

ISBN: 978-1-4549-3467-7

Distributed in Canada by Sterling Publishing Co., Inc.
c/o Canadian Manda Group, 664 Annette Street
Toronto, Ontario M6S 2C8, Canada

For information about custom editions, special sales, and premium and
corporate purchases, please contact Sterling Special Sales at 800-805-5489
or specialsales@sterlingpublishing.com.

Manufactured in China

2 4 6 8 10 9 7 5 3

sterlingpublishing.com

Design by Carlton Books
Picture credits – see page 128

MOON POWER

HOW TO HARNESS THE MAGIC OF THE MOON TO IMPROVE YOUR LIFE

LORI REID

STERLING ETHOS
New York

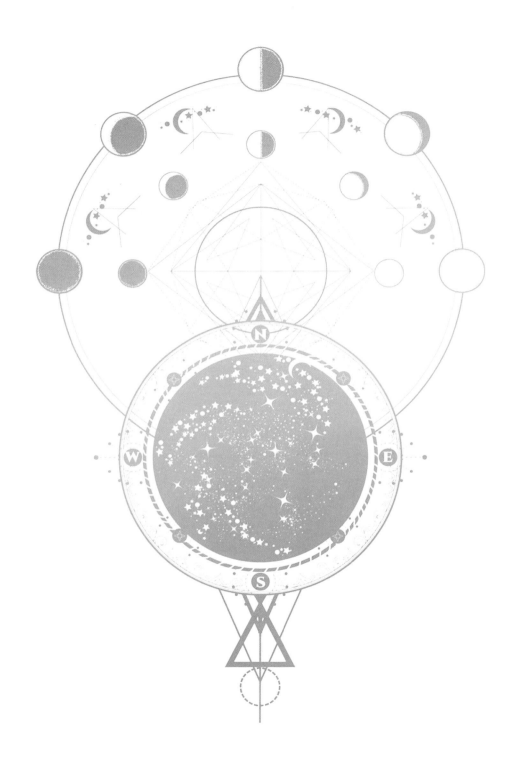

CONTENTS

INTRODUCTION
6

CHAPTER ONE
Lunar Rhythms
8

CHAPTER TWO
Tides and Eclipses
16

CHAPTER THREE
Goddess of the Night
22

CHAPTER FOUR
Sex, Fertility and Childbirth
28

CHAPTER FIVE
Crime and Passion
34

CHAPTER SIX
AstroMoon
38

CHAPTER SEVEN
Success in Business
90

CHAPTER EIGHT
Mind, Body and Health
96

CHAPTER NINE
Home Hints
104

CHAPTER TEN
Moon Lore
112

A PARTING THOUGHT
114

MOON CHARTS
115

INDEX / PICTURE CREDITS
128

INTRODUCTION

Since earliest times our ancestors have recognized that, just as the Moon has the power to move the great waters of the world's oceans, so she also exerts a profound influence on the lives of all things that live on this planet.

Now, more and more people are becoming increasingly aware of the fact that the ever-changing rhythms of the Moon affect our moods and emotions, our deepest impulses and our actions and behavior.

As she passes through her different phases, the Moon's rhythmic movement sets up a kind of "beat" – a dynamic and constantly changing energy that washes through us like the coming and going of the tides. How we behave and how we respond to the many stimuli around us springs from our personal interaction with that lunar beat.

Learning to tap into this tempo, to work in tune with the rhythm, means that we can capitalize on the energy of the moment. It means that, rather than fight against the trends, we can go with the flow and harmonize our efforts with the prevailing forces of Nature.

Falling out of step with these natural rhythms can all too often result in frustration, depression and a feeling of dislocation, as we waste large amounts of our time and energy struggling against the tide.

The angles that the Moon forms with the Sun, the relationships that she establishes with the other planets and her alignment with the astrological signs, all form a vital part of the rich pattern of natural energies that underlies everything we do in the course of our daily lives.

It is this natural pattern – essentially subtle and yet intense – that we all need to recognize in order to harness lunar energy, harmonize with our times and make the very most of every moment.

Through the pages of *Moon Power*, you will learn all about the fascinating lifecycle of the Moon. Discover just how the Moon exerts her power over our daily lives – from how she lights the night sky to how she influences the great tides of the world's oceans. Learn about eclipses and Moon phases and what they can mean in our lives – and, most of all, learn to capture the magic for yourself and improve your life.

CHAPTER 1

LUNAR RHYTHMS

Serene and romantic, the Moon's silver disc lights up the dark midnight skies and transforms everything she touches with her pallid, eerie beams. Inconstant, because of her ever-changing shape, the Moon fascinates and inspires artists, entrances lovers and illuminates the wanderer's path.

Time was when people could reckon the passing of time by a simple glance at the Moon – the cyclical pattern of her changing shape is as regular as precision clockwork. Today, huddled in our urban conurbations, city lights obscure our view of the night sky and we consult our hi-tech digital watches rather than the planetary patterns overhead. Yet the Moon's changing face repeats itself unfailingly every month. From New Moon, through First Quarter, to Full, to Last Quarter and back to New again, the cycle takes 29½ days in total to complete.

REFLECTED GLORY

The Moon actually emits no light of its own. It shines because it reflects light that it receives from the Sun. As the Moon circles the Earth, rays of sunlight strike its surface and illuminate different portions of its face. At that point in its journey, when it lies directly between us and the Sun, the Moon cannot reflect any light back to Earth since the Sun's rays strike the face of the Moon that is pointing away from us. This renders the Moon invisible from Earth – a point in its cycle known as the Moon's dark phase.

THE LUNAR PHASES

Four main lunar phases divide each month – New, First Quarter, Full and Last Quarter. But, since the Moon is constantly either waxing or waning as it travels around the Earth, changing shape each night, its cycle can be broken down further, into eight obvious stages. The first four stages are the waxing or increasing moons; the next four are the waning or decreasing moons; the ninth stage brings the cycle back to the beginning again, as follows:

1 New Moon
2 First/Waxing Crescent
3 First Quarter
4 Waxing Gibbous Moon
5 Full Moon
6 Waning Gibbous Moon or "Disseminating" Moon
7 Last Quarter
8 Waning Crescent or "Balsamic" Moon
9 And back to – the New Moon

Each stage lasts approximately three-and-a-half days.

Rays of Sun

Moon

Earth

The Moon circles the Earth and is lit by the rays of the Sun.

WAXING OR WANING?

Whichever stage it is in, the Waxing Moon takes the shape of a "D," and the Waning Moon of a "C." Say to yourself that the "D" equals Developing, or increasing, in size, while the "C" equals Contracting, or getting smaller.

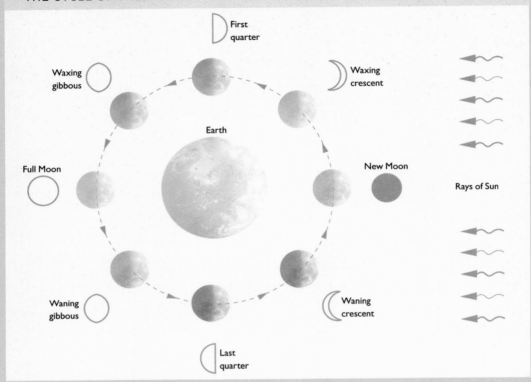

First
quarter

Waxing
gibbous

Waxing
crescent

Earth

Full Moon

New Moon

Rays of Sun

Waning
gibbous

Waning
crescent

Last
quarter

As the Moon moves out of direct line and begins to sweep around the Earth, the Sun's rays strike at an angle. The first sign of the New Moon, a slender silver eyelash in the darkened sky, begins to appear. This is the start of the Moon's waxing phase and, from now, as more and more of its face is illuminated by the Sun, the Moon appears to increase in size each night until it reaches halfway around the Earth. At this point, the Moon is at its farthest from the Sun, in direct opposition, so that its whole face is lit up by the sunlight. In this position, it is the Full Moon that is seen from the Earth.

From here, the Moon begins the second half of its journey around the Earth. As it sweeps around us in its approach to the Sun, it reverses its phases and, with less and less of its face lit up by the Sun, it appears to wane, or decrease. It wanes from Full to Last Quarter, to the Crescent and finally to invisibility again when it aligns itself between the Earth and Sun once more.

THE FULL MOON

There are 12 Full Moons in the year, one occurring each month, and different cultures have given each one a name. These names not only distinguish one from another, and therefore one month from another, but also act as tags that associate a certain month with the specific activities that always take place at that time of year. Harvest Moon and Hunter's Moon, for example, are the Full Moons that occur in September and October respectively, coinciding with harvests and hunting. Other cultures have names, such as Crow Moon and Big Winter Moon, to denote various times and events in their particular calendars.

ONCE IN A BLUE MOON...

Because the lunar cycle and the solar year are slightly out of sync with each other, once in a while we come across a month that contains two Full Moons. Since this is a fairly unusual occurrence, happening approximately every three years, we call the second Full Moon a Blue Moon. Hence the popular expression "once in a Blue Moon" – meaning something that happens only very infrequently. In these years there are 13 Full Moons.

The term "Blue Moon" is also used to refer to times when the Moon appears blue due to atmospheric pollution caused by a major volcanic eruption. This is an extremely rare phenomenon. For example, written records tell of a Blue Moon after the eruption of Krakatoa.

THE LUNAR PHASES

For many centuries, people right across the world have recognized that the Moon influences the affairs of all living things on the Earth. Some law enforcement agencies, for example, have noticed a significant rise in violent crime around the time of the Full Moon. In a totally different area of expertise, prominent surgeons have observed certain variations in the rate of blood flow. As far as they can see, these appear to tie in with different phases of the Moon's cycle.

The Waxing Moon appears to have a drawing, increasing and enhancing effect, whereas the waning Moon has a decreasing, receding and withdrawing effect. All things that come into being are stamped with the qualities of the prevailing Moon stage. So, for example, an individual who is born during the fortnight of the increasing Moon would be imbued with its corresponding waxing characteristics.

FINE DISTINCTIONS

Over the years, other observations have been made that refine these distinctions still further. So, it seems that people who are born during the other phases in the month – say, for example, the time of the Disseminating Moon – tend to share specific attributes with people also born during this time. In turn, their attributes will be subtly different from those of individuals born during any of the other stages in the Moon cycle – such as the First Quarter Moon period.

Knowing exactly which phase of the Moon you were born under gives you all kinds of extraordinarily valuable insights into your character, emotions, behavior and motivation in life. It can make you aware of your deepest underlying drives, the fundamental purpose that you feel you have in life and the contribution that you can make to society at large during the course of your lifetime.

Armed with the knowledge that these insights give you, you can begin to understand your responses and then attune yourself to a personal cyclical pattern that you go through each and every month. This will allow you to nurture your body's needs, cope with its ever-changing demands and channel all of your energies in the most propitious direction.

COSMIC CALENDARS

Since early times, people have used the movement of the stars and planets, and especially the movement of the Moon, with its precise sequences, as a great cosmic clock. First, the Moon marks the division of day and night. Then blocks of seven days, counted from one lunar phase to the next, create a week. From New Moon to Full Moon and Full Moon to the next New Moon forms two fortnights, so one entire cycle of the Moon constitutes a month. Indeed, the word "month" itself comes from an old Germanic term for Moon.

Throughout history, some civilizations have based their calendars purely on the movements of the Moon, while others used the Sun. The old Chinese calendar, for example, was based on the Moon, as is the Islamic month. The calendar currently in use in the West is mainly solar based, although it does incorporate elements of lunar timing. In this system, a year is calculated on the time it takes the Sun to return to exactly the same position in the sky. Months are loosely based on the phases of the Moon.

This mixture of solar and lunar influences in the Western calendar is best appreciated when looking at religious holidays. Christmas Day, for example, is fixed according to solar time and therefore always occurs on December 25th. Easter Sunday, however – a vestige of an old lunar calendar – is based on complex calculations revolving around the movement of the Moon and so falls on a different date each year.

LONG-TERM GOALS

Because this lunar pattern repeats itself every month, you will find that you can also pace yourself on a long-term basis. Soon you will be effectively targeting your efforts on periods of time that you know will be the most auspicious to you and your affairs.

WORKING WITH YOUR LUNAR CYCLE

You will find that your birth phase corresponds with the days of the month when you have plenty of energy and can generate new concepts with ease. During this period you should test out those ideas, process information, lay your plans, overcome obstacles, synthesize your thoughts and work toward a fruition of your efforts. Following this are the days in which you begin to take an objective view and look at your work and ideas retrospectively, making modifications if necessary to put right what might have gone wrong. At this stage you have the opportunity to spread your ideas wider and confer with like-minded people. This is the time to tie up loose ends and withdraw in order to muster your energies in anticipation of the new cycle that lies a few days ahead.

FIND YOUR LUNAR BIRTH PHASE

To discover how the Moon has shaped your character, find out which lunar phase was in effect at your birth by following the instructions below. Then look for the description of your Moon phase personality over the following few pages.

Discover your lunar birth phase by turning to the appropriate charts at the end of the book. These charts cover the Moon phases in every month of every year between 1950 and 2050 (charts for earlier years can be found online from various resources). Find the chart that refers to the year and month in which you were born. Next, find the phases closest to your date of birth. If you were born on the first day of that phase, or up to two-and-a-half days after it, then that will be your personal lunar phase. But if you were born up to three-and-a-half days before the date of the given Moon phase, you will belong to the preceding lunar phase.

Remember the order of all the phases:

1 New Moon
2 First/Waxing Crescent
3 First Quarter
4 Waxing Gibbous Moon
5 Full Moon
6 Waning Gibbous Moon or "Disseminating" Moon
7 Last Quarter
8 Waning Crescent or "Balsamic" Moon
9 And back to – the New Moon

Example:

The French film star and animal-rights campaigner, Brigitte Bardot, was born on September 28, 1934.

The listing for September 1934 looks as follows:

	Day	Hour	Min	Moon phase
1934 Sep	09	00	20	NM
1934 Sep	16	12	26	FQ
1934 Sep	23	04	19	FM
1934 Sep	30	12	29	LQ

NM = New Moon   FQ = First Quarter
FM = Full Moon   LQ = Last Quarter

The nearest Moon phase date given for this birth is 30 September, which is the day of the Last Quarter. As Brigitte's birthday is September 28th, she was born two days before the Last Quarter phase, so she falls within the previous phase of the Disseminating Moon.

A PERMANENT RECORD

Look up your lunar phase in the tables at the back of the book. Now use the space provided below to make a permanent record of this phase (along with the information needed to find it).

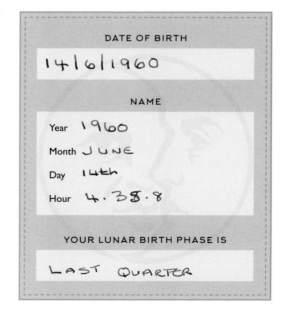

DATE OF BIRTH

14/6/1960

NAME

Year 1960

Month JUNE

Day 14th

Hour 4.38.8

YOUR LUNAR BIRTH PHASE IS

LAST QUARTER

Now that you know which lunar influences were operating at the time of your birth, and at certain times of each month, read on to find your lunar personality.

New Moon			First Crescent			First Quarter			Gibbous Moon			Full Moon			Disseminating Moon			Last Quarter			Balsamic Moon			
1	2	3	4	5	6	7	8	9	10	11	12	13	14	15	16	17	18	19	20	21	22	23	24	25	26	27	28	29

1 NEW MOON PHASE

If you were born during the New Moon phase, you have a childlike wonder and excitement about life. Open and demonstrative, you think and act spontaneously. With your bright, bubbling personality, you launch yourself into your work with tremendous enthusiasm. You are at your best when you are generating new ideas and beginning fresh projects, ever hopeful about their outcome. Your eagerness leads you to work fast and furiously, but with the attendant danger that you can all too often exhaust yourself before reaching your goal. On the negative side, you have a habit of seeing life from a purely subjective point of view. You are likely to make your mark in life when you are comparatively young and you will need to learn how to sustain that impulse throughout the rest of your life.

2 FIRST CRESCENT

As a First Crescent individual, you are assertive, adventurous and filled with joyous curiosity about life. Your creative disposition means that you have a need to expand your understanding and it also helps you look at problems from a fresh perspective. Because of this, you may often feel torn between the conventional approach and the desire to break new ground – a conflict between established and unorthodox approaches. You may also come up against restrictions to your plans and will need to find ways of overcoming these obstacles in order to achieve your aims in life. Your twenties and early thirties are likely to be especially productive and successful.

3 FIRST QUARTER

First Quarter people are positive and strong-willed. Physically and mentally active and expressive, you are constantly on the go, taking a healthy interest in everything that you come across. You were born with an actively questioning mind and an impulse to challenge the status quo. On the negative side, this can make you appear argumentative and demanding, Used constructively, however, this also enables you to come up with new solutions to old problems. Above all else you are a builder, and, if it appears that you have a compulsion to tear down existing structures, it is merely because you have the abilities to replace them with something that is not only more up-to-date, but is unquestionably an improvement on the past. You will produce some of your greatest endeavours in your thirties and early forties.

4 GIBBOUS MOON

Gibbous Moon individuals have a calming influence, a caring, constructive nature and a compulsion to help others. Your hope is that, through your life and work, you will contribute to the improvement of the world in some way. Whether consciously or unconsciously, this can become a "mission" with you – take care not to follow ideologies too blindly in your eagerness to accomplish your ends. Persevering in the face of obstacles will lead to maturity and will bring fulfilment and enlightenment. Look to your middle age for the recognition of your endeavours.

5 FULL MOON

Being born in the middle of the cycle means that your talents lie in bringing matters to fruition. You are adept at tempering logic with instinct and practicality with creativity. Moreover, this period acts like a bridge, linking you to the past but also protecting your ideas into the future. The negative side is that you may suffer guilt and irrational fears, especially when it comes to personal relationships. Only when you learn to take control of your own feelings, rather than taking your emotional cue from your partner, will you find a way of sustaining a mutually rewarding intimate relationship. Your best efforts will find their flowering after middle age.

6 DISSEMINATING MOON

Since "to disseminate" means to scatter seeds, your impulse is to sow your ideas and knowledge so that others may learn from your experiences – you are a communicator and a teacher. Dedicated to your ideals, if there is a touch of the revolutionary in your nature, then it is purely and simply an urge to reform the world. In your zeal to improve people's lives, however, you may need to find a compromise and learn how to reconcile your own vision with the needs of others. Your early fifties should bring a sense of achievement and contentment to your life.

7 LAST QUARTER

Your understanding, sympathy, maturity and poise transcend your years and so you excel in a counselling or advisory capacity. You help others to marshal their thoughts, expand their awareness, resolve their problems and organize their lives. Some may interpret your idealism as inflexibility. Prone at times to nostalgia or melancholia, you need to put aside the past and concentrate on the future. Contentment and fulfilment will come in your later fifties.

8 BALSAMIC MOON

This time is essentially one of transition, a chance to contemplate what has passed, tie up loose ends, journey inward and prepare for new beginnings ahead. You have inherited the meditative and introspective characteristics of this phase and yours is a dreamy and contemplative personality. Intuitive and far-sighted, you have innate wisdom and a mystical understanding of the workings of Mother Nature and of the human condition. For you, activity is spiritual and intellectual rather than physical. Your experiences involve endings and passings, so you are likely to live through many changes. Later life, rather than the earlier years, holds the key to your happiness and success.

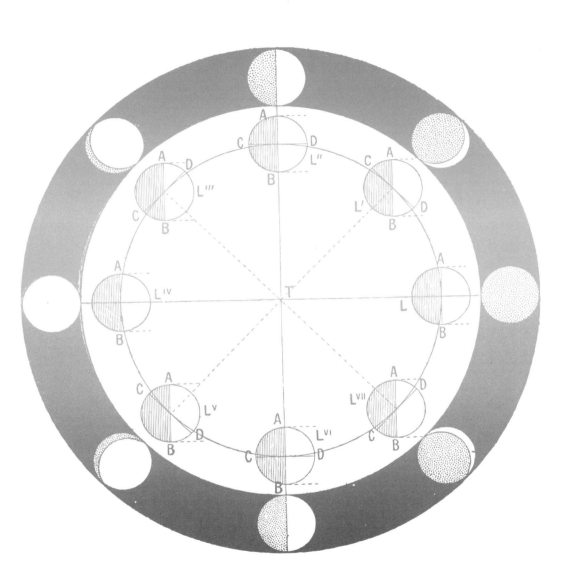

CHAPTER 2

TIDES AND ECLIPSES

THE TURNING OF THE TIDES

Of all the influences the Moon has upon the Earth, the one effect that is generally undisputed is the pull that the Moon exerts on our tides. Precisely how and why great oceans roll in and out was understood long ago by the ancient Chinese. The scholars of ancient Rome and Greece, however, failed to make the link between the Moon and the tides – simply because they had no need to, since the Mediterranean is virtually tideless. Julius Caesar, it is said, learned about the existence of tides only when he travelled to Britain.

Today the rhythmic ebbing and flowing of the oceans is common knowledge, even if the precise mechanism is not easily understood. In addition to the daily motion of high and low tides, there are also times each month when the tides are especially high (spring tide) or low (neap tide). This distinct monthly pattern strongly implicates the Moon's cyclical pattern.

THE PULL OF THE MOON

The Moon's gravitational pull upon the Earth is so strong that it draws the Earth and its waters toward it. This causes the seas to bulge at the point that is directly facing the Moon, producing a high tide at that location. At the opposite side of the Earth, the water is pulled less strongly than the land mass. This means that the oceans flow away from the surface of the Earth and form another bulge, and therefore another high tide, on the other side. As this occurs, low tide is experienced at those points of the Earth's surface that are in between – at 90° – to the bulges.

SPRING AND NEAP TIDES

Twice every month, the Sun, Moon and Earth align themselves at Full and New Moon times. With the Sun's extra draw added to the Moon's already powerful pull, the water bulges increase and produce the higher-than-normal swells that are called spring tides. Since spring tides can cause widespread flooding and danger to navigation and fishing, the ability to predict their occurrence has been of great value throughout history.

At the time of the Moon's quarters, each falling one week after the Full and the New Moons, the Moon is at 90° to the Sun and in this position its gravitational pull on the Earth counteracts that of the Sun. Consequently, at these times, the rise of the oceans will be minimized, producing the lesser high – or neap – tides.

EARTHQUAKES

Since it is believed that the gravitational pull of the Earth on the Moon is a significant factor in triggering Moonquakes, it would seem likely that a similar tension created by the Moon upon the Earth would have some bearing on the causes of earthquakes. And if the Moon has so much power to move the oceans, then it must also be capable of exerting stress upon the Earth's crust. Indeed, many scientists are coming to this conclusion and studies have shown a correlation between the incidence of earthquakes and volcanic eruptions and times of Full and New Moons. Moreover, they have detected a frequency pattern of seismic activity that recurs on an 18-year cycle – a sequence that corresponds to the Moon's eclipse cycle and which has been recognized since Babylonian times.

WEATHER

A connection between lunar phases and the weather has long been recognized. Those living in the country have been able to predict rain or to anticipate dry spells simply by observing the colour and formation of the Moon. One feature that most farmers understand well is a lunar halo – a ring around the Moon that invariably means that rain will follow. The scientific explanation of this phenomenon is that ice crystals in the atmosphere – the very ice crystals that will soon fall to Earth as rain – are lit up by reflected moonlight, and thus create the luminous halo.

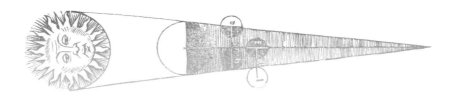

ECLIPSES

Eclipses occur when the Sun, Earth and Moon come into a particular alignment with each other at special times of either the New or Full Moon. A solar eclipse occurs at the New Moon phase, while a lunar eclipse can only take place at Full Moon. There are three types of eclipse – partial, total and annular. However, it very much depends upon where on the Earth's surface the observer is situated as to whether or not he or she will be able to view the eclipse. Only those who happen to be directly within the path of the eclipse can witness it.

Eclipses do not occur at each New and Full Moon because the tilt of the Earth's orbit prevents the three celestial bodies from coming perfectly into line every single month. Between two and five solar eclipses can occur in any one year, most of which are only partial. Total eclipses of the Sun are rarer. The Moon may be eclipsed either twice or three times per annum.

Both lunar and solar eclipses have been recorded since as far back as 3,000 BC. Eclipses follow an 18-years-and-11-days pattern that is known as the Saros cycle, a name given by the Ancient Greeks. This means that each eclipse will recur in approximately the same place as this regular interval.

ECLIPSE EFFECTS

Once feared as harbingers of doom that foreshadowed the sudden demise of a ruler, the destruction of crops, the maddening of livestock, pestilence and war, eclipses still fill us with awe and wonder. Moreover, many still believe that eclipses tie in with cyclical changes that are reflected on both a personal and political level.

Eclipses are said to trigger and foretell a critical turning point or challenges ahead. Turn to the eclipse charts at the end of the book for a date-list of solar and lunar eclipses between 1950 and 2050. Check through to find any dates that are personally significant to you. Perhaps an eclipse occurred on your birthday or close to the time you met your partner.

READING THE SIGNS

Take a note, too, of the sign in which the eclipse occurred, or will occur. Those that fall in either your Sun sign (your astrological sign) or in your Moon sign (see Chapter 6) are also likely to have a significant effect. Eclipses that fall in your Sun sign signal new experiences, whereas those that fall in your Moon sign refer to events that will affect you emotionally – perhaps marking the start of a new romantic interest.

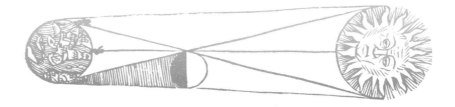

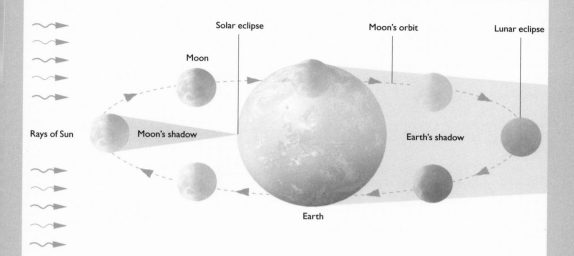

SOLAR ECLIPSES

An eclipse of the Sun occurs at New Moon time when the Moon passes between the Earth and the Sun. Viewed from the Earth, the Moon appears to travel across the Sun, covering either a part (partial eclipse), or sometimes all (total eclipse), of the Sun's face.

In a total eclipse, coldness and darkness descend on Earth for up to seven-and-a-half minutes. Frightening though this can be, it is relatively rare – only three lasting over seven minutes occurred during the twentieth century. Annular eclipses are spectacular and occur when the disc of the Moon appears slightly smaller in diameter than the face of the Sun. So, when the two are perfectly aligned, a ring of brilliant sunlight is seen around the eclipsed face of the Sun.

LUNAR ECLIPSES

The Moon can only be eclipsed when it is on the opposite side of the Earth to the Sun, since it is travelling through the shadow of the Earth. This shadow is known as the umbra and, as the Moon passes through it, sections of its disc are gradually dimmed. In a partial eclipse, only part of the Moon's face will be obscured; in a total eclipse, the Moon appears to go rapidly through its phases until it reaches totality, and then it reverses the process as more and more of its face gradually returns. It is rare for the Moon to disappear completely during an eclipse and even in a total lunar eclipse the Moon usually remains visible, taking on a reddish glow that is caused by "Earthshine," or light reflected off the Earth. From start to finish a lunar eclipse can last several hours.

ECLIPSE EFFECTS

In the case of the Sun, each hour of its eclipse is said to bring effects that last for one year. For the Moon, the ratio is one hour to one month. The effects may begin to unfold before or soon after the eclipse takes place. But the full implications might not make themselves apparent until months (with the Sun) or weeks (with the Moon) after the eclipse.

Eclipses have long been thought to affect national and political affairs. If a 12-sector astrological chart is drawn up for the time of an eclipse, the house (sector) of the chart in which the eclipse occurs will indicate which aspects of the nation are likely to be affected. An eclipse in the seventh house, for example, might indicate that international relations could reach crisis point. Alternatively, an eclipse falling in the 12th house could usher in penal reforms.

The sign of the Zodiac in which the eclipse takes place will throw further light on events still to unfold. Taurus, for instance, is associated with property, Gemini with telecommunications and Aquarius with new inventions. To find out more, see the box below.

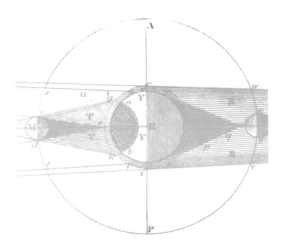

SIGNS OF THE TIMES

This gives a good idea of the areas of life affected when an eclipse occurs in a certain house or sign.

1st house	the state of the nation	11th house	committees, associations, local authorities, trade unions and allies
2nd house	finances, trade and general fiscal resources		
3rd house	communications and education	12th house	institutions, hospitals, prisons, secret service, criminality, public disgrace
4th house	the property market, women's affairs and the family		
5th house	cultural interests, the arts, leisure, gambling, children and childbirth	Aries	exploration, pioneering
		Taurus	property, real estate, wealth
6th house	employment and health matters	Gemini	communications, the media
7th house	international affairs, agreements and alliances, diplomacy, marriage	Cancer	home, the mother, the sea
		Leo	royalty, actors, the theatre
8th house	taxation, investments, morality, matters concerning death and regeneration	Virgo	servants, medicine, healing
		Libra	music, the arts
9th house	the law, the Church, science, higher education, publishing, foreign travel	Scorpio	sex, investigations, psychotherapy
		Sagittarius	publicity, travel, religion, education, ethics
10th house	the head of state, the monarchy, the government	Capricorn	business, power
		Aquarius	inventions, technology
		Pisces	dreams, illusions, the film industry

Here is an astrological chart drawn up for the total solar eclipse on 14 December, 2020. The path of this eclipse sweeps from the Pacific Ocean, over South America and across the Atlantic. The chart is set for Argentina, where maximum eclipse occurs, and is adjusted for local time at 1:17 p.m. What changes are hinted at by this chart? (See "A Possible Interpretation" below.)

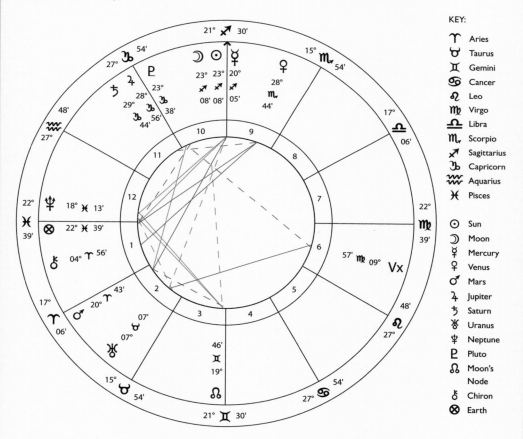

KEY:

♈	Aries
♉	Taurus
♊	Gemini
♋	Cancer
♌	Leo
♍	Virgo
♎	Libra
♏	Scorpio
♐	Sagittarius
♑	Capricorn
♒	Aquarius
♓	Pisces
☉	Sun
☽	Moon
☿	Mercury
♀	Venus
♂	Mars
♃	Jupiter
♄	Saturn
♅	Uranus
♆	Neptune
♇	Pluto
☊	Moon's Node
⚷	Chiron
⊕	Earth

A POSSIBLE INTERPRETATION

The eclipse falls in Sagittarius, the sign that rules international dealings and foreign affairs, politics, religion and the law. Expect important changes in these areas with matters that have been kept secret coming to light in the next few months. Other sectors that are likely to be affected concern travel, higher education, publishing, broadcasting, the media and the World Wide Web — all of which come under the dominion of the far-reaching Archer. In some cases, this will mark the end of an era with, down the line, the start of a new chapter.

CHAPTER 3

GODDESS OF THE NIGHT

Just as Yin is to Yang, so the Moon is to the Sun. Yin and Yang, light and dark, night and day, hot and cold, feminine and masculine, Moon and Sun – the complementary forces that permeate the universe, holding all things in a precise and dynamic balance. Each in opposition, yielding by turns one to the other.

So it is that civilizations have viewed existence since the dawn of our time. Our ancient ancestors looked up into the skies and saw the Sun as the life giver, bringing heat and light into the world. The Moon, they observed, had no light of its own but absorbed and reflected that of the Sun. Holding sway in the night, its cold rays were thought to have magical properties, casting their mysterious light on the land below.

BIRTH AND REBIRTH

Moreover, while the Sun appears as a constant golden orb, the Moon is inconstant, a shape-shifter that waxes and wanes from the finest silver sliver to a full-blown yellow disc, before reversing the process back to darkness again. The repeating cycle of the Moon has been likened to the pattern of birth, death and rebirth seen in the crops, in the seasons and in nature everywhere.

Soon people saw that the changing phases of the Moon were linked, not only to growth, destruction and regrowth in the vegetative world, but also to the female menstrual cycle that regulates human fertility, conception and birth. And so, just as the life-giving Sun became associated with masculine principles, so the Moon, his companion and receiver of life, became endowed with female qualities.

THE STUFF OF GODS

Throughout history, both the Sun and the Moon have been deified and venerated by civilizations and cultures throughout the world. Countless parallel myths grew up around the different functions of the two bodies, right across the continents.

Ra, Inti, Phoebus, Apollo, Tonatiuh, Kuat, Surya – these are just some of the incarnations of the Sun God that have been worshipped by ancient peoples. But while these mythologies center on one predominant image of the Sun deity, driving his flaming chariot gloriously across the midday sky, the Moon Goddess comes in many different guises that reflect the three main stages in her cycle.

As the New Moon, she is depicted in the form of a maiden or virgin – a nubile, seductive deity of burgeoning sexuality and emergent procreative powers. As the Moon increases to fullness, so the image becomes one of the fertile Mother, pregnant with life. In the last phase, as she wanes to darkness, she is portrayed as the witch or crone, the wise woman versed in magical arts, a sorcerer and mistress of disguise with powers to heal and transform all that passes through her hands.

MYSTICAL TRINITY

These three faces of the Moon Goddess represent Nature's cycles and fuse the conscious, subconscious and unconscious processes of the human mind – our material, emotional and spiritual faces. The Moon has become the archetype of creation, womanhood and the feminine psyche.

All major religions contain, in one form or another, evidence of this female trinity. Central to the ancient Greeks were Persephone, Demeter and Hecate with their Roman counterparts of Diana, Ceres and the Sibyl. In the Norse tradition, the Norns, or Weird Sisters, wove together the past, present and future. And for the Hindus, Kali incorporates the three-fold-goddess-in-one as "the light," "the dark" and "the mother of the world".

The maiden goddesses venerated in civilizations far and wide include Persephone, Aphrodite, Al-Uzza, Athene, Diana and Minerva. Mother goddesses of creation and of the Full Moon include Astarte, Demeter,

Ceres, Al-Lat, Kwan-Yin, Hathor, Isis, Selene and Wahini-Hai. And of the group belonging to the "dark" goddesses may be added Kali, Skadi, Hecate, Tlazolteotl, Circe, Hathor, Lilith, the serpent-headed Medusa and Nemesis, goddess of all retribution.

THE THREE FACES OF THE MOON

The three faces, or stages, of the Moon are symbolized by goddesses who, in turn, embody the powers of transformation through the processes of birth, growth and decay.

Among the first group, who display the qualities of innocence, creative energy, youthful hope and vigour, and who bring with them the promise of the new, are the Greek goddess Aphrodite, the Roman goddess Diana, and Freya, the Norse goddess of love and fertility.

APHRODITE

Tall, fair and lovely, Aphrodite is the symbol of beauty and the goddess of love and fertility. Born of the sea, she emerged from the waves with her feet treading the tide's white foam. Passionate, sensual and giving, she embodies seductive power, the joys of instinctive lovemaking and feminine love giving. Her name is synonymous with charm and grace and she is goddess and patroness of the arts. It is Aphrodite who has inspired artists through the centuries and who continues to inspire all those with a creative turn of mind.

Aphrodite holds sway over relationships, partners and lovers everywhere. Voluptuous and fertile, her connection with the waters of the oceans makes her a deity of the Moon. Her counterpart in Roman mythology is Venus, from whom the beautiful city of Venice, "Bride of the Sea," derives its name.

DIANA

Also known as the Greek goddess Artemis, Diana was the twin sister of Apollo, who was responsible for driving the Sun's chariot across the skies. She therefore stands for the feminine principle – the Moon to his Sun.

Usually portrayed in a short white tunic and with a distinctive headdress adorned with a Crescent Moon, Diana is the virgin huntress and the goddess of hunting. She is a young, free spirit who roams the woodlands far and wide, armed with her brow and arrow and accompanied by her trusty dogs and stags.

Like the Moon itself, Diana too is a skilled shape-shifter, adopting an animal guise at will to turn herself into a hare – the sacred animal of the Moon. A powerful deity, she was well versed in the healing arts and was known by many for her fierce protection of innocence, and of animals and young girls everywhere.

FREYA

Venerated by the ancient Scandinavians, Freya was the daughter of the sea god, Njord. Deity of love, she was the most beautiful of all the goddesses and, as a warrior queen, she led the Valkyries, the personal handmaidens of Odin.

Freya's name, which may also be written Freyja, means "Lady," and she stands as the feminine archetype and sister to the lord Frey. She was patroness of the oceans and has sometimes been known, rather poetically, as "She who shines over the sea."

Freya sweeps golden teardrops that fall like beads of amber into the water. This goddess's animal emblem is the cat, which is seen as a sacred link with the Moon, and she is often depicted riding a carriage pulled by two of her feline companions.

Of the goddesses who were extolled for their ability to nurture and who were held in great esteem for their fruitfulness and their powers to bring forth life are Isis, great priestess and goddess of the Egyptians; Selene, Moon goddess of the Greeks; and Ceres, Roman goddess of the ripened corn. All deities of the Full Moon and embodiments of motherhood and abundance, these goddesses were empowered with the gifts of growth and expansion, able to bestow fecundity and bring all endeavours to their fruition.

ISIS

Mother goddess of ancient Egypt, and both wife and sister to the great Lord Osiris, Isis was the deity of the Moon and ruled over home life, marriage, fertility and childbirth.

Often depicted suckling Horus, her son, and wearing the horns of a cow, a symbol of the Crescent Moon, Isis was known as the "Giver of Life." Versed in the arts of magic and healing, her personal emblems were the cow and the cat, both creatures being associated with the feminine archetype and sacred of the Moon.

Luna.

SELENE

As sister of Helios, the Sun god, Selene represents the Moon and, according to mythology, was responsible for guiding the Moon across the skies. It is said that, one night, Selene looked down and caught sight of Endymion, the handsome shepherd. She fell in love instantly. Unable to resist his beauty, she abandoned her nocturnal duties and crept down to lie gently beside her lover. Zeus, angered by the darkened sky, decided to punish Selene and ordered that Endymion should sleep forever. But even that could not break the love she had for her beautiful swain and, to this day, Selene slips away for a few nights each month to caress her sleeping lover, leaving behind her the darkened moonless skies.

It is from Selene that selenology, the term given to the scientific study of the Moon, is derived.

CERES

As goddess of the grain and an emblem of the harvest,

Ceres is often depicted holding a sheaf of corn. She is the Roman equivalent of the Greek goddess, Demeter, and her daughter is Proserpina, a parallel to Demeter's daughter Persephone. In both traditions, the daughters were abducted and taken away to the Underworld. The others, distraught by the loss, struck a very special bargain with the lord of the Underworld. Under the terms of this bargain, they could have their daughters returned to them at least for part of the year.

So it is that the sorrows of motherhood, when Ceres is parted from Proserpina, result in the bleakness of winter, and the joys that a mother experiences, when Ceres is reunited once more with her daughter, are celebrated in the delights and triumphs of the summer. Both Ceres and Demeter, goddesses of the Full Moon, embody the protective spirit of the mother and rule over vegetation and the fruitfulness of the crops, bringing forth increase and abundance.

In the natural cycle, everything is in constant flux, with each stage yielding inevitably to the next. So the Moon must inevitably decrease and disappear in order for the new cycle to begin all over again.

The next group of the goddesses reflects the wisdom and experience that have been gained through the process of birth and fruition. With their accumulated knowledge, these deities have developed an acute understanding of the transformational powers of Nature, and so have become seers – the guardians of mysticism, who are versed in the many magical arts.

Lilith, Kali, Hecate, goddesses of the Dark Moon and feared for their powers of destruction, possess great wisdom and maturity and teach us the need for reflection and spiritual enlightenment. Behind their darkest moods, they offer healing, solace, peace and rest. But, above all else, these goddesses of the Dark Moon bring with them the promise of rebirth and regeneration.

LILITH

Known long ago to the Sumerio-Babylonian people of the Middle East as the "Beautiful Maiden" who gave birth to the Moon, Lilith's legendary beauty and sexual charms were later distorted by Hebraic lore. This was done in order to subvert the popular Sumerian cult of goddess worship.

And so it was that the beautiful Lilith became transformed from the free-spirited and winged "Bird Goddess" into a female demon – a dangerous, evil beauty whose powerful eroticism drove men inevitably to total madness.

In her earlier incarnation, Lilith was associated with the owl – a strong symbol of wisdom, the night and the Moon. Her name itself is a translation of the word "screech" – the cry of the owl – but even this was later corrupted into the blood-curdling screech of the she-devil.

Lilith was transformed into an evil sorceress with powers of darkness. And yet, even in this dramatic transformation of identity, we see the pattern of the ever-changing Moon from New through Full to Dark again.

KALI

In Kali, (pictured opposite) the Hindu goddess of death, we see the destroyer. Depicted with a third eye in the center of a face that is smeared with blood and crawling with snakes, she wears a necklace of skulls and presents a truly terrifying image of destruction.

This fearsome and four-armed creature has a double-edged power – power both to deal out dreadful retribution and to offer love. Once she is bent on a frenzy of destruction, only Shiva – Kali's consort, whose seed she carries as the promise of new life – is able to control her insatiable lust for blood.

HECATE

In Hecate, the Moon goddess of the Ancient Greeks, we see the wise woman of the waning Moon, revered as the great mother figure who wore Nature itself as her mantle. As the deity of the dark hours and also known to some as "the distant one," she is often personified as a witch or a hag.

Versed in the black arts, Hecate is a shape-shifter par excellence, with the power to alter both her age and form at will – a fitting metaphor for her dominion over the changing stages of life. The owl and the bat, both well-known creatures of the night, as well as the dog and the toad – both symbols of conception – were her particular animal totems.

Drawn to tombs and crossroads, where opposing forces meet, she was worshipped in the hours of darkness with blazing torches to light up the black skies of the night.

CHAPTER 4

SEX, FERTILITY AND CHILDBIRTH

In a pioneering study, which was conducted by American doctors (Walter and
Abraham Menaker) over an eight-year period during the 1960s, and which took into
account half a million births, it was discovered that more babies are born during the
three days around the Full Moon than at any other time in the month.

Gathering statistics on the clustering of births is comparatively easy because hospital records are fairly accessible. But can this data tell us anything at all about the times of conception and, by implication, reflect any information on times of increased sexual activity? Dr. Walter Menaker and his team think it can, and their research has produced some interesting findings.

The first factor they addressed was the length of pregnancy, from conception to birth. Working on a lunar month of 29½ days, they found that the average period of human gestation takes 265½ days, or nine lunar months. The second factor they discovered was that birth takes place at the same lunar phase of the month as when conception took place. They found, in fact, that it corresponds to the very day.

REACHING A SEXUAL PEAK
This astounding piece of research shows that if more births take place during the Full Moon, then it must be that more women conceive when the Moon is full. These findings, in turn, suggest that this is the time in the month when sexual activity hits a peak.

Interestingly, the same study found that the smallest number of births occurs in the three-day period of the New Moon. So, by implication, it suggests that libido and sexual activity are generally reduced at that particular time of the month.

SEX AND THE SEA
People whose lives are closely linked to the sea have known since earliest times that sexual activity increases at the time of the Full Moon. For centuries it has been recognized that the mating cycles of sea urchins, shellfish and other aquatic creatures are regulated by the cycle

of the lunar phases. As far back as the first millennium BC, Aristotle observed that sea urchins tasted better if caught when the Moon was full. He also noted that the creatures were plumper and their ovaries heavier at that time of the month.

Over the years, similar observations have confirmed that many molluscs, crustaceans and other marine creatures spawn at Full Moon time. Their reproductive organs have been found to swell up gradually through the Waxing Moon phase as their gonads fill with eggs and sperm. These then mature halfway through the cycle and are released into the water as the Moon reaches fullness. Caught during the waning phase, the creatures are thinner and less plumped up and their sexual organs are considerably reduced in size and bulk.

BOILING WATERS
One of the best demonstrations of this mass Moon-triggered spawning can be seen around the islands of Fiji. Here, on two specific dates each year, the seas boil with swarming palolo worms as they come up to the surface to mate. So punctual are these creatures that the Fijians confidently await their coming at the appointed dates with fishing nets at the ready to catch their record hauls.

Similar evidence of lunar rhythms at work on aquatic life may be seen along the beaches of California. Here, a slender fish called the grunion comes ashore to mate and spawn during the breeding season – but only on the nights after either the New or the Full Moon. Indeed, so many grunion come ashore on those particular nights that the beaches shimmer in a luminous mass of silver, writhing bodies as far as the eye can see.

THE POWER OF THE MOON

Crabs, lobsters, scallops, oysters and many more creatures of the seas and oceans follow breeding cycles that can be timed according to lunar movements. Migratory journeys too, such as that of the eel, are undertaken at a precise time during the waning of the Moon. This means that they reach their spawning grounds at a time when the pull of the Moon is at its greatest. Ruled by the lunar tides, these journeys provide yet more persuasive evidence of the power of the Moon.

FERTILITY AND REPRODUCTION

THE FEMALE MENSTRUAL CYCLE

The human menstrual cycle, the process of ovulation, takes its name from the Latin word *mensis*, which means month. In fact, menstruation itself used to be called "the menses" – literally an event that occurred at monthly intervals. Menstruation and the very concept of a month are in turn linked to the Moon in that both the lunar cycle and a regular menstrual cycle last for 29½ days.

So much for regular menstrual cycles, but what about those women whose periods go haywire? How can erratic menstrual cycles be connected in any way with the Moon? This was the interesting conundrum that drew the attention, in 1967, of Edmond Dewan, a physicist working with the U.S. Air Force.

NATURAL RHYTHM

What Dewan suggested was that the Moon seems to act like a clock – it regulates the menstrual cycle and its light at Full Moon triggers ovulation. So, under natural circumstances, a woman's menstrual pattern would always be governed by the lunar phases. The existence of electric lighting, however, has confused many women's sensitive biological rhythms and is thought to disturb the regularity of their natural cycles.

Working on this theory, Dewan proposed an experiment. He suggested that women with irregular periods could set up artificial "Full Moon" conditions for themselves by leaving the light on in their bedrooms for three consecutive nights, starting from the 14th day after their last period. In terms of lunar phases, the 14th day marks a mid-point between one New Moon and the next and, thus, is equivalent to the period of a Full Moon.

The results were astounding. Without exception, every women who took part in the experiment found that her menstrual cycle became as regular as clockwork – even if her electricity bills increased in the process!

CONCEPTION AND CONTRACEPTION

It was in the 1960s that the gynaecologist from what is now Slovakia, Dr. Eugen Jonas, set up a clinic and research center that dealt with the problems of fertility and contraception. What was unique about Dr. Jonas' approach was that, while much of the world was beginning to use the pill as a form of birth control, he was advocating a system which, medically speaking, smacked of quackery and superstition. And yet his method seemed to be 98 percent effective. Moreover, it was natural, inexpensive, simple to use, totally drug-free and, more importantly, it had no side effects. This system was based on the workings of the lunar cycle. What Dr. Jonas had "discovered"' was a method of family planning that had actually been recognized and used by women for centuries. Essentially, the method is based on the idea that a woman is at the peak of her fertility at that time of the month when the Moon is in the same phase as it was at the time of her own birth. So, if she was born during the Gibbous Moon, for example, then it would be during the three days around that same period of each month that she would be at her most fertile and have the best chance of conceiving.

DISCOVERING THE SEX OF YOUR CHILD

For the majority of expectant parents, part of the excitement of pregnancy has been the anticipation of finding out whether the baby will be a boy or a girl. The advent of scans, however, has taken much of the uncertainty away, and now, weeks before the actual birth, a doctor can inform the parents-to-be, with a good degree of accuracy, what sex the baby will be at birth.

But what about following the phases of the Moon to ascertain what sex your child-to-be could be even before conception takes place? All kinds of theories and possible future products have been suggested to help people to do this, but there may be a more natural method that we have actually known about all along. Perhaps we simply have to get in sync with the movements of the Moon.

FEMININE AND MASCULINE PRINCIPLES

For centuries it has been recognized that astrological signs tend to be either masculine or feminine. Every month, the Moon travels through all of the signs, spending about two-and-a-quarter days in each one. One research team discovered that the sex of the child tends to be determined by whichever gender of sign the Moon is in when conception takes place. You might like to try this theory out for yourself. Turn to the charts at the end of the book and work out which sign the Moon is in on the days you think you are likely to conceive.

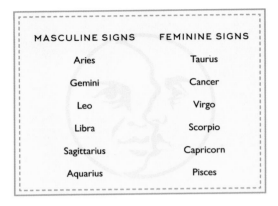

MASCULINE SIGNS	FEMININE SIGNS
Aries	Taurus
Gemini	Cancer
Leo	Virgo
Libra	Scorpio
Sagittarius	Capricorn
Aquarius	Pisces

MAKE YOUR OWN FERTILITY CALENDAR

If you have been trying unsuccessfully to have a baby, and there are no medical reasons preventing you from conceiving, perhaps you have simply been unlucky with your timing and may have been missing your personal fertility peak. Learning to tune in to your own body rhythms and synchronizing your cycle with that of the Moon may well provide the answer. By following a few simple steps each month (see below), you can make your own fertility calendar and target those few days in your cycle when you are at your most fertile.

1. Buy or download a calendar that displays a whole month on one page (or use the sample month below).
2. Turn to the charts at the end of the book to find the Moon Phases for each month of each year. Find the Moon Phases for the current month and mark them on your calendar.
3. Look back to the year in which you were born and find out which Moon phase prevailed at the time of your birth. Now, using a colored pen, color in the equivalent Moon Phase on your current calendar. This phase will be your peak fertility period.
4. Now, using the charts at the end of the book once again, work out which astrological sign the Moon will be in on each day of the month. Using two different colors to distinguish the masculine from the feminine signs, color in each two-and-a-quarter day block in your calendar with the appropriate color.
5. Exactly which astrological sign coincides with your peak fertility period? If it is a traditionally masculine sign and you conceive, you are more likely to conceive a boy during this period; if it's a feminine sign, you may be more likely to conceive a baby girl.

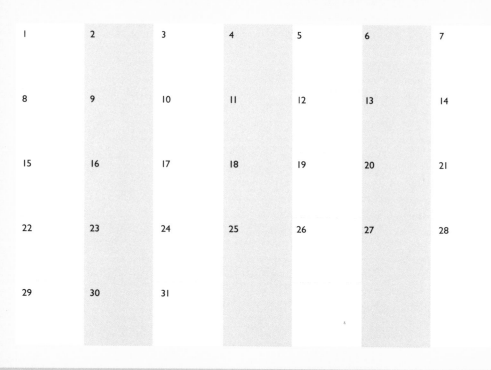

1	2	3	4	5	6	7
8	9	10	11	12	13	14
15	16	17	18	19	20	21
22	23	24	25	26	27	28
29	30	31				

CHAPTER 5

CRIME AND PASSION

"Experts" have stated publicly time and again that the Moon and her cycles have absolutely no influence on human behavior. Despite this, many people's personal experiences tell a very different tale – and a growing number of psychiatrists and law enforcement agents also have plenty of reasons to believe otherwise.

Members of police forces across the world are only too aware of the rise in violent crimes around the time of the Full Moon. At this same time in the lunar cycle, nurses and doctors in psychiatric institutions have also observed that many of their patients become more agitated than usual. Calls to emergency or crisis centers increase, as do road traffic accidents and acts of general mindless vandalism.

Those on the ground, so to speak – officers on the beat, firefighters and intake clerks working on hospital receptions – recognize these trends and acknowledge that there is some kind of monthly pattern. One senior police officer was recently quoted as saying that people seem to go out of control on a regular basis every 28 days when, to use his words, "they start acting and drinking like idiots."

A FORCE FOR GOOD OR EVIL?

Curiously, despite the fact that we think of the Moon as a serene presence in the night sky, astrologically speaking, the Moon represents instability. The effects of the strong gravitational pull that the Moon exerts, not only on our tides and on our weather, but also on the state of our minds, were being noted as far back as the days of Hippocrates, the Greek physician now regarded as the father of medicine.

What all this points to is that at certain times in the Moon's cycle, we experience its influence more strongly than usual. The periods of the Full Moon, when Moon, Sun and Earth are aligned, are particularly significant, since at those times the Sun's gravitational pull is added to that of the Moon. And it is then that the pressure can have an adverse effect on us, heightening tensions and bringing emotions to the boil.

This is when people start to act irrationally. They can get edgy and jumpy, blowing things out of all proportion, become prone to accidents and start acting violently toward other people.

CRIMES OF PASSION

As the police officer mentioned above observed, irrational behavior, that can lead to crimes of passion and violence of a bizarre nature, occurs on a monthly basis, coinciding with the Full Moon.

Another lunar event that can exert a very powerful influence on our behavior is known as the Moon reaching perigee (see p.37 for a full explanation). This event takes place every few years and, when it occurs at the same time as the Full Moon, the effects can be extremely dramatic. So, just what form does this link between the Moon and our darker passions take?

MOON-INFLUENCED CRIMES

While records show a normal distribution of what might be termed "straightforward" crimes throughout the month, those that occur around the time of the Full Moon tend to be especially unpleasant.

Behavior at Full Moon time becomes psychotic, and criminal acts bear all the hallmarks of mental imbalance. The following are just some of the examples that various people have noted:

- Athletes incur more penalties during events that take place at the Full Moon than at other times of the month.
- Those who are the worse for wear after heavy drinking might wander home and sleep it off during the Moon's First Crescent, but they can all too easily become aggressive and dangerous at Full Moon.

THE MOON

- Motorists can literally go into dangerous overdrive at this time, becoming irate and unreasonably intolerant of other drivers on the road.
- Attacks on people and burglaries show psychopathic tendencies around this phase of the Moon.
- Records have shown that the Full Moon, especially when it is combined with the Moon at perigee (see below), creates a dangerous climate where assassinations occur, racial tensions are inflamed and riots are sparked.

REACHING PERIGEE

Because the Moon's orbit is elliptical, there is a point in its cycle when it is at its farthest distance from the Earth. There is also a point when it is at its nearest. The farthest point is known as apogee, while the closest point to Earth is called perigee.

This process of traveling farther out and coming closer in is simply part and parcel of the Moon's monthly cycle around the Earth, but when perigee coincides with the Full Moon, then the fireworks can really begin. It is at these times that all kinds of extreme weather conditions and freak natural phenomena are often produced. Passions are also inflamed to fever-pitch and crimes involving unusual or widespread violence, such as riots, tend to occur.

CRIMES AND THE NEW MOON

Records suggest that, although crimes at and following the New Moon either show a slight decline or are at what might be considered a more normal level, there does seem to be a slight increase in crimes in the days preceding the New Moon. However, this minor peak is minimal in comparison with the sharp peak that occurs when the Moon is full. It seems that the Moon does indeed have a strong pull on the very deepest of our passions and emotions.

CHAPTER SIX

ASTROMOON

Most of us know which sign of the Zodiac we belong to. When we say we are
Taurean or Libran, what we mean is that the Sun was in that particular sign on the
day we were born. And the sign we belong to is a shorthand method of describing
our personalities and the trends in our lives.

SUN AND MOON

In astrological terms, we say that the Sun travels roughly
one degree per day, moving through each sign in 30 or
31 days, and through all 12 in one year. The Moon,
however, is much swifter of foot. While the Sun spends
roughly one month in each sign, the Moon whizzes
through in about two-and-a-quarter days and passes in
and out of the whole lot in just four weeks.

Because the Sun spends a comparatively lengthy
time in each sign, it is fairly easy for each of us to know
where it was positioned at our time of birth – apart, that
is, from those born on the cusp (the end of one sign and
the beginning of the next). Though we probably know
our Sun signs, few of us know the sign through which
the Moon was passing at our birth – yet this is just as
important to our understanding of ourselves.

SUN SIGN VERSUS MOON SIGN

Your Sun sign describes how you present yourself to
others and the impression that they have of you. It
underlines your ego, your mannerisms and idiosyncrasies,
the strength of your willpower and the impact you have
on your environment – in fact, everything to do with
your façade, the outer you, is contained within the
parameters of your Sun sign.

Your Moon sign, on the other hand, describes the
fundamental inner you – the private person you know
yourself to be. It reveals your passive role in life, how
you express your feelings and deal with your emotions.
It reflects how you interact with people, the sort of
relationships you are likely to form and how you come
across to others emotionally. By understanding your
Moon sign, you will gain a deeper insight into your
moods and personal sensitivities.

Your Moon sign describes and affects:

- your instinctive responses
- your deepest longings and needs
- your secret wishes and desires
- your innermost loves and hates
- your emotional highs and lows
- your jealousies and joys
- your imaginative potential
- your fears and obsessions
- how other people perceive you
- how you behave in private
- how you react to others on first meeting
- how you interact emotionally with the people
  you love
- your daily habits and preferred routines
- your home environment and domestic lifestyle
- your family history
- your security dependencies
- your relationship with your mother or guardian
- the relationship you have with other important
  females in your life
- your creative and artistic inclinations
- the areas in life in which you find emotional
  satisfaction
- the ups and downs you experience on a cyclical basis
- your subconscious memories
- your nurturing instincts
- your early conditioning
- your unconscious programming
- your family influences
- the behavior you learned as a child and which affects
  you as an adult

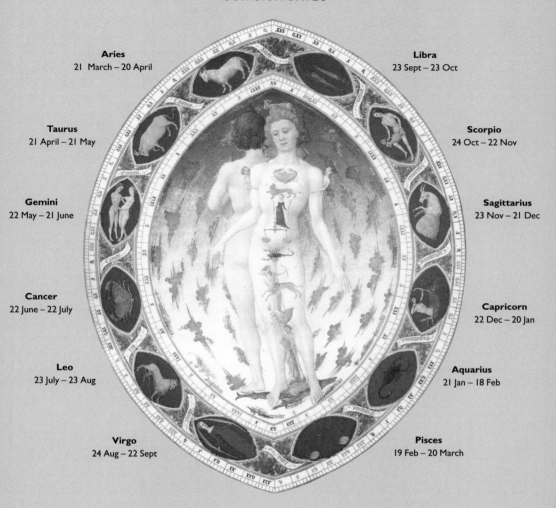

Aries
21 March – 20 April

Taurus
21 April – 21 May

Gemini
22 May – 21 June

Cancer
22 June – 22 July

Leo
23 July – 23 Aug

Virgo
24 Aug – 22 Sept

Libra
23 Sept – 23 Oct

Scorpio
24 Oct – 22 Nov

Sagittarius
23 Nov – 21 Dec

Capricorn
22 Dec – 20 Jan

Aquarius
21 Jan – 18 Feb

Pisces
19 Feb – 20 March

FINDING YOUR MOON SIGN

Because the Moon stays in each sign for just under two and a quarter days, simply knowing your date of birth may be enough to find out where it was when you were born. But if you were born on one of the days when the Moon was changing from one sign to another, you may need to know your time of birth fairly accurately to be sure of the exact sign.

The Moon sign tables at the end of the book give a step-by-step guide to help you discover your personal Moon sign by calculating the Moon's position on the day you were born. You can also find out which Moon sign prevails on the days of special importance, such as your wedding day. Work out signs for yourself and for the people you love and then read on to find out how the Moon affects you all.

EARTH

TAURUS · VIRGO · CAPRICORN

If your Moon is in an Earth sign, your emotions are stable and well balanced. In relationships, you are practical and solid as a rock. Down-to-earth and unpretentious, you take a sensible, no-nonsense attitude to affairs of the heart. Partners find you reliable but also predictable and stubborn. Rarely prone to verbalizing your feelings, your actions speak louder than words. Routine is important in your life and you need a settled, structured framework in which to live and work.

FIRE

ARIES · LEO · SAGITTARIUS

Warm, vibrant, outgoing and physically expressive describes your emotional disposition if your Moon is placed in one of the Fire signs. You are passionate by nature and an enthusiastic and often lusty lover. Characteristically fiery, you generate a lot of heat – physically, emotionally and mentally, and in some situations there is the risk that you might overheat! You like to be where the action is and preferably center stage. A feisty, challenging, loving partner maintains your interest.

AIR

GEMINI · LIBRA · AQUARIUS

If your Moon is situated in one of the Air signs, you are a bright and breezy lover. Friendship is important to you and you need to be on the same mental wavelength as your partner. Curious about how people tick, you take an intellectual interest in sexual matters, and probably find it easier to express your feelings verbally than physically. Indeed, partners can find you cool and detached, sometimes off-hand and unpredictable. Not over-fond of too much body contact, you need your own freedom and your own space.

WATER

CANCER · SCORPIO · PISCES

Having your Moon in one of the Water signs mean that you are inherently sensitive and ruled by your emotions. Indeed, your feelings, never very far from the surface, sweep over you in great tidal waves of emotion, often taking you by surprise and sometimes threatening to overwhelm you altogether. Mostly, you tend to be inward-looking and subjective in outlook, and so are easily hurt by the merest slight. Nurturing and deeply caring, you are emotionally clinging and have lots of love to share with an empathetic partner.

YOUR ELEMENT AND NATAL CHART

Each Zodiac sign is associated with one of the four elements – Earth, Air, Fire and Water. People of the same element group are said to be more compatible with each other than with members of other element groups.

A natal chart is a map of the positions of the planets in the sky at the moment of an individual's birth. The chart is divided into 12 sectors (houses), and each is governed by a Zodiac sign. Each sector represents a region of the skies, and the planets are plotted into the sectors according to their actual positions above.

Analysis of a person's character and possible future events in their life is made by considering the planets'

position and the relationships they form with one another. These relationships are known as "aspects" and the patterns that they create suggest either harmonious or challenging energies within a person's psyche.

The position of the Moon in the chart is crucial to understanding a person's emotional nature, unconscious motivations, moods and attitudes to relationships. First, the sign that the Moon inhabits, as well as its element and house position, are considered. Next, the Moon's relationship with the Sun is assessed in order to gauge the person's physical/emotional integration. Lastly, the aspects between the Sun, the Moon and the rest of the planets are brought into play.

YOUR PERSONAL CHART

To have a complete astrological chart drawn up, you need to consult a professional astrologer, who will ask you for three vital pieces of information: your date, time and place of birth. Astrologers use glyphs (universally recognized symbols; see page 21 and Prince William's chart), to represent the planets and Zodiac signs.

BIRTH CHART FOR WILLIAM, DUKE OF CAMBRIDGE

Just as physical characteristics are handed down through the family, so distinct patterns of similarities can been seen to run through the charts of parents and their children. William, for example, may be second in line to the British throne but as a son and a Cancerian he has inherited his nurturing, family-oriented qualities from his mother, Diana, who was also born under the same sign of Cancer. His father, Charles, is a Scorpio – no surprise, then, that this sign appears on William's tenth house of rulership placing him firmly in line, through his father, to the succession of the British throne. At the top of his skies Jupiter, symbol of wisdom and far-sightedness, holds sway. As such, William's reign will hark back to his great-grandfather, George VI, who also had Jupiter at the top of his chart and whose fortitude, intelligence and good judgement won the respect of the people and proved a noble asset to his country through troubled times.

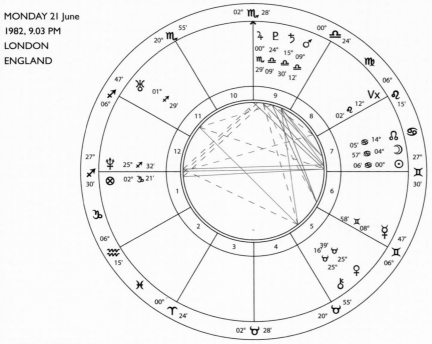

MONDAY 21 June
1982, 9.03 PM
LONDON
ENGLAND

KEY:

♈	Aries
♉	Taurus
♊	Gemini
♋	Cancer
♌	Leo
♍	Virgo
♎	Libra
♏	Scorpio
♐	Sagittarius
♑	Capricorn
♒	Aquarius
♓	Pisces

☉	Sun
☽	Moon
☿	Mercury
♀	Venus
♂	Mars
♃	Jupiter
♄	Saturn
♅	Uranus
♆	Neptune
♇	Pluto
☊	Moon's Node
⚷	Chiron
⊕	Earth

NOW READ ON …

The following pages contain information about you and your life according to your Moon sign. First, work out your Moon sign by using the charts at the end of the book, then turn to the section that deals with your sign.

MOON IN ARIES

KEY CHARACTER POINTS

Your instinctive response is:	enthusiastic and positive
Your best characteristics are:	courage and strength of character
Your negative qualities are:	impatience and sensitivity
You dislike:	weakness or indecision
You need:	a constant supply of new interests to keep your mind active and alive
You must:	learn to consider other people.

THE ESSENTIAL YOU

The Moon in this sign reveals an independent spirit with a dynamic, outgoing personality. You have a fundamental need to excel, so you are by nature competitive and you work hard to achieve your ambitions in life. It is leadership, making decisions and taking charge of situations that brings you the greatest satisfaction in life. Since this Moon placement confers courage, you also enjoy the thrill of challenging situations and adventure and are usually to be found right at the front of the action.

LIFESTYLE

THE ARIES MOON AT HOME

Because the Moon in Aries imbues you with masses of physical stamina, there will be much evidence of sporting activities around your house. Travel, too, is a leisure-time passion so there are likely to be souvenirs, artifacts and memorabilia from past excursions around the world.

YOUR SUN AND MOON SIGN COMBINATION CHART

This shows just how well your outward persona (Sun sign) and inner personality (Moon sign) are integrated.

YOUR MOON IN ARIES WITH:

YOUR SUN IN...	COMBINATION KEYNOTES	STAR RATING
Aries	Strong, robust, insensitive	*
Taurus	Conflicting desires	***
Gemini	Dynamic, but short attention span	****
Cancer	Push and pull	**
Leo	Powerful	*****
Virgo	Spirited	***
Libra	Ups and downs	**
Scorpio	Deep and intense	***
Sagittarius	A winning combination	*****
Capricorn	Ruthlessly determined	****
Aquarius	Charismatic	***
Pisces	Strong, yet shy	**

* Highly subjective
** At odds with yourself
*** Need to work toward achieving inner balance
**** In harmony
***** Strongly integrated

YOU AND YOUR FAMILY

You were probably encouraged to stand on your own two feet from a very young age and although your parents were supportive, they were highly ambitious for you too. In turn, you are likely to become a pushy parent, anxious that your own children do well in life. You may have had difficulties relating to your father, and the women in your family are likely to be strong and dominant characters, with seemingly inexhaustible energy.

AT WORK

With a mind that teems with original and far-sighted ideas, and the courage to see your projects through to their conclusions, it is inevitable that sooner or later you will make a success of your career. Moreover, you are ambitious and thrusting and will not allow obstacles to stand in your way when you are in pursuit of your goals. A born leader, you have the gift to inspire those who work under you.

UNWIND BY:

driving, hiking, going on survival training, traveling to foreign lands.

MONEY MATTERS

As an Aries-Moon subject you are likely to possess a nose for good investments and are always ready to spot a bargain.

HEALTH NOTES

Aries-Moon born people are usually robust individuals. However, because they also have a tendency to be impulsive, they are prone to accidents, especially cuts and burns.

CHILDREN BORN WITH THE MOON IN ARIES

Noisy, active and adventurous, these youngsters are bursting with life and constantly on the go. They are born with an innate competitive spirit that will usually find its true forte out on the sports field. Much happier leading rather than being led, they will always be found at the front of the queue or wherever the action is at its thickest.

The Moon in Aries can produce loveable firebrands, but look out for any signs of early aggression – these need to be channeled smartly into creative pursuits.

RELATING TO OTHERS
YOUR EMOTIONAL PATTERN

In a tough, rugged, independent and egocentric sign such as Aries, there is little room for sentiment, or any patience for subtle sensitivities. Here, the softness and nurturing instincts of the Moon's influence are overlaid by a feisty, robust approach to life. As an Aries-Moon subject, therefore, you do not appreciate weakness or dilly-dallying of any kind. In fact, you may actually find it difficult to deal with emotions – your own or those of other people. You are a spontaneous sort of person. Decisions must be made instantly and life must be lived now because, in your scheme of things, it is important to keep ahead of the game.

Your passion, too, is immediate: loving or loathing at a glance. Indeed, there is a tendency among most Aries-Moons to fall in love all too hastily and to pursue the object of their desire with such zeal that it can actually frighten off potential partners, who may need more time to allow their feelings to develop. Sooner or later, natives of this Moon sign learn to control their ardor and find, often to their surprise, that a little patience will yield just the response they want.

Belonging to this sign means that you like to take the lead in intimate relationships. You are a fiery lover, easily aroused and with desires that need to be satisfied urgently. And though you may be quick to anger, you are unlikely to bear grudges or to seethe with lasting resentment. Aries-Moon subjects readily forgive and forget.

In life, your ideal partner needs to be as fiery and passionate as you yourself are. A person who is adventurous, and who has plenty of stamina to keep up the pace you set, would gain your admiration and respect.

ARIES

Sharing this Moon sign means you both feel the same emotions in equal intensity. You are both fiery and adventurous but also as independent as each other. Neither is likely to give in to the other and the lack of compromise is bound to cause conflict.

TAURUS

This partner was not born to rough it in life, for it is luxury and ease that the Taurus-Moon craves. You, on the other hand, prefer life with a sharper edge and plenty of grist to hone the senses. Needless to say, there is a fundamental discrepancy here in your outlooks.

GEMINI

Both restless and curious, your Aries-Moon and your partner's Gemini-Moon will keep each of you searching for adventure. Whether you are on the same quest, however, is debatable. Perhaps you may have to agree to disagree.

CANCER

Not an easy pairing since Cancerian-Moon people are cuddly individuals while you are uncomfortable with too much billing and cooing. Additionally, this partner is a natural homebody while you prefer the rugged outdoors.

LEO

An exciting partnership, whether intimate or professional. There is masses of energy in this combination and together you should have tremendous fun. Entertainment, adventure and an active sexual life will color your days – and nights.

VIRGO

The Virgo-Moon's need for order, tidiness and discipline will undoubtedly contrast markedly with your cavalier attitude to domestic life. Sex, too, is likely to be a problem since your ardor may not be reciprocated quite so eagerly.

LIBRA

You will be enchanted by the grace of your Libra-Moon companion and would do well to allow some of that charm and elegance to smooth your rougher edges. You are opposites but, in relationships, opposites can so often attract!

SCORPIO

The jealousy and intense emotions that are so characteristic of a Scorpio-Moon will impinge on your compulsive need for independence and personal freedom. Despite this, the passion and desire between you will be red-hot.

SAGITTARIUS

Both adventurous and highly charged, both seeking challenge and distant horizons, this partnership offers excellent prospects and very few dull moments – in or out of bed.

CAPRICORN

The chances of this combination lasting will be greatly improved if you and your partner happen to be in business together, because you will be able to channel your considerable, but disparate, passions into the success of your company.

AQUARIUS

Moon-Aquarians are the first to respect one another's need for independence and personal freedom, so this partnership promises tolerance and understanding from the outset.

PISCES

For this relationship to work, you would need the patience of a saint and your Pisces-Moon partner would have to develop a very thick skin – and fast! Miracles are rare so this combination may prove unrealistic.

MOON IN TAURUS

KEY CHARACTER POINTS

Your instinctive response is: cautious and pragmatic
Your best characteristics are: charm and tenacity of purpose
Your negative qualities are: stubbornness and self-indulgence
You dislike: anything or anybody that makes you uncomfortable
You need: physical, emotional and financial security
You must: learn to let go.

THE ESSENTIAL YOU

People who are born with the Moon in Taurus are noted for their reliability, strong sense of responsibility and level-headedness. You have your feet firmly on the ground and you know just what you want and what will make you happy in life.

Fundamentally, you are driven by a need for personal security, something that will influence almost everything you do in life. You have innate artistic talents and are endowed with immense charm.

LIFESTYLE

THE TAURUS MOON AT HOME

Because you are unashamedly sensual by nature, comfort and plush surroundings will be given top priority when it comes to furnishing and decorating your home.

PEOPLE WHO SHARE YOUR MOON SIGN

Keira Knightley
Carrie Fisher
Donald Glover
Lindsay Lohan
Demi Lovato
Christina Aguilera
Cameron Diaz
Demi Moore
Sigourney Weaver
Prince Harry
Rafael Nadal
Robert Downey Jr.
Frida Kahlo
Kobe Bryant
Chris Pratt
Elton John
Meryl Streep
Bob Dylan
Che Guevara
Mick Jagger

YOUR SUN AND MOON SIGN COMBINATION CHART

This shows just how well your outward persona (Sun sign) and inner personality (Moon sign) are integrated.
YOUR MOON IN TAURUS WITH:

YOUR SUN IN...	COMBINATION KEYNOTES	STAR RATING
Aries	Gutsy	***
Taurus	Solid, but stolid	*
Gemini	Surface tension	**
Cancer	Emotionally together	****
Leo	A united front	****
Virgo	Mental harmony	*****
Libra	A happy mean	****
Scorpio	Powerful	***
Sagittarius	Mismatched	**
Capricorn	Totally together	****
Aquarius	Certain discrepancies	**
Pisces	Self-oriented	***

* Highly subjective
** At odds with yourself
*** Need to work toward achieving inner balance
**** In harmony
***** Strongly integrated

YOU AND YOUR FAMILY

The generation gap that causes problems in so many families has never really been an issue between you and your parents because your mature attitude has always ensured that you get on well with older people. It is quite possible that one of your parents was strict, but your shrewdness and charm helped you to find a way to cope.

In your own turn, you make a fiercely proud and protective parent, and the more responsible, polite and well mannered your children are, the happier you will be.

AT WORK

Practical, hard-working and down to earth, you are never afraid to pitch in wherever you are needed and, in your drive for security and prosperity, it is not unusual for you to take on several jobs at once.

Any occupations involving music and the arts draw you, although the fashion and financial industries will attract you, too. You are usually quite stubborn in the way that you work and tend to resist the slightest hint of enforced change.

UNWIND BY:

having a relaxing aromatherapy massage or a session of reflexology.

MONEY MATTERS

You are a hoarder of money and will save diligently throughout your whole life. You choose your investments extremely wisely and are careful to make sure that you never put all your eggs in one basket.

HEALTH NOTES

Putting on weight can be a major problem for people born in this group as the pear body shape is often associated with a Taurus-Moon placement. You may also find that you are prone to throat infections, laryngitis and various other ailments that affect this part of the body.

CHILDREN BORN WITH THE MOON IN TAURUS

Nice plump babies are often born when the Moon is in the sign of Taurus. As long as they are warm and well fed, these infants are usually perfectly contented and undemanding. Taurus-Moon children tend to be born either to parents who are well-to-do, or who have a rural or agricultural background. They have a strong sense of family and healthy appetites and grow into happy, helpful and positive young people.

RELATING TO OTHERS
YOUR EMOTIONAL PATTERN

Emotionally stable and solid as a rock, you take a sensible, pragmatic approach to life. Security is perhaps your most important consideration, so you soon develop a cautious nature underpinned by an extremely strong sense of self-preservation.

So vital is your need for security that Taurus-Moon people tend to surround themselves with material possessions, which they feel give their lives structure and support. Many, too, grow over-possessive, jealously – even neurotically – guarding what (or whom) they believe to be theirs.

You are not the sort of individual who leaps blindly into a new relationship. Before you give your affections, you will carefully weigh up all the pros and cons in order to satisfy yourself that this individual is really trustworthy and will offer you the stability you require, as well as providing the physical, financial and emotional anchors that are essential to your wellbeing.

To your relationships you pledge commitment and loyalty. You work hard to make your partnership successful, comfortable and prosperous and your domestic environment a pleasant place in which to live. Innately sensual, you like to indulge yourself and your loved ones whenever possible, so ensuring that you and your family have all the creature comforts you need will be high on your list of priorities.

Sociable and outgoing, you enjoy people and get-togethers. But with such strong nurturing instincts, you are a formidable nest-builder and like to tuck your loved ones, and your possessions, under your wing to keep them safe from harm.

ARIES

Your love of comfort and ease does not match the Aries-Moon subject's driving need to experience the challenges at the sharper end of life. Sexually, though, the atmosphere can be hot and satisfying.

TAURUS

A splendid combination, with both partners sharing identical emotional needs. You will feel comfortable in each other's company and will grow happy and prosperous together.

GEMINI

Certainly you both have plenty to say but you may not exactly speak the same language. Your Taurus-Moon demands stability but your partner likes to be loose and fancy-free.

CANCER

A Moon in Taurus matched with a Moon in Cancer makes a delightful combination. You are both loving, gentle and attentive to each other and to your family and friends.

LEO

Apart from the occasional battle of wills, there is every potential here to form a vibrant and enduring relationship together.

VIRGO

With both Moons in strong, reliable and earthy signs, you will have plenty in common. This has all the makings of a sexy, stable and lasting union.

LIBRA

Shared creative tastes offer excellent prospects for a successful combination. You and your gentle Libran-Moon partner will forge an artistic and highly sensual relationship together.

SCORPIO

Your Moon is in an Earth sign, that of your partner is in Water. Earth and water mixed can produce a muddy swamp. Alternatively, they can form the basis of creation. The choice is yours.

SAGITTARIUS

As a Taurus-Moon individual, you need a sense of permanence and stability under your feet. But your partner's Sagittarian-Moon hates to be tied down. There is little in common between you, it appears.

CAPRICORN

There is a wonderful meeting of hearts between these two Moon signs, which bodes extremely well for a compatible and lasting relationship together. Top marks for a solid and stable union.

AQUARIUS

A Taurus Moon has little in common with an Aquarian Moon since each has different needs and wants different things from life. Consequently, there is no real meeting ground here.

PISCES

With these two Moon placements there are potentially good spin-offs from one to the other. You two, therefore, could be very good for each other.

MOON IN GEMINI

KEY CHARACTER POINTS

Your instinctive response is:	flexible and sociable
Your best characteristics are:	wit and a generally youthful outlook on life
Your negative qualities are:	a tendency toward superficiality and craftiness
You dislike:	routine
You need:	lots of intellectual stimulation
You must:	learn to see your projects through to the end.

THE ESSENTIAL YOU

Bright as a button, as well as being both clever and amusing, you are blessed with a wit that is razor-sharp. Communications are your forte and, ever-questioning, you take a lively interest in everything around you – from how a gadget might work to precisely what makes a person tick. But you also suffer from a very short attention span, flitting like a butterfly from one interest to another, without giving yourself time to learn a subject in depth or to finish the projects you undertake.

LIFESTYLE

THE GEMINI MOON AT HOME

All the latest in technological wizardry will be very much in evidence in this home – anything to take the tedium out of all of those routine domestic chores. And since you are so restless and have a strong need to experience new environments, you are likely to move house several times in your life.

YOUR SUN AND MOON SIGN COMBINATION CHART

This shows just how well your outward persona (Sun sign) and inner personality (Moon sign) are integrated. YOUR MOON IN GEMINI WITH:

YOUR SUN IN...	COMBINATION KEYNOTES	STAR RATING
Aries	On the go	****
Taurus	Creative and clever	***
Gemini	Young at heart	*
Cancer	Caring but too easily bored	**
Leo	Charismatic	****
Virgo	Inventive	***
Libra	Persuasive	*****
Scorpio	Cool customer	****
Sagittarius	Restless	**
Capricorn	Ambitious	***
Aquarius	Visionary	*****
Pisces	Whimsical	**

*Highly subjective
** At odds with yourself
*** Need to work toward achieving inner balance
**** In harmony
***** Strongly integrated

YOU AND YOUR FAMILY

You treat everyone close to you as your friend, in a brotherly or sisterly way – including your own offspring and parents. And, because the Moon in Gemini means you are young at heart, when it's your turn to be a parent, there is unlikely to be a noticeable generation gap between you and your children – you really enjoy the outlook of young people and are happy to share their interests, their music, their games and their fun.

AT WORK

Moon-Gemini people are quick with their brains and dextrous with their hands. You can pick up new skills as fast as lightning – all you need to do is have something demonstrated or explained once and you are able to grasp the essentials immediately.

Your versatility lends itself to a wide variety of occupations although communications, entertainment, the media and travel industries will be the most appealing to you.

UNWIND BY:

Surfing the net and browsing social media.

MONEY MATTERS

You need to curb your tendency to spend, spend, spend.

HEALTH NOTES

With your nervous and tense disposition you, more than any of the Moon signs, really do need to take some time out to relax. Make sure this isn't an area that you overlook.

CHILDREN BORN WITH THE MOON IN GEMINI

True to their Mercurial Moon sign, children belonging to this group develop language skills from a very early age and, once they begin to talk, never seem to stop again!

Highly socially skilled, Moon-Gemini youngsters tend to be very amusing. They are fascinated by anything that moves and they can drive their parents mad with a constant bombardment of questions.

RELATING TO OTHERS
YOUR EMOTIONAL PATTERN

It has been said that those born with the Moon in this sign display the characteristics of a chameleon. Whichever crowd they happen to be with, they find a way of blending in, reflecting the mood of their companions and saying what they think other people want to hear rather than revealing their own true opinions or feelings. As a member of this sign, it is hardly surprising, then, that many people find it rather hard to get to know the real you.

Since variety is the spice of life to a Gemini-Moon, you tend to be emotionally changeable, or perhaps whimsical might be a better description. You like to feel free – light as the air that is the Geminian element. Commitments, in particular, overwhelm you and too many responsibilities leave you champing at the bit. In fact, any situation that bogs you down, for example a relationship that you feel restricts your movements, will soon become suffocating and intolerable.

If truth be told, you are a monumental flirt, whether you are in or out of a relationship, for neither constancy nor fidelity are particularly strong suits where this Moon sign is concerned.

Just as you need a good supply of interests for mental stimulation, so you also need a wide social network of friends and acquaintances that you can call up whenever you begin to feel bored. An address book brimming over with the phone number of friends, acquaintances – and even various past lovers – is an absolute must for anyone who has the Moon in Gemini.

You may flit from one thing to another and from one person to the next, but you do tend to have good control over your emotions. You are usually able to rationalize your feelings and work out precisely what it is that's affecting you. A Gemini-Moon individual will very rarely let their heart rule their head.

A partner who is intelligent will intrigue you. But for a truly successful relationship, he or she must also be clever enough to recognize that, just as long as you are given enough freedom, you will always want to come home.

ARIES

Both restless and curious, your Gemini-Moon and your partner's Aries-Moon will keep you both searching for adventure. Whether you are on the same quest, however, is debatable. Perhaps you may have to agree to disagree.

TAURUS

Certainly you both have plenty to say but you may not exactly speak the same language. Your partner's Taurus-Moon demands constancy – something which, alas, would bore you rigid.

GEMINI

A bright and breezy union with many intellectual interests in common but little sticking power, since the Moon in Gemini exacerbates restlessness.

CANCER

Cancerian-Moon individuals like to be close to hearth and home while Gemini-Moon people are only happy when they are out and about. You and your partner, therefore, seem to be at odds.

LEO

A light and airy combination, full of fun and frivolity. If you can keep laughing with each other and not at each other, this relationship could be amusing as well as sexually exciting.

VIRGO

Differences of attitude and opinion between your Moon sign and that of your partner make the divide just too great to guarantee lasting romance and happiness with this union.

LIBRA

Definitely on the same emotional wavelength. Gemini-Moon combined with a Libran-Moon make one of the best matches in the Zodiac. This is a potentially brilliant relationship.

SCORPIO

Your Gemini-Moon demands freedom whereas your partner's Scorpio-Moon is jealous and possessive. Consequently, this makes for a highly volatile situation.

SAGITTARIUS

Despite the fact that Sagittarian-Moons are at the opposite end of the spectrum to Gemini-Moons, this combination has been known to work very nicely.

CAPRICORN

There is very little meeting of minds and heart between Gemini-Moons and Capricorn-Moons. As a result, you and your partner would irritate each other and trying to stay together could prove an uphill struggle.

AQUARIUS

A splendidly amicable relationship, where each partner is cool and independent, yet both see eye to eye. An easy pairing with a very good chance of long-term success.

PISCES

A Pisces-Moon is perhaps the most emotionally clinging of the Moon signs. A Gemini-Moon is the most elusive. Neither has a true grasp of the other's feelings.

MOON IN CANCER

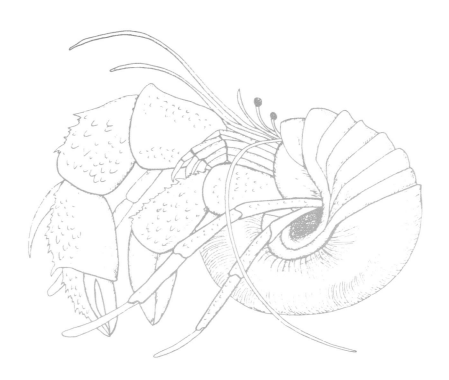

KEY CHARACTER POINTS

Your instinctive response is:	emotional and sensitive
Your best characteristics are:	good intuition and a nurturing instinct
Your negative qualities are:	a tendency toward defensiveness
You dislike:	throwing anything away
You need:	the security of a happy and settled home life
You must:	learn to take less seriously whatever other people say to you.

THE ESSENTIAL YOU

Just as the crab has a hard external shell into which it climbs for protection, so you have learned to hide your tender feelings behind a tough facade. This is essentially because Cancer-Moon people are very, very sensitive. Being born under this sign means that you are by nature intuitive, and you characteristically feel your way through life. If you sense that something is right, you do it. If you feel it is wrong, you don't. For you, home is where the heart is and you are at your happiest in your own environment, surrounded by all the people that you love.

LIFESTYLE

THE CANCER MOON AT HOME

An innate homemaker, but also a terrific collector, your home will be cosy and comfortable but crammed with all the things you cannot bear to throw away. Domesticity pleases you and, with your creative talents, you have the knack of turning the humblest hovel into a palace.

PEOPLE WHO SHARE YOUR MOON SIGN

George Orwell
Igor Stravinsky
Harrison Ford
Liza Minnelli
Taylor Swift
Kate Middleton
Shakira
Penélope Cruz
Prince William
Colin Farrell
Keanu Reeves
Robert Pattinson
Pierce Brosnan
Heath Ledger
Michael Schumacher
Isaac Newton
Kurt Cobain
Drake
Emilia Clarke
Chrissy Teigen
Franklin D. Roosevelt

YOUR SUN AND MOON SIGN COMBINATION CHART

This shows just how well your outward persona (Sun sign) and inner personality (Moon sign) are integrated.
YOUR MOON IN CANCER WITH:

YOUR SUN IN...	COMBINATION KEYNOTES	STAR RATING
Aries	Restless spirit	**
Taurus	Practical sense	*****
Gemini	Gossip, gossip, gossip	**
Cancer	Cuddly	*
Leo	Warm-hearted	****
Virgo	Solid and sensible	****
Libra	Charming and eloquent	***
Scorpio	Hidden depths	****
Sagittarius	A searching soul	***
Capricorn	Responsible	**
Aquarius	Divided	**
Pisces	Super-sensitive	*****

* Highly subjective
** At odds with yourself
*** Need to work toward achieving inner balance
**** In harmony
***** Strongly integrated

YOU AND YOUR FAMILY

All Moon-in-Cancer subjects are both strongly family-oriented and nurturing by instinct, so you will delight in looking after the people you love. As a child, you felt responsible for your brothers and sisters, even if they were older than you, and it is this tender, caring role that you carry through to your partner and your own offspring. Your mother is a very significant figure in your life and you are unlikely ever to lose the close attachment you formed with her as a child.

AT WORK

Cancer-Moon individuals are life's carers, so you would do well in the medical or counselling fields. Charity work, the voluntary sector and working with children would also appeal. Since you are happiest in your own environment, working from your own home might well give you immense satisfaction. Setting up your own business as an interior decorator, landscape designer or an antiques dealer would all be suitable pursuits.

UNWIND BY:

Creating an elaborate dish for the family to enjoy.

MONEY MATTERS

You are a compulsive hoarder, so saving money will come naturally to you. Something among your eclectic possessions is bound to prove valuable one day.

HEALTH NOTES

You are physically tougher than you appear, although you are sensitively attuned to every ache and pain. But it is your habitual worry that tends to lay you low.

CHILDREN BORN WITH THE MOON IN CANCER

Cancer-Moon babies are loving and cuddly and especially bonded to their mothers – features they take with them into adulthood. They readily demonstrate their feelings and emotions and, when little, they tend to cry easily. As a consequence they may be bullied or teased at school – a possibility that all parents of these Cancer-Moon children need to keep in mind.

RELATING TO OTHERS
YOUR EMOTIONAL PATTERN

Soft and sentimental, you are a consummate romantic with a tendency to slip on rose-tinted spectacles at every opportunity. Born with an innate nurturing instinct, your caring nature will reach out to help anyone in need. Protective of the people and possessions that belong to you, your family and home are the center of your universe and you tend to fret if you are kept away from your own environment for too long.

Because the Moon is in her own sign here, her sensitivity is especially strong, so you are likely to find your emotional response to others intensified. Instinctively, you are able to tap into other people's feelings and pick on their moods, something that can affect you deeply. Indeed, so infectious do you find the emotions of those you are with that you become happy or sad according to the prevailing atmosphere around you. And, of course, it is this intuitive capacity that makes you such an understanding and sympathetic companion to your partner, your family and your friends.

Cancer-Moon and mother-figures are inseparably associated with each other. For a start, whether male or female, you have a close rapport with your own mother, taking after her in some notable way or sharing particular physical or mental characteristics. And when choosing a mate, you may be drawn to someone who will "mother" you in the same way that your own mother did when you were a child. Or else, because of your own nurturing instincts, you will naturally gravitate toward a partner who, for some reason, needs to be "mothered" and the relationship will enable you to assume the role you know so well, and which brings you so much satisfaction in your life. But perhaps the greatest fulfilment of all for you is the creation of your own family and the opportunity of watching your children grow into happy, well-rounded individuals.

ARIES

You prefer to reminisce rather than look forward, but your Aries-Moon partner wants to live in the present and not the past. You like cuddling, but your partner cannot tolerate too much body contact. These are the sort of differences that will come between you.

TAURUS

A Moon in Cancer matched with a Moon in Taurus makes a delightful combination. You are both loving, gentle and attentive to each other and to your family and friends.

GEMINI

Gemini-Moon people like to be out and about while Cancerian-Moon individuals are only happy when they are close to hearth and home. You and your partner, therefore, seem to be at odds.

CANCER

A lovely combination, producing a gentle, quiet union and a somewhat old-fashioned relationship, reminiscent of lavender and lace. You are loving, tender and solicitous of one another.

LEO

Here is a relationship that could just work – but only if you are all-adoring and your Leo-Moon partner refrains from being too bossy and overbearing.

VIRGO

Pairing up with a Virgo-Moon partner has all the ingredients of a mutually beneficial relationship. You could find this match stimulating and enriching for both of you.

LIBRA

Your Libra-Moon partner is much too cool and aloof for your liking while he or she will probably find you too physically and emotionally demanding. Altogether, then, an uphill struggle.

SCORPIO

Intense feelings and deep love will underlie this union, despite occasional moods and temperamental outbursts. There will be plenty of passion and sex will be both satisfying and rewarding.

SAGITTARIUS

With different attitudes and disparate ambitions, you and your partner are unlikely to want the same things in life. At the end of the day, neither finds the other truly understanding.

CAPRICORN

Despite the fact that your Moons are in opposite signs, this combination has all the makings of a highly successful partnership. All in all, a splendid romantic match.

AQUARIUS

Cancer-Moons and Aquarius-Moons are poles apart emotionally – one is clinging and dependent, the other is distant and remote. Such differences are difficult to reconcile.

PISCES

Moons in Cancer and Pisces produce gentle, caring people with a loving and affectionate nature, so there will be shared feelings and understanding here. This is an ideal match.

MOON IN LEO

KEY CHARACTER POINTS

Your instinctive response is:	dramatic and enthusiastic
Your best characteristics are:	warmth and generosity
Your negative qualities are:	egotism and a tendency to boast
You dislike:	being ignored
You need:	to be admired
You must:	learn to see through empty flattery.

THE ESSENTIAL YOU

The Moon in Leo endows you with a happy, sunny nature that makes you a charismatic, popular and attractive figure among your contemporaries. You come across as honest, warm-hearted and generous to a fault. In fact, extravagance can be your downfall since you tend to have expensive tastes. You like to live life to the full and, if you can live it in luxury, then all the better! With the Moon in this placement, you feel your natural role in life is center stage. Being overshadowed or pushed to the sidelines would profoundly rock your inner confidence.

LIFESTYLE

THE LEO MOON AT HOME

There is invariably a sense of grandeur about a Leo-Moon's house. Here, luxury will be much in evidence, with vibrant colors and rich textures that give an overall effect of opulence and style. To be complimented on their homes gives Leo-Moon subjects tremendous satisfaction.

YOUR SUN AND MOON SIGN COMBINATION CHART

This shows just how well your outward persona (Sun sign) and inner personality (Moon sign) are integrated. YOUR MOON IN LEO WITH:

YOUR SUN IN...	COMBINATION KEYNOTES	STAR RATING	
Aries	A ball of fire	*****	
Taurus	Luxury-loving	****	
Gemini	Colorful	***	
Cancer	Very affectionate	****	
Leo	Self-centered	*	
Virgo	Fussy	**	
Libra	Stylish	****	* Highly subjective
Scorpio	Unpredictable	**	** At odds with yourself
Sagittarius	Plenty of charisma	*****	*** Need to work toward
Capricorn	Upwardly mobile	***	achieving inner balance
Aquarius	Passionate ideals	**	**** In harmony
Pisces	Creative	**	***** Strongly integrated

YOU AND YOUR FAMILY

Individuals belonging to your Moon sign often have mothers who are colorful, demonstrative and flamboyant figures, and you respond well to this warmth.

Fathers, however, are often a different kettle of fish, possibly authoritarian or difficult in some way. They were deeply proud of, and ambitious for you, and you have the same feelings for your own offspring. As a parent you are very generous and have a tendency to indulge your children's every whim.

AT WORK

Better in the limelight than in the shadows, and at the top of the hierarchy than at the bottom, whatever your line of work, you quickly establish yourself in a position of leadership and control. With your ambitious, upwardly mobile drive, you soon attract recognition and success. Whenever possible, you will mix business with pleasure. In particular, you have a talent for transforming any hobby into a thriving and lucrative business.

UNWIND BY:

joining a local amateur dramatics group.

MONEY MATTERS

Because of your extravagant nature, you may tend to be a big spender. If you have anything at all left over to invest, then you should put your money into luxury goods or blue chip companies.

HEALTH NOTES

The heart and spine are this sign's weak links, so you need to watch your diet carefully and ensure that you take regular exercise.

CHILDREN BORN WITH THE MOON IN LEO

These children come into the world equipped with a regal bearing that seems to command respect when they are still tiny. So much so that, whatever the financial status of the family, they tend to be treated almost like royalty. Because of this, and their formidable, precocious talent, there is a danger that these youngsters may become arrogant or boastful, showing off in front of their friends.

RELATING TO OTHERS
YOUR EMOTIONAL PATTERN

Because Leo is the sign of the King of the Zodiac, to be born with the Moon in this placement means that you have a great need for recognition, or for others to treat you as a special person of some importance. Consequently, you project a high profile and give off an air of authority which, you find, most people do respect. Above all else, you need constant reassurance, so it is essential that you get lots of praise from those around you. To be appreciated, to be patted on the back for your achievements or to be thanked for your trouble, is as important to you as the air that you breath.

Emotionally demonstrative and openly affectionate, you come across as warm and loving. You are outgoing and extroverted, and happier in the limelight than in the shade, so you seek a crowd where you can be the center of attention. It is important that people like you and that you feel loved. But in your search for praise, you must be careful not to fall for empty flattery, nor for the ingratiating compliments of the sycophant.

In love, you are warm and generous, spontaneously affectionate and enthusiastic in your lovemaking. You can be fiery and passionate, giving your love joyfully and voluptuously, but you do expect your feelings to be reciprocated just as eagerly and abundantly as they have been given. If this doesn't happen or if, for any reason, your partner withholds his or her love from you, then you will instantly shut down all feelings and cut yourself off from that person altogether.

In relationships generally, you like to take charge and, in an ideal world, you would choose a partner who allows you to shine and who is content to bask in your reflected glory. All in all, you are a happy and outgoing person – and you take the greatest pleasure in making those you love happy, too.

ARIES

An exciting partnership, whether intimate or professional. There is masses of energy in this combination and together you should have tremendous fun. Entertainment, adventure and an active sexual life will color your time together.

TAURUS

Apart from the occasional battle of wills, there is every potential in these two Moon placements to form a vibrant and enduring relationship together.

GEMINI

A light and airy combination, full of fun and frivolity. If you can keep laughing with each other and not at each other, this relationship could be amusing as well as sexually exciting.

CANCER

Here is a relationship that could feasibly work – but only if your Cancer-Moon partner is all-adoring and you refrain from being bossy and overbearing.

LEO

A fiery and highly combustible combination. Although there is a great deal of passion at the start of the relationship, you are each much too competitive and self-oriented to make this union viable in the long term.

VIRGO

The Leo-Moon is emotionally driven while your Virgo-Moon partner is all reason and analysis. Such contrasting needs and approaches suggest that this relationship is not highly rated for lasting success.

LIBRA

With a Leo-Moon and a Libra-Moon in the same house, it has to be five-star living all the way. This is certainly a fun-loving combination, but the relationship will only work with give and take on both sides.

SCORPIO

Though emotionally very different types, there is a powerful and magnetic attraction that draws the two of you together. Sexually sultry, your union will sizzle and smoulder on.

SAGITTARIUS

What a fiery, dynamic duo you two make! This has all the ingredients of a powerful love affair. With your shared interests and similar ways of experiencing the world, you are bound to go far together.

CAPRICORN

Not the easiest of pairings since a Capricorn-Moon will unhesitatingly deflate your pride and your Leo-Moon generosity would affront your economically-minded partner.

AQUARIUS

In many ways chalk and cheese, this combination has been known to work surprisingly successfully. Though you come from opposite ends of the spectrum, there is much to unite you.

PISCES

Although this might appear a strange combination on the surface, there is a great deal of romance and enchantment between you and your Pisces-Moon partner that will bind you together.

MOON IN VIRGO

KEY CHARACTER POINTS

Your instinctive response is: cool and off-hand

Your best characteristics are: practical know-how and attention to detail

Your negative qualities are: fastidiousness and a tendency to worry

You dislike: flamboyance and ostentation

You need: a well-ordered routine

You must: learn to relax in general and, in particular, don't worry about what the neighbors might think.

THE ESSENTIAL YOU

If you were born when the Moon was in the sign of Virgo, you may be described as serious in outlook and modest of demeanor. Though you possess quick and instinctive reactions, there is, nevertheless, something quiet and retiring about your nature that, rather than push yourself forward, you prefer to take a step back. But onlookers would do well not to be deceived, for this quietness belies an intelligent and incisive mind, a wise and critical judgement and a clever, discriminating eye that can sort the wheat from the chaff from a mile away.

LIFESTYLE

THE VIRGO MOON AT HOME

People born with the Moon in Virgo tend to change residences several times in their lives, often uprooting themselves from their early environment and setting up home far away from where they grew up. Drawn to the country rather than to an urban setting, their homes are usually neat and tidy and many are quite happy living completely on their own.

PEOPLE WHO SHARE YOUR MOON SIGN

J F Kennedy
Stephen Hawking
Madonna
Benjamin Britten
Leo Tolstoy
Jack Kerouac
J K Rowling
Jodie Foster
Natalie Portman
Nicki Minaj
Serena Williams
Zayn Malik
Zac Efron
Blake Lively
Michael Fassbender
Channing Tatum
Gloria Vanderbilt
Lorde
Chris Hemsworth
Samuel L Jackson

YOUR SUN AND MOON SIGN COMBINATION CHART

This shows just how well your outward persona (Sun sign) and inner personality (Moon sign) are integrated.

YOUR MOON IN VIRGO WITH:

YOUR SUN IN...	COMBINATION KEYNOTES	STAR RATING
Aries	Sharp and decisive	**
Taurus	Level-headed	*****
Gemini	Silver-tongued	***
Cancer	Caring	****
Leo	Warm but reserved	**
Virgo	Critical	*
Libra	Discerning eye	***
Scorpio	Determined	***
Sagittarius	Wise and thoughtful	***
Capricorn	Serious	*****
Aquarius	Intelligent	****
Pisces	Medically minded	**

* Highly subjective
** At odds with yourself
*** Need to work toward achieving inner balance
**** In harmony
***** Strongly integrated

YOU AND YOUR FAMILY

Early family life may have been strict or difficult in some way. As a result, the relationship between you and your parents may have been strained. As a parent yourself, you approach family life in a cool, dispassionate manner, expecting your home to run like clockwork and taking a firm but fair and disciplined control over your offspring.

AT WORK

With your clever, methodical approach to work, you would find both satisfaction and success in any occupation that demands precision skills coupled with a keen eye for detail. Several areas draw your interest. The first might be in the technological, mechanical or engineering industries. The second includes the medical or scientific fields. And, because of your green fingers, the third involves gardening or horticulture. Lastly, any form of research, whether in these areas or in academic life, would also suit you well.

UNWIND BY:

going for a walk in the countryside.

MONEY MATTERS

You are as organized and careful in your financial affairs as you are in all other areas of your life, so you will undoubtedly have made some wise investments as well as sound provisions for your future.

HEALTH NOTES

Tension headaches from poring over intricate detail, or because you get wound up worrying about your work, seem to be the Virgo-Moon bugbear.

CHILDREN BORN WITH THE MOON IN VIRGO

Whether male or female, children born with the Moon in Virgo tend to be timid and shy, in some cases even nervous and withdrawn. Mostly self-resourceful and self-contained, they often need encouragement to express their inner talents. They possess excellent powers of concentration and can work away diligently and systematically until they are satisfied that they have achieved their objective.

RELATING TO OTHERS
YOUR EMOTIONAL PATTERN

Having the Moon in Virgo means you were born with a sense of service and a deep-seated instinct for helping others. Above all else, you need to be needed. Sometimes, though, there may be a danger that you will take on too much and then find yourself over-burdened by commitments or by other people's problems.

Perhaps it is because you are innately shy, or maybe because you are afraid of being let down and hurt, that you tend not to express your innermost feelings openly to others. This means that, emotionally, you come across as cool and reserved. For whatever reason, you are cautious about giving your love and trust to others. In addition, you have very high standards of excellence that you impose on yourself as well as on those with whom you interact. Always searching for perfection, you fuss over details, scrupulous about your own appearance and behavior and expecting others to feel the same.

In truth, the Moon in this placement is not in the most passionate of signs. Rather, it imbues you with a logical and practical approach to relationships. You say to yourself that, if you enter a partnership with your eyes wide open, then you cannot be disappointed.

The key for you, however, is finding the right partner. You need someone who you can respect and who is on your wavelength; a person who will not criticize you or pick holes in the things you do. Someone who appreciates your cool efficiency and tidy mind; who will encourage you to articulate your feelings and remind you to let your hair down and relax. A partner, above all else, who knows how to make you laugh. With such a partner as this at your side, you will discover the true solace of your heart. For this soulmate will help you to flower and reach the heights of joy.

HOW YOUR VIRGO–MOON RELATES TO YOUR PARTNER'S MOON IN:

ARIES
Your Virgo-Moon calls for order, tidiness and discipline, which is not at all well matched with your partner's cavalier attitude to domestic life. Sex, too, is likely to be a problem, since you do not always appreciate the Aries-Moon's need for urgency when it comes to satisfying passion and desire.

TAURUS
With both Moons in strong, reliable and earthy signs, you two will have plenty in common. This has all the makings of a sensual, stable and lasting romantic relationship.

GEMINI
Differences of attitude and opinion between your Moon sign and that of your partner make the divide too great to guarantee lasting romance for this particular union.

CANCER
Pairing up with a Cancer-Moon partner has all the ingredients of a mutually beneficial relationship. You could find this match stimulating and enriching for both of you.

LEO
The Virgo-Moon is all reason and analysis, while your partner is emotionally driven. Such contrasting needs and diverse approaches suggest that this relationship is not highly rated for lasting success.

VIRGO
Though you undoubtedly have plenty in common, there is the danger that, with both your Moons in this sign, your relationship could become a touch too stolid. You work hard, but neither of you knows how to relax.

LIBRA
Verbal communications between you will be very satisfying, with long conversations and debates well into the night. But when it comes to passion, you each look for different things.

SCORPIO
Potentially, a relationship together could be a scorcher in more ways than one. In reality, however, Scorpio-Moons are physically demanding while Virgo-Moons can be prudish. So sex can be a problem here.

SAGITTARIUS
Virgo-Moons like to feel that they have their feet on terra firma, but Sagittarius-Moons dislike being pinned down. You are both too self-sufficient in your own ways to expect this relationship to work in the long term.

CAPRICORN
With both Moons in Earth signs, you both know exactly what the other wants and needs. This, therefore, is a splendid combination, with excellent chances for durability and success.

AQUARIUS
Your Virgo-Moon delights in the punctilious. Your partner's Aquarius-Moon relishes the unpredictable. Unless you both find a compromise, the odds would seem to be stacked against you.

PISCES
There is no doubt that friendship between you and your Pisces-Moon companion is a sure bet. But when it comes to a more intimate relationship, you may find that each soon loses patience with the other.

MOON IN LIBRA

KEY CHARACTER POINTS

Your instinctive response is:	affable and charming
Your best characteristics are:	tact and strong sense of fair play
Your negative qualities are:	indecision and a tendency to pass the buck
You dislike:	unpleasantness of any sort
You need:	to be surrounded by beauty and aesthetic harmony
You must:	learn to take the rough with the smooth.

PEOPLE WHO SHARE YOUR MOON SIGN

Malala Yousafzai
Maya Angelou
Bruce Springsteen
Michael Caine
Ella Fitzgerald
Pierre Cardin
Sylvester Stallone
Agatha Christie
Josephine Baker
Edwin "Buzz" Aldrin
The Duchess of Sussex
Kate Winslet
Anne Hathaway
Kristen Stewart
Ariana Grande
Leonardo DiCaprio
Dr. Dre
Justin Bieber
Harry Styles
Jay-Z
Emma Stone
Tom Hardy

THE ESSENTIAL YOU

With the Moon in the sign of the balance, you will find yourself constantly weighing up everything and everyone you come across, and invariably finding that you simply cannot make up your mind either way! Others see you as an indecisive fence sitter. In reality, you simply want to please everyone and be for them what they want you to be. Harmony is essential to your wellbeing. Peace, beauty and tranquility is what you strive to achieve, for ugliness and discord upset you profoundly. Elegant, charming, suave and sophisticated, you are a genuine class act.

LIFESTYLE

THE LIBRA MOON AT HOME

All Libran-Moon natives have a sharply honed sense of aesthetics and a beautiful home environment takes priority over comfort. Design is a strong feature, with furnishings and interiors that are stylish and elegant. A home that might be featured in *Vogue* is what you aspire to achieve.

YOUR SUN AND MOON SIGN COMBINATION CHART

This shows just how well your outward persona (Sun sign) and inner personality (Moon sign) are integrated.
YOUR MOON IN LIBRA WITH:

YOUR SUN IN...	COMBINATION KEYNOTES	STAR RATING	
Aries	Impatient	**	
Taurus	Loves an easy life	****	
Gemini	Witty but superficial	*****	
Cancer	Gracious	***	
Leo	Extravagant	****	
Virgo	Analytical	***	
Libra	Indecisive	*	* Highly subjective
Scorpio	Sophisticated	***	** At odds with yourself
Sagittarius	Conciliatory	***	*** Need to work toward
Capricorn	Status-conscious	**	achieving inner balance
Aquarius	Fascinating	*****	**** In harmony
Pisces	Easygoing	***	***** Strongly integrated

YOU AND YOUR FAMILY

Characteristically, people who are born with the Moon in this sign belong to families who are creatively talented in some way – either well read or musically or artistically inclined. The mother tends to be very feminine, an attractive and indulgent personality who takes a great interest in the life and career of her Libra-Moon son or daughter. As a parent, you instil good manners in your children, and encourage their musical or artistic skills.

AT WORK

It is important that the environment in which you work is graceful and aesthetically pleasing. If it is, then you will be able to function at your most creative. You dislike stress and conflict, so any discord between yourself and your colleagues will have an adverse effect on your output. Since you are people-oriented, you tend to excel in teamwork rather than working in an individual capacity. The world of the arts appeals to you but so, too, does the diplomatic service or any occupation where counselling, negotiating or mediation is required.

UNWIND BY:

sitting in a glorious setting and listening to your favorite music.

MONEY MATTERS

Because you have an eye for quality and expensive tastes in general, you need a substantial amount of money simply to survive. You would prefer to inherit or win it on the lottery but, if you must work for it yourself, you will try your best to find an occupation that brings the least stress for the maximum gain.

HEALTH NOTES

Your system simply cannot tolerate too much conflict and you may succumb to glandular or kidney infections when under stress.

CHILDREN BORN WITH THE MOON IN LIBRA

These infants are the sweetest babies with the most delightful manners. They soon learn that their smiles and charming ways are a winning formula for achieving their own ends. You might think that butter simply wouldn't melt in their mouths! With such an engaging personality, Libra-Moon children become consummate psychologists from a very young age and soon learn to handle people with apparent ease.

RELATING TO OTHERS
YOUR EMOTIONAL PATTERN

Charming, affable, easy-going, you're always prepared to please. This is because harmony and a peaceful existence are quintessentially important to your wellbeing. And because, in relationships, any ill-feeling or the merest hint of an argument upsets you to the core, you immediately become conciliatory and do your best to find a compromise, so long as it leads to an easy life.

People with this Moon placement are able to intellectualize their emotions and so, although immensely sociable and friendly, they can also be cool and aloof. With the right partner, they make delightful companions – chatty, amusing and graciously entertaining. But many may also be described as fair-weather friends, cordial for as long as everything goes well, but quick to distance themselves in times of difficulty.

In truth, you go through life in love with love itself. You idealize a world of honor and gallantry, of fair damsels and courtly knights. It is not so much fiery passion that moves you, it is romance that you seek. For natives of a Libran Moon are essentially romantic creatures who wish to live their lives in a permanently euphoric state of being. Alas, euphoria is by nature tenuous and, when the initial romantic magic of a new relationship inevitably settles into the humdrum realities of everyday life, then Libran-Moon subjects tend to feel total disillusionment.

As a member of this sign you probably know that you have exquisite tastes and, when it comes to choosing a partner, looks and presentation will be high on your list. So your ideal partner must be attractive, well groomed and well dressed. Nothing turns you off faster than coarseness, boorish behaviour or poor hygiene. But good manners, refinement, a noble bearing, and the promise of keeping the romance alive will be the first steps toward winning your heart.

ARIES

When it comes to making decisions you like to take your time in order to consider all the parameters. Your Aries-Moon partner, however, demands instant action. Despite your differences, there is a lot you can learn from each other.

TAURUS

Shared creative tastes offer excellent prospects for a successful combination. You and your Taurus-Moon partner will forge an artistic and highly sensual relationship together.

GEMINI

Definitely on the same emotional wavelength. Gemini-Moon combined with a Libra-Moon makes one of the best matches in the Zodiac. This is a potentially brilliant relationship.

CANCER

Your Cancer-Moon partner needs a lot of cuddling but you, on the other hand, prefer to keep your distance since you dislike too much physical contact. Altogether, then, an uphill struggle.

LEO

With a Leo-Moon and a Libra-Moon in the same house, it has to be five-star living all the way. This is certainly a fun-loving combination, but the relationship will only work with give and take on both sides.

VIRGO

Verbal communications between you will be very satisfying, with long conversations and debates well into the night. But when it comes to passion, you each look for different things.

LIBRA

A splendid meeting of minds, both with highly sophisticated tastes. But since you are both indecisive, with two Libra-Moons under the same roof, how would decisions ever get made?

SCORPIO

An interesting match in which each can learn a great deal from his or her partner. However, a Scorpio-Moon needs more devotion than a Libra-Moon is prepared, or even able, to offer.

SAGITTARIUS

You both like your freedom so that is something you have in common. A little knowledge of when to share and when to leave well alone will go a long way in this relationship.

CAPRICORN

Your Moon tends toward indolence and your partner's Moon is dedicated to hard work. You are light-hearted while Capricorn-Moons can be stern moralists. There are many fundamental differences here.

AQUARIUS

Fun, friendship, understanding. You share so many characteristics and have such a wide variety of interests in common that life will be led in peaceful co-existence. A terrific combination.

PISCES

Both creative, both lovers of beauty, both needy of harmony and tranquility. Sex can be sweet and gentle between you, but ultimately you will each blame the other for faults of your own respective making.

MOON IN SCORPIO

KEY CHARACTER POINTS

Your instinctive response is:	penetrating and intense
Your best characteristics are:	shrewdness and an ability to focus exclusively on the task in hand
Your negative qualities are:	jealousy and irritability
You dislike:	disloyalty in any form
You need:	to feel in control of your environment and of the people you are with
You must:	learn to take yourself less seriously.

THE ESSENTIAL YOU

Cool, sexy, mysterious, mean and broody – these are a few of the adjectives that describe an individual born with the Moon in Scorpio.

A born survivor, you are blessed with tremendous strength of character, an ability to focus your total attention upon a task and a tenacity of purpose that will not be deflected until your objective has been reached.

With these kinds of indomitable qualities, you tend to be a formidable personality to deal with. A master or mistress of control, you usually like to take charge of a situation – and always play your cards close to your chest.

YOUR SUN AND MOON SIGN COMBINATION CHART

This shows just how well your outward persona (Sun sign) and inner personality (Moon sign) are integrated.

YOUR MOON IN SCORPIO WITH:

YOUR SUN IN...	COMBINATION KEYNOTES	STAR RATING
Aries	Athletic	***
Taurus	Stubborn	**
Gemini	Sharp and perceptive	***
Cancer	Deeply emotional	*****
Leo	Fiercely loyal	***
Virgo	Vocational instinct	***
Libra	Animal magnetism	**
Scorpio	Obsessional	*
Sagittarius	Idealistic	**
Capricorn	Single-minded	***
Aquarius	Insightful	**
Pisces	Psychologically aware	*****

* Highly subjective
** At odds with yourself
*** Need to work toward achieving inner balance
**** In harmony
***** Strongly integrated

LIFESTYLE

THE SCORPIO MOON AT HOME

Traditionalist at heart, you go for honest-to-goodness quality and comfort when it comes to furniture and fittings. Antique is usually preferable to modern and darker, richer colors chosen rather than lighter hues. Since Scorpio is a water sign, living by a river or overlooking the sea would be a great draw.

YOU AND YOUR FAMILY

Your admiration of feisty women probably stems from early memories of your mother who, if she is typical of a Scorpio-Moon parent, may well have been either strong or manipulative, or both. You are likely to be loyal and supportive to your brothers and sisters and feel a close kinship with them. As parents, members of this Moon sign are usually loving but strict.

AT WORK

Scorpio-Moon individuals are unlikely ever to find themselves on Skid Row, since they have an uncanny sixth sense that leads them to employment of one sort or another. If you belong to this sign, you will operate more successfully as a boss rather than an employee for, in most situations, you like to be the one who gives the orders. With your intuitive abilities and investigative mind, psychological or psychiatric work will appeal. Surgery, the police force, or research of any kind will also attract.

UNWIND BY:

taking part in a karate class.

MONEY MATTERS

You are a canny investor, intuitively picking the policy or saving scheme that will yield the highest dividends.

HEALTH NOTES

Problems with the reproductive organs can sometimes be the weak link in the Scorpio-Moon system.

CHILDREN BORN WITH THE MOON IN SCORPIO

According to an old saying, when one Scorpio dies, another one is born. A baby whose chart shows the Moon in Scorpio, then, may well be born into a family that has recently lost one of its members.

The household of a Scorpio baby seems to revolve around him or her, more than with any other sign. Children with the Moon in Scorpio have big egos and make their demands known from the very beginning of their lives. They simply have to be noticed.

RELATING TO OTHERS

YOUR EMOTIONAL PATTERN

Intense is the appropriate adjective to describe the emotions of a Scorpio-Moon subject. You may well appear glassy-smooth on the surface, but your feelings will run in virtually unfathomable, labyrinthine channels down to your very core. So deep, in fact, that others find you quite enigmatic. But this is precisely what gives you the air of mystery that makes you so fascinating and magnetically alluring. Indeed, potential love interests fall over themselves to get close enough to you in an attempt to unlock your secrets.

Interestingly, though, while you yourself tend to be secretive, you have an innate ability to see through others, which makes you a brilliant psychologist and master of the art of subtle manipulation.

With your razor-sharp intuitive capacity, you can spot an untruth, a sycophant or a fraud a mile away. For, in your books, sincerity is what counts. Life for you is either black or white – with very little room for grey areas in between. You either take to someone on first meeting, or you dislike them on sight. Few people get a second chance.

Forever riding an emotional rollercoaster, you know the heights of joy and the depths of misery. Sex is very important in your scheme of things and it is a deep, meaningful relationship that you seek to achieve with your chosen partner in life.

You cannot resist a challenge, so your ideal life partner needs to be spunky and passionate, prepared to give as good as they get. To this relationship you pledge total commitment. You are prepared to give 100 percent loyalty, but you also demand 100 percent in return. When you are completely sure of your ground, then you prove honest, supportive and deeply caring. A constant and faithful companion, you give your heart and soul willingly and totally to the one you love.

ARIES

If you can curb your jealous impulses and respect your partner's need for personal freedom, the rewards, in terms of your shared passions, will more than make up for your differences.

TAURUS

Your Moon is in a Water sign, that of your partner is in Earth. Earth and water mixed can produce a muddy swap. Alternatively, they can form the basis of creation. The choice is yours.

GEMINI

Your Scorpio-Moon is jealous and possessive whereas your partner's Gemini-Moon demands freedom. Consequently, this makes for a highly volatile situation.

CANCER

Intense feelings and deep love will underlie this union, despite occasional moods and temperamental outbursts. Passion will be plentiful and sex will be both satisfying and rewarding.

LEO

Though emotionally very different types, there is a powerful magnetic attraction that draws the two of you together. Sexually sultry, your union will sizzle and smoulder on.

VIRGO

Potentially, a relationship together could be a scorcher in more ways than one. In reality, however, Scorpio-Moons are physically demanding, while Virgo-Moons can be somewhat prudish. So sex can be a problem here.

LIBRA

An interesting match in which each can learn a great deal from their partner. However, a Scorpio-Moon needs more devotion than a Libra-Moon is prepared, or even able, to offer.

SCORPIO

Deep, and with a tendency to introspection, two Scorpio-Moons in the same house would produce a relationship that is crackling with tension – and where neither partner is willing, or able, to diffuse the situation.

SAGITTARIUS

Your Moon is possessive and demands complete devotion. Your partner's Sagittarius-Moon needs freedom and a looser framework. You will constantly be chasing different goals.

CAPRICORN

There is great attraction between you that augurs well for a lasting union. However, both of you are dedicated in your own way but in different directions. You must try to find a common path.

AQUARIUS

Your Scorpio-Moon is insistent; your partner's Aquarius-Moon is cold and distant. There is little agreement between you and this can lead to tension and discord.

PISCES

Emotionally, you two make an ideal match. Able to experience life's highs and lows with the same heart, you are magnetically drawn to each other. A brilliant liaison.

MOON IN SAGITTARIUS

KEY CHARACTER POINTS

Your instinctive response is: open and friendly
Your best characteristics are: enthusiasm and far-sightedness
Your negative qualities are: irresponsibility and tactlessness
You dislike: being confined
You need: freedom – to say and do what comes naturally to you
You must: learn to curb your restlessness.

THE ESSENTIAL YOU

Being born with the Moon in the sign of Sagittarius means that you are blessed with a cheerful nature and a good-humored, happy-go-lucky disposition. You are optimistic and enthusiastic, eager to experience everything that life has in store. Perhaps that is why you are so restless, always looking for new challenges and adventures. Fortunately, you are adaptable and will bend according to the situation or company you find yourself in. Though you may appear superficial, you are, in fact, deeply philosophical, and your wisdom and understanding of life are without equal.

LIFESTYLE

THE SAGITTARIUS MOON AT HOME

Sagittarian-Moon natives are not by nature the most domesticated of people, so your home will permanently have that relaxed and lived-in look about it. If you have a preference it will be for modern rather than antique. There is every chance that you will set up home in a different country to your native land, perhaps in a university town, or close to a cathedral.

PEOPLE WHO SHARE YOUR MOON SIGN

Albert Einstein
Yoko Ono
Mozart
Beethoven
Vincent van Gogh
Friedrich Nietzsche
Nicole Kidman
Jennifer Aniston
Freddie Mercury
Michael Jordan
Sharon Stone
Emma Watson
Al Pacino
Richard Gere
Oprah Winfrey
Adele
Naomi Campbell
Justin Timberlake
Liam Neeson
Zlatan Ibrahimovic
Michael Phelps
Vin Diesel

YOUR SUN AND MOON SIGN COMBINATION CHART

This shows just how well your outward persona (Sun sign) and inner personality (Moon sign) are integrated.

YOUR MOON IN SAGITTARIUS WITH:

YOUR SUN IN...	COMBINATION KEYNOTES	STAR RATING
Aries	A born explorer	*****
Taurus	Research interests	****
Gemini	Constantly restless	**
Cancer	Divided	**
Leo	Sunny-natured	*****
Virgo	Philosophical	**
Libra	Sociable	****
Scorpio	Investigative mind	**
Sagittarius	Nomadic	*
Capricorn	Successful	***
Aquarius	Inspirational	****
Pisces	Drawn to foreign lands	**

* Highly subjective
** At odds with yourself
*** Need to work toward achieving inner balance
**** In harmony
***** Strongly integrated

YOU AND YOUR FAMILY

The Moon in Sagittarius is somehow associated with foreign lands, so perhaps you have mixed or immigrant parentage, or parents who travelled abroad extensively when you were young. Certainly, your parents had strong views on education and brought you up to be confident and independent. You see your family members as a united group, a team, with each member pulling in the same direction. When it comes to your own children, you are more like a friend to them than a parent.

AT WORK

If your company allows you to work flexi-time, you will be in your element, getting all your tasks completed in double-quick time. Otherwise, since you buck against a rigid nine-to-five regime, and because you tend to be a law unto yourself, perhaps you would be better off self-employed, so that you can choose when and how you work. You're a born teacher, lecturer or demonstrator, would make a brilliant sports person, or delight in the travel industry.

UNWIND BY:

throwing an informal party for all of your friends.

MONEY MATTERS

Carefree by nature, the Moon-in-Sagittarius individual can also be carefree about money. As long as you have enough to see you through the next adventure that you have lined up, that is fine by you.

HEALTH NOTES

Being overweight can present a problem with this sign, particularly after middle age and especially around the hip and thigh area!

CHILDREN BORN WITH THE MOON IN SAGITTARIUS

Youngsters of this sign are curious and adventurous. They seem to take an interest in anything and everything that moves. Interestingly, they are often born into easygoing families, of parents who are connected with clerical, religious or academic institutions. They are outgoing children, full of sunshine, who love the outdoors and tend to excel at sports and foreign languages.

RELATING TO OTHERS
YOUR EMOTIONAL PATTERN

"Don't fence me in" is the cry of the Moon-in-Sagittarius sign. Belonging to this group, then, means that you value your freedom more than just about any other aspect of life. So, when it comes to romantic relationships, you have a habit of becoming restless the moment you feel you are getting in too deeply. For a start, you dislike clingy or over-dependent partners. Not especially the jealous type yourself, you resent anyone who is jealous of you or who tries to tie you down. In the company of such people you become off-hand and insensitive to their feelings.

As a lover, you are spontaneous and passionate, but you must learn to give others space to develop their own feelings in their own time. If you do tie the knot, it should be to a partner who is as emotionally uncomplicated as you are yourself but also someone who passionately shares your beliefs and philosophical views. However, Sagittarius-Moon natives can actually live quite happily without an intense love relationship in their lives – but only so long as they have a wide network of supportive friends around them.

Honest as the livelong day, you are emotionally open and frank. Little embarrasses you, least of all talking about your most intimate feelings or experiences, and you are constantly surprised to find that others are not as candid or forthright as yourself in these matters. Consequently, you have a tendency to put your foot in it, or to embarrass those less thick-skinned than yourself with insensitive questions or tactless disclosures.

But, full of bonhomie, cheerful and carefree, you have the knack of infecting everyone you meet with your own enthusiasm and optimism, which means that you make friends wherever you go. You are an adventure par excellence and at your happiest when you are, literally, or metaphorically, on the road.

ARIES

Both adventurous and highly charged, both seeking challenge and distant horizons, this partnership offers excellent prospects and very few dull moments – in or out of bed.

TAURUS

As a Taurus-Moon, your partner needs a sense of permanence and stability under his or her feet. But your Sagittarian-Moon hates to be tied down. There is little in common between you, it appears.

GEMINI

Despite the fact that Sagittarian-Moons are at the opposite end of the spectrum to Gemini-Moons, this combination has been known to work nicely.

CANCER

With different attitudes and disparate ambitions, you and your partner are unlikely to want the same things in life. At the end of the day, neither finds the other truly understanding.

LEO

What a fiery, dynamic due you two make! This has all the ingredients of a powerful love affair. With your shared interests and similar ways of experiencing the world, you are bound to go far together.

VIRGO

Virgo-Moons like to feel that they have their feet on terra firma, but Sagittarius-Moons dislike being pinned down. You are both too self-sufficient in your own ways to expect this relationship to work in the long term.

LIBRA

You both like your freedom, so that is something you have in common. A little knowledge of when to share and when to leave well alone will go a long way in this relationship.

SCORPIO

Your partner's Scorpio-Moon is possessive and demands complete devotion. You need freedom and a looser framework in which to relate. You will both constantly be chasing different goals.

SAGITTARIUS

An understanding and richly philosophical relationship. You will know how to get the most out of life and even the most insignificant experience together will prove deeply rewarding.

CAPRICORN

You might as well face it, Capricorn-Moons and Sagittarian-Moons live on completely different planets. Making this relationship work can be an uphill struggle.

AQUARIUS

Your Moon signs have a lot in common, not least that you both recognize the other's need for space. In many ways, though, this is likely to be a highly unconventional pairing, and perhaps that is precisely what gives this partnership its momentum.

PISCES

Not the easiest of relationships for the reason that your Sagittarian-Moon is so freedom-loving whereas your partner's Pisces-Moon is clingy and dependent.

KEY CHARACTER POINTS

Your instinctive response is:	cautious and reserved
Your best characteristics are:	industrious and a strong sense of responsibility
Your negative qualities are:	a certain snobbishness and emotional detachment
You dislike:	childish behavior
You need:	status, position and recognition for your efforts
You must:	learn to moderate your cynicism.

THE ESSENTIAL YOU

Efficient, down-to-earth and hard-working, you take a serious, mature attitude to life. Other people sometimes interpret your ultra-cautious nature incorrectly as pessimistic. Ambition is a positive spur and you put in long hours to achieve the position and status to which you aspire. Your staying power and willingness to work your way up the ladder means that, sooner or later, you will gain the power, respect and recognition you seek.

LIFESTYLE

THE CAPRICORN MOON AT HOME

Traditional and formal are your tastes in furniture and architecture. Preferring to keep your environment simple, you do not appreciate ornate furniture or over-embellished interiors. People with this Moon placement tend to be house-proud, so at home there is a place for everything, and everything in its place.

YOUR SUN AND MOON SIGN COMBINATION CHART

This shows just how well your outward persona (Sun sign) and inner personality (Moon sign) are integrated. YOUR MOON IN CAPRICORN WITH:

YOUR SUN IN...	COMBINATION KEYNOTES	STAR RATING	
Aries	Determined	****	
Taurus	Very sound	*****	
Gemini	Well-organized	***	
Cancer	Home-oriented	**	
Leo	A born leader	****	
Virgo	Methodical	*****	
Libra	Class-conscious	**	*Highly subjective
Scorpio	Powerful	****	** At odds with yourself
Sagittarius	Charitable	**	*** Need to work toward
Capricorn	Workaholic	*	achieving inner balance
Aquarius	One step ahead	***	**** In harmony
Pisces	Self-effacing	**	***** Strongly integrated

YOU AND YOUR FAMILY

Capricorn-Moon subjects often take after their fathers. Their mothers are likely to have been forceful individuals, never overtly affectionate, but achievement-motivated and ambitious for their children. Indeed, this is something you carry through to your own offspring, for you dearly want to see them succeed in life. You expect them to knuckle down and work as hard as you do. If they don't, you are quick to show your disapproval.

AT WORK

Perhaps the hardest-working and most industrious Moon sign, you excel in efficiency and organizational skills. You are practical and logical, using your initiative to get things done. Colleagues and employers soon learn that you are steady, reliable, responsible and always prepared to go the extra mile. You work such long hours that you are in danger of becoming a workaholic. The financial sector, civic or corporate management and local politics would suit your talents well.

UNWIND BY:

watching a funny movie.

MONEY MATTERS

You work hard and save your money. You have frugal tastes so your money stays in the bank and grows steadily. Capricorn-Moon natives have been known to make fortunes by dint of their industriousness.

HEALTH NOTES

Natives of this Moon sign have a wiry constitution, so although they may look lean and spare they tend to be long-lived. The bones and joints may give them problems in later life, however – particularly rheumatism or arthritis, and especially in the knees.

CHILDREN BORN WITH THE MOON IN CAPRICORN

These children are born with an old head on young shoulders, which is just as well since, for whatever reason, they have to grow up fast. Sometimes, this placement can indicate that the parents are elderly and the child feels responsible for the family from an early age. Family life tends to be restricted and children of this sign often suffer a lack of demonstrative affection, which may mar their own ability to form loving relationships later in life.

RELATING TO OTHERS
YOUR EMOTIONAL PATTERN

If you were born with the Moon in Capricorn, you are a cool customer and you come across as distant and aloof. You're not given to overt displays of feeling, don't care for too much body contact, and sloppy sentimentality turns you off completely. But, although your head rules your heart, you do have a generous nature and, when it comes to relationships, you are practical and mature.

Never the sort to play silly games or to go in for one-night stands, no-one could ever accuse you of being a flighty lover. On the contrary, you take your responsibilities seriously and, once you have given your word, you will remain faithful and true. Before embarking on that solemn commitment you will have thought through the consequences very carefully, for you are emotionally cautious and never rush into a relationship.

Customs and social conventions must be observed in your world. Although maintaining proprieties may indeed inhibit the free flow of spontaneous emotion, you feel that there is a correct way to go about things and you like to think that you follow the right path and thereby do your duty. If you didn't, you would worry dreadfully about what other people might think of you.

And then, of course, there is the question of status and position. These are fundamentally important to a Capricorn-Moon individual. Either you are busy climbing your own ladder of success, or you will want a partner with drive and ambition to root for, encourage – or push, if need be.

Sometimes you try to convince yourself that, as long as you are financially secure and in a good occupation with a prestigious position in life, love and affection are not really necessary. But, when you sit down and think about it, you soon come to the conclusion that life is pretty bleak without someone special to share all your troubles and your triumphs.

ARIES

The chances of this combination lasting will be greatly improved if you and your partner happen to be in business together, since you will be able to channel your considerable, but disparate, passions into the success of your company.

TAURUS

There is a wonderful meeting of hearts between these two Moon signs, which bodes extremely well for a compatible and lasting relationship together. Top marks for a solid and stable union.

GEMINI

There is very little meeting of minds and hearts between Gemini-Moons and Capricorn-Moons. As a result, you and your partner would irritate each other, and trying to stay together could prove an uphill struggle.

CANCER

Despite the fact that your Moons are in opposite signs, this combination has all the makings of a highly successful partnership. All in all, a splendid match.

LEO

Not the easiest of pairings, since your partner's extravagance would affront your ideas about domestic budgeting and your Capricorn-Moon would not hesitate to puncture your partner's Leo-Moon pride.

VIRGO

With both Moons in Earth signs, you each know exactly what the other wants and needs. This, therefore, is a splendid combination with excellent chances for durability and success.

LIBRA

Your Moon is dedicated to hard work, while your partner's Moon tends toward indolence. Libra-Moons are light-hearted. You can be a stern moralist. There are too many fundamental differences here.

SCORPIO

There is great attraction between you that augurs well for a lasting union. However, both of you are dedicated in your own way but in different directions. You must try to find a common path.

SAGITTARIUS

You might as well face it, Capricorn-Moons and Sagittarian-Moons live on completely different planets. Making this relationship work will call on all your resources, and more besides.

CAPRICORN

A strong match since both of you experience the world in the same way and share similar ambitions. You are both heavily work-oriented, which will bring success and rewards, especially so if you are in business together.

AQUARIUS

There are undeniable differences between you, yet Aquarius-Moon can lift your spirits and you can help to ground your partner.

PISCES

Problems, problems, problems... Capricorn-Moons may be described as rock-hard, while Pisces-Moons are soft as putty. The equation simply does not add up.

KEY CHARACTER POINTS

Your instinctive response is:	cool but friendly
Your best characteristics are:	sincerity and humanitarian zeal
Your negative qualities are:	eccentricity and a tendency to deny your feelings
You dislike:	maintaining the status quo
You need:	a mission in life
You must:	learn to give yourself emotionally to those you love.

THE ESSENTIAL YOU

Having the Moon in the sign of Aquarius means that you are endowed with extraordinary flair and originality. With your far-sightedness, you have a rather unusual imagination and often come up with ideas that others consider odd or eccentric. Odd though they may seem now, these are the very ideas that in 10 or 20 years' time become accepted standards. Driven by humanitarian instincts to improve the world, you enjoy immersing yourself in issues of global importance.

LIFESTYLE

THE AQUARIUS MOON AT HOME

Ultra-modern is the Aquarius-Moon preference when it comes to the home and domestic environment. Here, there will be experimental shapes or color schemes and the whole look will be quite different to other houses in the street. Housework is not your forte, your attitude being that there are too many other interests in life to waste time on cleaning up.

YOUR SUN AND MOON SIGN COMBINATION CHART

This shows just how well your outward persona (Sun sign) and inner personality (Moon sign) are integrated.
YOUR MOON IN AQUARIUS WITH:

YOUR SUN IN...	COMBINATION KEYNOTES	STAR RATING
Aries	Controversial	***
Taurus	Provident	***
Gemini	Electric	*****
Cancer	Compassionate	**
Leo	Impulsive	**
Virgo	Tender-hearted	**
Libra	Easygoing	*****
Scorpio	Insightful	**
Sagittarius	Original	****
Capricorn	Far-seeing	**
Aquarius	Eccentric	*
Pisces	Flights of fancy	**

* Highly subjective
** At odds with yourself
*** Need to work toward achieving inner balance
**** In harmony
***** Strongly integrated

YOU AND YOUR FAMILY

Family life in your household is likely to be as unconventional as your Aquarian-Moon character. For example, you may have called your parents by their first names. Or perhaps there was a wide age difference between your parents, or is now between you and your partner. Or possibly your parents had unusual occupations – astronauts, professors, or geniuses of some sort.

AT WORK

Scientific work is a natural occupation for you, but a job that is not run-of-the-mill tends to draw your interest. You might join the media as a correspondent or go into film-making. Your certainty and far-sightedness would certainly pay off in the fashion industry or in dealing in the futures market. And because you are brilliant at logical thinking and delight in giving advice, belonging to an advisory team or think tank would suit you well. But it will be the charitable organizations, or working for the good of the community, that will appeal to you most.

UNWIND BY:

playing chess or computer games with your friends.

MONEY MATTERS

Money per se holds no great fascination for you and if you do invest, you will be highly discriminating, choosing to put your money only into those companies with a proven ecological or ethical track record.

HEALTH NOTES

Ankles, shins and calves are the vulnerable areas for Aquarius-Moons. Circulatory problems, such as high blood pressure, may develop later in life.

CHILDREN BORN WITH THE MOON IN AQUARIUS

A child born with this Moon placement may seem like the cuckoo in the nest. It may be that he or she does not physically resemble any other family member, or that his or her tastes, preferences or behavior will be markedly different to the rest. These youngsters develop into very bright or exceptionally gifted children who, because of their friendly nature and love of people, should never be isolated, but left to work as part of a team.

RELATING TO OTHERS
YOUR EMOTIONAL PATTERN

Being born with the Moon in this sign does not encourage you to forge deep attachments. In fact, because you are such a gregarious person, you prefer a large network of friends and acquaintances rather than a serious all-encompassing one-to-one type of relationship. You are very open about your feelings, and truly genuine in your sentiments, but curiously surprised when you find that others are not quite as dispassionate when it comes to matters of the heart as you yourself are.

The problem, if there is one, lies in your views and attitudes about human emotions which, like your progressive intellectual ideas, may be described as radical or advanced.

You possess an innate tolerance and open-mindedness, and so your approach to relationships is somewhat unconventional in comparison to the norm. For example, open marriages or *ménage à trois*, both of which many people find totally unacceptable, seem to be quite normal to you. It is precisely this kind of unorthodox character trait that makes others often see you as being unemotional and detached.

The Moon in this placement, as in Gemini and Libra, the other two Air signs, shows that you are a multi-faceted character – a chameleon who changes shape and color according to your environment and company. You live in the present. What you were last month, yesterday – even half an hour ago – was then. Now is now and that is all that counts. For the Aquarius-Moon person, it is always the moment that is to be experienced.

With this philosophy, then, it is not surprising that your friends and partners find you unpredictable, as you suddenly and for no apparent reason change your mind or your feelings, turning yesterday's belief on its head in favor of today's ideology. And this is exactly what makes you so fascinating, so original and so exciting to be with. One thing is certain – life can never be dull if it is shared with a partner who has an Aquarian Moon.

ARIES

With the Moon in this sign, you will find it easy to respect your partner's need for independence and personal freedom. In return, your Aries-Moon partner will appreciate your need for privacy. In this partnership there is enough tolerance and understanding to make it work.

TAURUS

An Aquarian Moon has little in common with a Taurus Moon, since each has different needs and wants different things from life. Consequently, there is no real meeting ground here.

GEMINI

A splendidly amicable relationship where each partner is cool and independent, yet both see eye-to-eye. An easy pairing, with every chance of long-term success.

CANCER

Aquarius-Moons and Cancer-Moons are emotionally poles apart – one is distant and remote, the other clinging and dependent. Such differences are difficult to reconcile.

LEO

In many ways chalk and cheese, this combination has been known to work surprisingly successfully. Though you come from opposite ends of the spectrum, there is much to unite you.

VIRGO

Your Aquarius-Moon relishes the unpredictable. Your partner's Virgo-Moon delights in being punctilious. Unless you both find a compromise, the odds would seem to be stacked against you.

LIBRA

Fun, friendship, understanding – you share so many characteristics and have such a wide variety of interests in common that life will be led in peaceful co-existence. A terrific combination.

SCORPIO

Your partner's Scorpio-Moon is insistent. Your Aquarius-Moon is cold and distant. There is little agreement between you and this can lead to tension and discord.

SAGITTARIUS

Your Moon signs have a lot in common, not least that you both recognize the other's need for space. In many ways, though, this is likely to be a highly unconventional pairing, and perhaps that is precisely what gives your partnership its momentum.

CAPRICORN

There are undeniable differences between you, yet Capricorn-Moon can ground you while you can help to lift your partner's spirits. This is, however, a sobering relationship for both concerned.

AQUARIUS

An unconventional couple with an unorthodox attitude to life and relationships. Of all the signs, an Aquarius-Moon individual is likely to marry later in life rather than earlier.

PISCES

Aquarius-Moon coupled with Pisces-Moon is likely to produce a somewhat turbulent union. Each, however, has immense curiosity about what makes the other tick and the mystery will draw the two of you together.

MOON IN PISCES

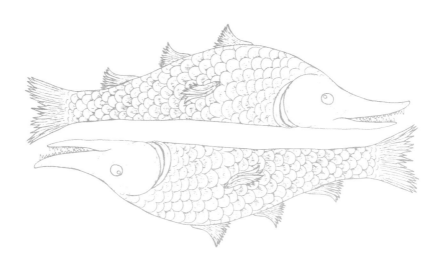

KEY CHARACTER POINTS

Your instinctive response is: gentle and sympathetic

Your best characteristics are: creative talent and an ability to empathize with others

Your negative qualities are: moodiness and a tendency to play the victim

You dislike: aggression in any form

You need: understanding and support

You must: learn to live in the real world.

THE ESSENTIAL YOU

People who are born with the Moon in Pisces are tender flowers who need careful nurturing and protection. Belonging to this sign means that you are trusting and somewhat naive. Dreamy, romantic and compassionate, you fantasize a fairytale world that is as far removed from the harsh realities of everyday life as you can make it. The Moon in this placement works on your emotions, making you ultra-sensitive by sending overwhelming tidal waves of feeling through your heart. To hurt or offend others is your greatest fear. To find love and serenity is your dearest wish.

LIFESTYLE

THE PISCEAN MOON AT HOME

With the strong creative talents that are bound up with your Moon sign, your home will be tastefully decorated and artistically inspired. Love of music and an appreciation of the arts will be in evidence. You are drawn to water and ideally should try to live by a river or near the sea.

PEOPLE WHO SHARE YOUR MOON SIGN

Elvis Presley
Kim Kardashian
Grace Kelly
J R R Tolkien
Hillary Clinton
P D James
Marie Stopes
Michelle Obama
Rita Ora
Catherine Zeta-Jones
Rachel Weisz
Sarah Michelle Gellar
Leonard Cohen
Axl Rose
Leonardo da Vinci
Michelangelo
Martin Luther King
Che Guevara
Edgar Allan Poe
Usain Bolt

YOUR SUN AND MOON SIGN COMBINATION CHART

This shows just how well your outward persona (Sun sign) and inner personality (Moon sign) are integrated.
YOUR MOON IN PISCES WITH:

YOUR SUN IN...	COMBINATION KEYNOTES	STAR RATING
Aries	Resilient	**
Taurus	Creatively talented	***
Gemini	Storyteller	***
Cancer	Nurturing instinct	*****
Leo	Romantic	***
Virgo	Perceptive	**
Libra	Dreamy	****
Scorpio	Psychoanalytical	*****
Sagittarius	Far-ranging	***
Capricorn	Reserved	**
Aquarius	Committed	**
Pisces	Vulnerable	*

* Highly subjective
** At odds with yourself
*** Need to work toward achieving inner balance
**** In harmony
***** Strongly integrated

YOU AND YOUR FAMILY

For some reason you may not have been as close to your mother as you think a parent and child should be. There may have been difficulties and disappointments or rejections early in your life and, since it is crucial for you to feel strongly bonded to a family group, this apparent lack of understanding or acceptance would have bruised your tender sensitivities and diminished your self-confidence. To your own family, you are selflessly loving, and happiest when you are sharing everything you have with those you love.

AT WORK

Employees with the Moon in Pisces make invaluable team members, always eager to help and to please their colleagues. As one of these, you positively flower in a supportive group of people. A creative environment is essential for you, and so work in the music industry, the fashion business or in the arts would be ideal. Alternatively, you are also drawn to counseling, psychology or psychotherapy. Fringe medicine or alternative therapies also suit your talents.

UNWIND BY:

meditating or taking a walk.

MONEY MATTERS

The least money-conscious of all the Moon signs, when you have any cash you tend to give it away to those you think are more deserving than yourself. A partner who will wisely take your finances in hand for you would be greatly appreciated.

HEALTH NOTES

In one way or another, the feet are frequently a source of problems for the Pisces-Moon individual.

CHILDREN BORN WITH THE MOON IN PISCES

The Moon in Pisces produces sweet and gentle babies who are easily pleased and no trouble to rear. They grow into children with a passive nature and a fertile imagination, able to create a fantasy world into which they withdraw whenever they are upset. Often shy and sensitive, they tend to daydream in class. Tougher kids may find them "drippy" and consequently may tease or bully them. They excel in writing stories and in art.

RELATING TO OTHERS
YOUR EMOTIONAL PATTERN

Sensitive, emotional and sentimental, you are the most romantic of all the signs. Moreover, you have a tender heart that can easily get hurt and this gives you an instinctive understanding of the suffering of others. And, because you are so gentle and compassionate, you make a caring partner, always ready to listen and to lend a helping hand. With your kind nature and dreamy, idealistic approach to relationships, you can be influenced all too easily by other stronger, and sometimes less scrupulous, individuals, who may take advantage of your tender heart.

Criticism and harsh words deeply wound you and crush your spirit. Quarrels and aggressive behavior of any kind literally make you feel ill. If you are caught in the crossfire of conflict – for example – a row in the family, your natural reaction would be to run away, find a job to do in another room perhaps, or go for a long drive, and hope that the storm will have blown itself out by the time you return.

It is possible that others will interpret your withdrawal as pure petulance and accuse you of going into "one of your sulks." In reality, disengaging yourself from the scene of battle is simply your natural defence mechanism, somewhat similar to burying your head in the sand – if you don't see it, it can't possibly be happening, so all is right again with your world. For you desperately want a world that is nice and pleasant, where people live in peace and harmony with each other, where there is no cruelty or suffering, but only love and compassion and empathy for one another.

These are the qualities that you yourself are prepared to give and these are the same qualities that you need a partner to offer to you. In addition, someone who will know how to boost your ego and encourage you to believe in yourself would be ideal.

ARIES

Your tender feelings get short shrift in this relationship, since you find an Aries-Moon partner abrasive and impatient. Passions are certainly steamy between you, but you could end up the one who gets seriously burnt.

TAURUS

With these two Moon placements there are potentially good spin-offs from one to the other. You two, therefore, could be very good for each other.

GEMINI

A Pisces-Moon is perhaps the most emotionally clinging of the Moon signs. A Gemini-Moon is the most elusive. Neither has a true grasp of the other's feelings.

CANCER

Moons in Pisces and Cancer produce gentle, caring people with a loving and affectionate nature, so there will be shared feelings and understanding here. This is an ideal match.

LEO

Although on the surface this might appear a strange combination, yet there is a great deal of romance and enchantment between you and your Leo-Moon partner that will bind you together.

VIRGO

There is no doubt that friendship between you and your Pisces-Moon companion is a sure bet. But when it comes to a more intimate relationship, you may find that each soon loses patience with the other.

LIBRA

Both creative, both lovers of beauty, both needy of harmony and tranquility. Sex can be sweet and gentle between you, but ultimately you will each blame the other for the faults of your own respective making.

SCORPIO

Emotionally, you two make an ideal match. Able to experience life's highs and lows with the same heart, you are magnetically drawn to each other. A brilliant liaison.

SAGITTARIUS

Not the easiest of relationships because your Pisces-Moon is clingy and dependent whereas your partner's Sagittarian-Moon is freedom-loving.

CAPRICORN

Problems, problems, problems. Capricorn-Moons may be described as rock-hard while Pisces-Moons are soft as putty. This equation simply does not add up.

AQUARIUS

Aquarius-Moon coupled with Pisces-Moon is likely to produce a somewhat turbulent romantic union. Each of you, however, has immense curiosity about what makes the other tick and the mystery will draw you together.

PISCES

A dreamy, idealistic and blissful romance. In reality, you lack the necessary worldly practicality that is essential to keep body and soul together.

CHAPTER 7

SUCCESS IN BUSINESS

As any comedian or stockbroker knows only too well, timing is of the essence. Being on the right spot at exactly the right moment can make all the difference between success and failure. This applies to all areas of our lives, but it is especially true in the world of business. It really pays to know just when to schedule meetings in order to reach an amicable consensus; when to begin projects to ensure a really satisfactory completion; when to sign contracts, target publicity campaigns, ask for a raise or go for promotion, apply for a new job, set up on one's own, expand the business, seek a bank loan, employ and dismiss staff – and so on.

STAYING AHEAD OF THE GAME

The key to really successful timing can be found in the movements of the Moon as its daily cycles influence the tide of events, affect moods and expectations, and generally alter the whole tempo of life. To make sure that you really stay ahead of the game, you must learn to adapt to and work with the shifting requirements that are imposed by the changing lunar phases.

SOME GOLDEN RULES OF GOOD TIMING

In general, any new ventures launched during the two weeks in which the Moon is increasing are more likely to meet with success than those begun after the Full Moon. If you try to put a new scheme into motion under a waning Moon, the wheels will grind very slowly indeed and the project is likely to fizzle out before it even begins to gather steam.

On the other hand, the period from Full to New Moon is propitious for anything to do with bringing matters to a close. This might include:

- slimming down operations
- shedding staff
- clearing up
- researching new lines
- investigating competitors.

WORKING WITH THE TIMES

Those who keep an eye on the money markets may be interested to know of a powerful cycle of highs and lows that is linked to the lunar phases. There are, of course, other cycles, such as the Jupiter-Saturn planetary combination, which also have important triggering effects on the rise and fall of the markets. Some are long-term cycles affecting world economies over a period of several years. The lunar cycle may not be as dramatic, but it has a very definite effect on a monthly basis.

It appears that a downturn occurs both at the time of the New Moon and at the Full Moon, while a significant rise may be expected eight and nine days after the New Moon. Perhaps keeping notes, comparing a few statistics, or plotting monthly graphs may bear this out and help decision-making when it comes to investments and trading.

HEEDING THE SIGNS

In addition, there seems to be some evidence that whichever sign the Moon is in at these sensitive times may also affect market trends, as each sign has its own unique "nature." Use the tables at the end of the book to discover what sign the Moon is in at any given time and consult the box headed "Signs of the Times" (pp.93–4) to learn how to work with this important influence.

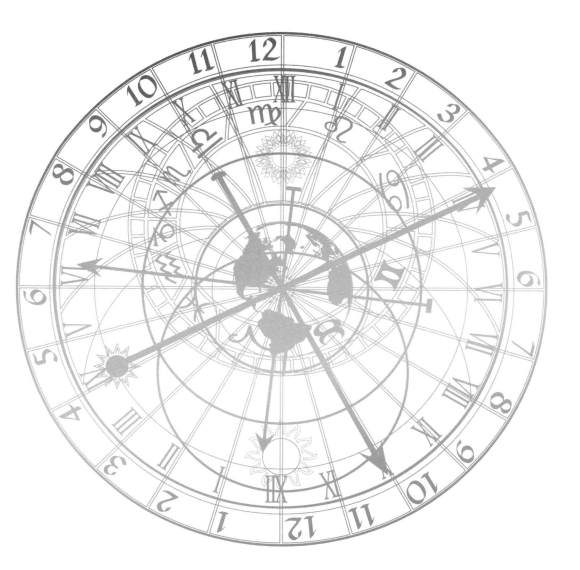

NEW MOON DAY

Think of the day on which the New Moon falls as a Dynamic Day, or D-Day for short. This is the point in the month when the Moon begins to grow again, redoubling her light and reflecting new creative energy on all worldly things. This is a time to move up a gear and plan our aspirations for the future – personal and business ones. Write down five to 10 key objectives, register them consciously and then work to bring them to fruition – in the short term, over the next four weeks or, in the longer term, over the next few months.

1. Generate ideas and begin all new projects from the day after the New Moon up until the day before the next Full Moon.
2. The two weeks following the New Moon are periods of expansion and high-profile activities. Use them to promote yourself, your work or your company.
3. Make plans, set objectives and start the ball rolling on the day of the New Moon.
4. Evaluate and reassess your agenda and business plans after the Full Moon.
5. It is unwise to seek work, apply for a new position or put a new product on the market in the two weeks between the Full Moon and the next New Moon.

NEW MOON TO FIRST QUARTER

- initiate new deals
- draw up contracts
- sign documents and agreements
- catch up on correspondence
- make new contacts
- apply for a promotion or seek a new job
- introduce new ideas/submit proposals
- announce takeover bids
- enter into partnerships
- set projects in motion
- sue for damages
- start new construction work
- arrange important board meetings
- stand for election
- elect new members
- interview people, draw up shortlists, hire staff
- publish or broadcast favorable performance figures

FIRST QUARTER TO FULL MOON

- launch advertising ventures
- pursue all high-profile activities, such as promoting the company's image
- seek legal or financial advice
- lend money
- inform workforce of pay rises or bonus schemes

DAY OF THE FULL MOON

- switch gear, and assess progress
- concentrate on bringing existing projects to fruition over the next two weeks
- if necessary, plan to eliminate all time-consuming and unproductive procedures

FULL MOON TO THIRD QUARTER

- undertake all investigative, undercover work or projects of a secret nature
- concentrate on doing useful research
- explore new markets
- undertake profile studies of customers or clients
- prepare budgets and costings
- take stock
- carry out maintenance work
- write up reports

- review company policies
- draw up new agendas
- go on study courses

THIRD QUARTER TO NEW MOON

- stand down or resign
- downsize
- demote or dismiss staff
- inform workforce of pay cuts
- restructure
- delegate
- dissolve partnerships
- take out a loan
- fight a lawsuit
- publish or broadcast poor performance figures
- call a strike
- clean, paint or refurbish work premises
- clear decks
- tie up loose ends
- prepare to implement new projects during the next phase of the Moon

MOON IN ARIES

Conducive to: Trading, buying, selling, making decisions on the spur of the moment, implementing tough measures, taking advantage of situations, launching new schemes, setting up new businesses (especially those of a risky or pioneering nature)

Avoid: Going in with all guns blazing, acting on impulse, skipping over the essentials

Beware: Other people's bad tempers

Important days for activities concerning: The automobile industries, mechanical trades, sports, pioneering enterprises

MOON IN TAURUS

Conducive to: Making investments, leasing or renting property, taking on new staff, decorating/refurbishing business premises, showing empathy to one's colleagues

Avoid: A tendency to sit back, digging in your heels, missing good opportunities

Beware: Other people's inflexibility

Important days for activities concerning: The building industries, home furnishings, interior designs, farming, agriculture, horticulture, garden design, confectionery trade

MOON IN GEMINI

Conducive to: Trade, buying, selling, making business trips, generating new ideas, correspondence, decorating, reorganizing/refurbishing business premises, introducing new machinery/technology, giving presentations, crisis management

Avoid: Distractions from the main issue, a shallow appreciation of the situation, being underhand or economical with the truth, having too many irons in the fire

Beware: Con artists

Important days for activities concerning: The media, audio-visual technology, communications industries, printing trade, news outlets and magazines, newsagents, postal services, toy manufacturers

MOON IN CANCER

Conducive to: Signing documents, setting up a company nursery, bringing unsatisfactory conditions to an end

Avoid: Thinking too narrow-mindedly, a reluctance to take risks, being oversensitive to criticism, being influenced by other people's negative moods

Beware: People who think the world owes them a living

Important days for activities concerning: Domestic goods, property and real estate, furniture manufacturers, childcare products, marine and fishing industries

MOON IN LEO

Conducive to: Leasing or renting property, taking control of the situation, money deals, eliciting support, lucky breaks

Avoid: Overspending, a domineering attitude to your colleagues/workforce, forming intimate relationships with fellow workers

Beware: Other people's indiscretions

Important days for activities concerning: Luxury goods, designer brands, cosmetics industries, first-class travel, hotel trade, the theatre, children's goods, lotteries and gambling industries

MOON IN VIRGO

Conducive to: Trade, buying, selling, business trips, reorganization, presenting detailed accounts, practical demonstrations, methodical reviews of mail-shots, taking stock

Avoid: Missing the overall picture while worrying about details, being overcritical, making judgemental errors

Beware: Other people's fussiness

Important days for activities concerning: Hospitals, the medical profession, the veterinary services, the pharmaceutical industries, statisticians, precision-tools manufacturers, health and wellness outlets, diet and fitness outlets, complementary health practitioners, pet food manufacturers

MOON IN LIBRA

Conducive to: Decorating, refurbishing business premises, disclosing information, forging new business alliances, marketing, human resources, public relations, signing contracts, negotiations, settling disputes, going on a company outing, office parties

Avoid: Sitting on the fence, expecting others to take your share of the responsibility, making open enemies, any hint of underhandedness

Beware: Other people's indecisiveness

Important days for activities concerning: The diplomatic corps, the music and entertainment industry, the arts, haute couture, bridal and wedding outfitters, advertising groups, public relations

MOON IN SCORPIO

Conducive to: Signing documents, leasing or renting property, painting business premises, projecting confidence, solving problems, making discreet enquiries, stealing a march on competitors, making major deals while mental faculties are acute

Avoid: A reluctance to disclose all the facts, playing cards too close to one's chest, becoming too intense, operating a secret agenda, pretending to know more than one does

Beware: Other people's resentment, making enemies

Important days for activities concerning: The police force, surgical procedures, research companies, the secret service, butchery trade, mining, investment management, funeral directors, mortuaries

MOON IN SAGITTARIUS

Conducive to: Trade, promotions, advertising, important correspondence, travel, business meetings, lending or borrowing money, legal or judicial matters

Avoid: Becoming blind to detail, restlessness, financial irresponsibility, slapdash work

Beware: Other people's carelessness

Important days for activities concerning: Publishing, the law, travel industries, foreign trade and communications, religious institutions, teaching, higher education

MOON IN CAPRICORN

Conducive to: Getting down to brass tacks, working overtime, high finances, rearranging the filing system, drawing up new schedules, administration, asking for promotion, setting up new business, entertaining the boss

Avoid: An inflexible attitude, overworking, depression, a lack of compassion toward your colleagues/workforce

Beware: Other people's ruthless ambition

Important days for activities concerning: Banking and financial services, real estate, the local council, political parties, the head of state, royalty, superstars

MOON IN AQUARIUS

Conducive to: Leasing or renting property, improving working conditions, money transfers, decorating/refurbishing business premises, eliciting cooperation from colleagues, think tanks, future projections

Avoid: Favoring the group at the expense of the individual, taking an overly detached point of view, going off on a tangent

Beware: Interruptions

Important days for activities concerning: The power industries, scientific research institutions, trade unions, new inventions, manufacturers or electronic or hi-tech equipment, clubs, groups and societies, social services

MOON IN PISCES

Conducive to: Signing documents, drawing up financial agreements, sending out mass mailings, making any necessary repairs to equipment, taking stock

Avoid: Looking at your prospects through rose-colored glasses, being too easily influenced, illogical reasoning, self-doubts

Beware: Other people's unrealistic expectations, behind-the-scenes machinations

Important days for activities concerning: Film and television, petrochemical industries, oil refineries, the brewery trade, shipping, chiropody, shoe manufacturers

COMPANY PROFILES

No matter how big or small the company, whether it is well established or just being set up, drawing up its own astrological chart would be of enormous benefit in highlighting the company's progress. Of greatest importance to any business is the significance of the Moon, as the factors she represents will yield especially invaluable insights – not only about the day-to-day running of the business, but also about its future prospects and standing in the commercial world. For a start, company fortunes tend to run in cycles: the 7th/8th, 14th/15th, 21st/22nd, 28th/29th years being significant either in terms of an upturn or downturn in yearly figures, expansion, contraction, introduction of new lines and so on. Note that these intervals correspond to lunar timing. Recognizing these patterns in the affairs of the company means that products and new developments can be targeted to take advantage of the forthcoming trade.

THE PUBLIC VIEW

Apart from the company's progress, the Moon in the chart will also, and most importantly, represent the public, including how the company is perceived in the outside world and how the markets will respond to its products. Consequently, studying the position and aspects that the Moon makes within the charts will give a fair indication of the company's fate in the years to come.

CHAPTER EIGHT

MIND, BODY AND HEALTH

Have you noticed how some days you wake up feeling so full
of positive energy that you could climb a mountain?

On other days, though, all you want to do is curl up and sleep. If you start to take note, you will find that these moods come and go on a cyclical basis. This pattern can often be matched to the Moon phases, and the particular astrological sign through which the Moon is travelling.

What happens is that the lunar phases and sign placements interact to affect our minds and bodies. As the Moon moves signs every two and a quarter days, so the nature of the influences changes, which also alters our mood – our perception of our situation.

YOUR HEALTH AND THE MOON

From the New Moon to the Full Moon is a time for new initiatives. Full Moon is the time for reaping rewards from our hard labors. With the waning Moon we should review endeavors and correct mistakes. Through the dark of the Moon it is advantageous to meditate, research, draw inner strength and lay plans in preparation for the new energies that appear with the emergence of the New Moon.

FROM NEW MOON TO FULL MOON

- A productive time when efforts will grow visibly
- Begin new projects
- Put ideas in motion
- Get medical treatment
- Have beauty treatments
- Have your hair cut if you want fast regrowth
- Become engaged/decide to live together/get married
- Make long-term relationship plans

FIRST QUARTER MOON

If you are trying to locate a lost phone number or hoping to meet someone whose address you've mislaid, look for these things around the Moon's First Quarter and they should simply fall into your lap.

FULL MOON

- Feelings are heightened
- Matters appear larger than life
- Delay all decisions to another day
- Have your hair cut if you want it to grow back thicker

FROM FULL MOON TO NEW MOON

- Pluck eyebrows
- Have hair cut if you want to slow its growth
- Have hair dyed
- Use depilatory treatments
- Have dental work
- Begin health regime
- Settle disputes with friends and family

LAST QUARTER MOON

- Get rid of clutter and everything that is causing an obstruction
- Throw out anything (or anyone) you no longer want or need
- Rest and recuperate
- Good time for self-analysis

MENTAL HEALTH AND PHYSICAL HEALTH
MOON MADNESS

That the Moon influences our state of mind has been recognized throughout history. Medical staff in mental institutions have been especially convinced of this phenomenon and attempted suicides, psychotic behavior and admissions to special care units tend to increase around Full Moon. The link between madness and the Moon has even been incorporated into several languages – the Italian phrase, *avere la luna*, which means "to be angry," translates literally as "having the Moon."

SURGERY AND THE FULL MOON

If possible, avoid surgery around the Full Moon. Studies have revealed that blood flows more freely at this time of the month and is slower to clot. In fact, carrying out operations on Full Moon days has been banned by medical authorities in certain parts of the world. Since blood flow is more sluggish around the Last Quarter and New Moon times, these phases are more conducive to the healing process following surgery because the likelihood of hemorrhaging is reduced. The same advice applies to any dental work that involves extractions.

ILLNESS AND THE LUNAR CYCLE

If you fall sick between New Moon and Full Moon, your illness will normally be worse and take longer to shake off than illness contracted during the waning period (Full Moon to New Moon).

INTOXICATING EFFECTS

Have you ever wondered why the same amount of alcohol sometimes has a greater effect on you than at other times? This may be because the strength of alcohol is intensified on the day of the Full Moon.

BODY IMAGE

Take advantage of the enhancing influences of the Moon in Taurus, Leo or Libra and have beauty treatments, facial makeovers or massages. These are also excellent times to change your image, hairstyle and wardrobe.

A health regime that involves "shedding" in some way – such as losing weight, getting rid of physical or emotional clutter, or giving up smoking or chocolate, for example – is more likely to be successful if it is begun when the Moon is decreasing, so plan to start after the Full Moon. It also helps if this coincides with the Moon being in the signs of Aries, Gemini, Leo, Virgo, Sagittarius or Aquarius.

MARRIAGES MADE IN HEAVEN?

It would be ridiculous to expect people to arrange to meet their prospective partners, or even to choose to fall in love, only when the planetary patterns are auspicious. If we all did that, relationships would be pretty thin on the ground.

On the other hand, we do give considerable forethought and planning time to the arrangements of a wedding, so why not also give some thought, when wedding plans are being made, to the movements of the Moon? Try to arrange the ceremony for a day when the influences are especially beneficial to the ongoing contentment and stability of a relationship.

GOOD VIBRATIONS

In general, setting up home together or getting married are best begun during an increasing Moon period – that is, from New Moon to the day before the next Full Moon. The good auspices at this time will help the relationship to develop and prosper.

Avoid the days around the Full Moon when increased tension is likely to strain the occasion and throw a shadow of volatility and restlessness over the union. The waning Moon period should also be avoided, as this brings with it a decrease in fortune and diminishing prospects.

If you want to understand the nature of the union itself, then you should examine the qualities of the Moon sign in operation at the time of the wedding. Read on…

THE EARTH SIGNS –
TAURUS, VIRGO, CAPRICORN

Permanence, endurance and security underlie marriages begun when the Moon is in one of the Earth signs. Under Taurus, the couple will be staunch and persevere together through thick and thin. With a Virgo rulership, the couple will be conscientious and hardworking, but expect some critical nitpicking, too. A Capricorn Moon denotes an ambitious pair who are solid, stable and looked upon as pillars of society.

THE AIR SIGNS –
GEMINI, LIBRA, AQUARIUS

Tying the knot under one of the Air signs endows a bright and breezy character to the relationship, but perhaps one that is not renowned for its permanence. If any fickleness can be curbed, then marriage under a Gemini Moon can be amusing and lighthearted. An elegant and sophisticated union can be expected with the Libra Moon – a sign that, in fact, rules marriages and partnerships in general. Friendship will characterize the Aquarius Moon marriage, although each individual will insist firmly on acting independently of the other.

THE FIRE SIGNS –
ARIES, LEO, SAGITTARIUS

Passion typifies marriages made when the Moon is in a Fire sign. Desire will be impulsive with an Aries Moon at the helm but the ardor may consume itself as rapidly as it began. The auspices for married life are excellent under the romantic and fun-loving Leo Moon. There is room for spiritual growth when the Moon is in Sagittarius but this couple will resent the least hint of being tied down.

THE WATER SIGNS –
CANCER, SCORPIO, PISCES

The Water signs are fundamentally nurturing and with the Moon placed here, the sensual and strongly procreative urges of these signs will also be brought out. A Cancer Moon is one of the most auspicious placements for marriage. Under the sign of Scorpio, jealousy and possessiveness may mar the union. With a Pisces Moon, on the other hand, there will be tenderness and empathy in abundance but, unless addressed, co-dependency might be the cause of problems.

END OF THE AFFAIR

Separation and divorce are, sadly, a fact of life these days. Unhappy though these events may be, if the split is inevitable, then choosing an appropriate time to end the relationship officially can ensure that parting occurs with the least amount of acrimony and rancor. Trying to end the relationship during a Waxing Moon will simply drag out proceedings and increase bad feelings. The Last Quarter, however, is generally thought to ease endings of all kinds and, with the prospect of the New Moon in sight, adds hope for fresh beginnings to come.

RECOMMENDED ACTIVITIES DURING THE WAXING MOON PHASE	RECOMMENDED ACTIVITIES DURING THE WANING MOON PHASE
ARIES • Set yourself a new challenge • Take up a martial art or self-defense discipline • Begin a new exercise regime	• Get your hair cut • Have an eye test • See the dentist
TAURUS • Cook a new recipe • Go to the theater • Make some new cushion covers • Start a savings scheme • Take out a new insurance policy • Work on the garden	• Plan a new color scheme for your bedroom • Put your finances on a firmer footing • Give your lover a massage • Have a relaxing aromatherapy bath • Paint • Play music
GEMINI • Write emails to your friends • Phone up your siblings • Take a computer course • Join a debating society • Make a start on that book you've always wanted to write	• Play a board game with your children • Go to the library • Buy books and writing materials • Put your feet up and read a magazine • Go for a drive in the country
CANCER • Visit your parents • Join an upholstery class • Paint your lounge • Move house • Look up your ancestry • Cook your family's favorite meal	• Take a walk along a river or seashore • Go swimming • Rearrange your furniture • Take a trip down memory lane • Plant a shrub or a tree
LEO • Take the afternoon off and spend it with your partner • Make love • Be creative – paint, write, sew, sculpt, go to the theater/concert/opera • Go to the races/casino • Buy someone a present	• Take the children to the cinema • Tell those you love that you love them • Watch a funny television program • Hang a gilt-framed mirror in your hallway • Be conscious of your own happiness • Sunbathe
VIRGO • Start to eat more healthily • Read up on alternative medicines/therapies • Join a health club • Seek medical diagnoses and treatments • Make new plans • Give your pet an extra cuddle	• Review your daily routine • Cut out bad habits • Have a clean-out day • Go through your wardrobe and pack/give away anything you no longer wear

THINGS TO AVOID	HEALTH TRENDS TO WATCH
• Rashness • Driving too fast • Rushing a job • Wanting to get your way at all costs	• Headaches • Scalds and burns • Cuts • Accidents
• Eating too much • Wanting things you do not have • Being overly possessive	• Sore throat • Laryngitis
• Being too easily distracted • Beginning one job before finishing another	• Nervous tension • Agitation • Restlessness
• Meddling in other people's affairs • Being overly clingy	• Worry • Moodiness • Stomach upsets • Skin problems
• Feelings of insignificance • Resentment • Imagining no one appreciates you	• Backache • Circulatory problems
• Fussing over detail • Being overcritical • Fads	• Irritability • Gastric or dietary upsets

STAYING IN TUNE

As the Moon enters each new sign, the characteristics associated with that sign are "triggered," allowing their influences to color our states of mind and health. Certain activities will harmonize with the prevailing energies; others will prove counter-productive.

As the Moon travels through all the signs in turn each month, a little understanding of these characteristics and their effects means that we can tune in to the changing influences and requirements of each day. We can channel our activities in harmony with the flow, recognizing which tasks will bring satisfaction, which habits we should curb, which part of our body is susceptible and which behavior must be avoided.

RECOMMENDED ACTIVITIES DURING THE WAXING MOON PHASE	RECOMMENDED ACTIVITIES DURING THE WANING MOON PHASE
LIBRA <ul><li>Get married</li><li>Invite friends round</li><li>Go to a concert</li><li>Stream some new music</li><li>Send your partner red roses</li><li>Buy an exquisite item for the house – it needn't be expensive but it must be lovely</li><li>Go on a romantic weekend with your partner</li></ul>	<ul><li>Take your lover out to an intimate restaurant for dinner</li><li>Create a space where you can go for peace and relaxation</li><li>Go to a museum/art gallery</li><li>Make an ikebana flower arrangement</li></ul>
SCORPIO <ul><li>Join a psychology course</li><li>Go for a boat ride</li><li>Look for items that you have mislaid</li><li>Take up a new therapy</li><li>Call up a debt</li><li>Go on a murder-mystery weekend</li><li>Visit an astrologer</li><li>Learn about hypnosis</li></ul>	<ul><li>Seek answers to questions that have been on your mind</li><li>Read a thriller</li><li>Psychoanalyze yourself</li><li>Clear out the cellar</li><li>Watch a spy movie</li><li>Solve a puzzle</li></ul>
SAGITTARIUS <ul><li>Enrol at a college</li><li>Set off on your holidays/travels</li><li>Arrange a camping weekend</li><li>Contact friends/family abroad</li><li>Ride a horse</li><li>Attend a lecture on philosophy</li></ul>	<ul><li>Read a travel book</li><li>Contemplate, meditate or pray</li><li>Go to church</li><li>Take the dog for a walk in the country</li><li>Write up a list of your future aspirations</li></ul>
CAPRICORN <ul><li>Join the local political party</li><li>Spring-clean the house</li><li>Climb a mountain</li><li>Invite your boss to lunch</li><li>Get down to some serious work</li><li>Start a new business</li><li>Buy a smart business suit</li></ul>	<ul><li>Write up a list of the 10 things you want to achieve in your lifetime</li><li>Talk to your partner about your ambitions</li><li>Count the money in your piggybank</li><li>Go on an economy drive</li><li>Tell your lover how you feel about him/her</li></ul>
AQUARIUS <ul><li>Paint your kitchen cabinets electric blue</li><li>Invent something the world needs and doesn't have yet</li><li>Organize a surprise party for a friend's birthday</li><li>Join a club</li><li>Upgrade electronic devices</li><li>Learn a new dance</li></ul>	<ul><li>Rearrange the furniture before you go to bed</li><li>Offer your help at the local school/hospital</li><li>Meet friends for lunch</li></ul>
PISCES <ul><li>Write a romantic story</li><li>Go swimming</li><li>Drink champagne in the bath</li><li>Compose a piece of music</li><li>Take your partner to a dance</li><li>Paint a scene in watercolors</li></ul>	<ul><li>Have reflexology treatment</li><li>Write down your dreams</li><li>Snuggle up to your lover</li><li>Have an early night</li><li>Listen to your favorite music</li></ul>

THINGS TO AVOID	HEALTH TRENDS TO WATCH
• Feelings of being unloved • Loneliness • Stress	• Kidney ailments • Biochemical imbalances
• Jealousy • Spite • Wanting to take control of people and situations • Brooding	• Problems with the reproductive organs • Hemorrhoids
• Boredom • Taking unnecessary risks • Overindulgence	• Liver disorders • Putting on weight
• Worrying about money, position or status • All work and no play	• Toothache • Skin abrasions • Problems of the joints – especially the knees
• Breaking the rules • Rebeling just for the sheer hell of it • Giving notice at your job	• Ankle sprains • Circulatory disorders
• Falling in love with the first person you meet • Changing your mind • Feeling inadequate	• Physical and mental sensitivity • Problems with the feet

MANY HAPPY RETURNS!

Each month, when the Moon returns to your own Moon sign, it is like a little birthday – a marker that sets the tone for the four weeks to come. How you are feeling at that time will find echoes throughout the coming month. Ideally, it would be best to know the exact degree your Moon was in at the very moment of your birth, but that requires a natal chart drawn up by an astrologer. Failing that, knowing the Zodiacal sign in which the Moon was placed when you were born will give a good enough approximation to indicate the trends that will affect you in the month to come. If you have got this far in the book and still don't know your Moon sign, turn to the tables at the end.

CHAPTER 9

HOME HINTS

To keep your home at its best, coordinate your domestic activities with
the appropriate lunar phases, or take advantage of the trends that come
into force as the Moon travels through the different signs.

SPRING-CLEANING

Tackle major cleaning jobs after the Full Moon. The
few days following the Last Quarter are excellent for
thorough cleanings.

BAKING

If you bake your own bread, you might notice that dough
tends to rise higher during the weekend of the increasing
Moon (from New to Full) than in the second half of the
lunar cycle.

BREWING

Many home brewers observe strict rules for when to
bottle their wines and beers. There are two specific times
in the lunar cycle that are especially recommended:
on the day of the Full Moon and on the day of the Last
Quarter. Ideally, the Moon should also be in one of the
water signs – Cancer, Scorpio or Pisces.

DESIGN AND DIY

Paint your house on the days around the Last Quarter
and preferably when the Moon is in Taurus, Leo or
Aquarius. Avoid both the New Moon and times when the

Moon is in Cancer, Scorpio or Pisces – Water signs that
may slow the drying process. Interior design, including
purchasing materials, fares well under a Waxing Moon,
especially one in Taurus, Cancer, Leo, Libra and Aquarius.
Times when the Moon is in Taurus or Cancer are ideal
for working on anything associated with interiors and
soft furnishings, especially furniture and upholstery. If
DIY is involved, schedule your work for when the Moon
is in Capricorn. Get electrical equipment fixed when the
Moon is in Aquarius.

SMART MOVES

Seek and/or buy your new house when the Moon is in
the "home" sign of Cancer. Buying it when the Moon
is in Taurus will give you a sense of security, while the
Moon in Leo will bring love and laughter into your home.
Aquarius will ensure amicable relationships and a house
that is always full of friends. For moving house, choose
the period between the New Moon and the day before
the Full Moon, with the Moon in Taurus, Leo, Scorpio
or Aquarius. If you are building a house, begin to lay
the foundations when the Moon is in Taurus, Leo or
Aquarius, preferably on the day of the Full Moon.

Whether you are throwing a huge party or having a couple of friends over for supper, try checking the planetary favors first:

THE MOON IN ARIES
Ensure you provide some spills and thrills – lay on some games or go out for a champagne picnic – to make it a memorable occasion.

THE MOON IN TAURUS
Provide a prodigious amount of food with several different desserts. Make sure everyone has somewhere to sit – comfort is an absolute must.

THE MOON IN GEMINI
Parties go with a really sociable swing – especially surprise ones.

THE MOON IN CANCER
Go for traditional family get-togethers.

THE MOON IN LEO
Luxury and opulence are very much the key words here. Black tie wll be essential for any social occasion that you organize tonight.

THE MOON IN VIRGO
Healthy eating and the Virgo Moon go hand in hand, so make it a garden party with energy-packed salads and fresh fruits.

THE MOON IN LIBRA
Elegance is the hallmark here, so think quality rather than quantity, and pay attention to presentation. Play soft music and drift into cultured conversation with your guests.

THE MOON IN SCORPIO
The Scorpio Moon is a seductive Moon, so there is bound to be a frisson of sexual tension to the occasion, even when you don't expect it.

THE MOON IN SAGITTARIUS
Informality is the key – create a relaxed, convivial atmosphere, add lots to eat and drink and then just sit back and watch the company mellow.

THE MOON IN CAPRICORN
Capricorn is the sign of status, authority and success, so invite the boss round or book a table at the very best restaurant in town. Formal functions are also highly recommended.

THE MOON IN AQUARIUS
Think up something totally different and imaginative to turn the occasion into a real experience under the Aquarian Moon. A fireworks and bonfire party might be ideal, or else rig up a music and light show and dance the night away.

THE MOON IN PISCES
Illusion is the name of the game when the Moon is in dreamy Pisces – how about a fancy-dress party or a masked ball?

THE MOON IN ARIES

Shopping tip: Excellent for shopping because energies and enthusiasms are at a peak
Buy: Sports clothes and gear, hats, sunglasses, glasses, tools, anything made of metal, cars, DIY materials, anything red
Avoid: Buying on impulse
Timely advice: Have your hair done

THE MOON IN TAURUS

Shopping tip: You'll want value for money with every purchase you make
Buy: Anything practical, consumer durables, luxury goods, cosmetics, chocolates and other delicacies, flowers, plants and garden furniture/equipment, seating, beds and bedding
Avoid: Gimmicky goods
Timely advice: Open a new investment account

THE MOON IN LEO

Shopping tip: Make sure you save up for this shopping expedition – you will be in an extravagant mood
Buy: Jewelery, luxury goods, silk lingerie, children's clothes, presents for your youngsters, theater tickets, leisure wear, items for your hobbies and spare time activities, champagne, caviar, anything made of gold
Avoid: Buying essential groceries
Timely advice: Place a bet or buy a lottery ticket

THE MOON IN VIRGO

Shopping tip: You will have a keen eye for detail
Buy: Anything you need for the medicine cupboard, diaries, personal organizers, organic foods, vitamin and mineral supplements, cleaning materials, toiletries, a subscription to the local health club, a surprise treat for your employees, local services
Avoid: Anything that does not have a practical purpose
Timely advice: Look into health insurance policies

THE MOON IN SAGITTARIUS

Shopping tip: A brilliant time for a shopping spree as you won't mind parting with money and you'll be delighted with the bargains you find
Buy: Imported goods, casual clothes, travel books, binoculars, a compass, hiking boots, camping equipment, maps and atlases, presents for your in-laws, relics or religious items, anything secondhand
Avoid: Shopping in your own locality
Timely advice: Book your holiday flight now

THE MOON IN CAPRICORN

Shopping tip: Not the best time to shop as there could be all kinds of problems
Buy: Practical household items, good-quality clothes, consumer durables, professional tools, items for elderly relatives, office equipment, uniforms, hardware, DIY materials
Avoid: Making frivolous purchases – you will regret having parted with your money
Timely advice: Buy a burglar alarm now

SHOPPING TIPS

Juggling our busy lives, as we all do today, means that few of us can choose when to buy the essential things we need, but you might like to take note of the favorable lunar phases when it comes to making the more important purchases in life.

THE DAY OF THE NEW MOON THROUGH TO THE FIRST QUARTER

Choose this period for researching products, window shopping, seeking advice and either picking up or sending off for samples. You will find there is plenty of energy about at this time, people are sharp and willing to help and you will amass all the information you need in double-quick time.

THE MOON IN GEMINI

Shopping tip: An excellent couple of days for window shopping and buzzing around from store to store
Buy: Computers, gadgets, gimmicky goods, writing materials, books, telephones and other communications equipment, toys, dictionaries and encyclopedias
Avoid: Long or far-flung shopping expeditions
Timely advice: Buy your car under this sign

THE MOON IN CANCER

Shopping tip: Excellent for monthly essential shopping, buying for the home and for those you love
Buy: Food and other general provisions to replenish your store cupboards, kitchen equipment, presents and greetings cards, household knickknacks, china, linen and lace, souvenirs, antiques, boats, anything white or silver
Avoid: Shopping anywhere near your place of work
Timely advice: Look for and/or buy a house

THE MOON IN LIBRA

Shopping tip: You may have problems making up your mind, so take a friend alone to help you choose
Buy: Haute couture, anything beautiful, expensive or elegant, accessories, embellishments or decorations for the house, presents for your partner, concert tickets, music, perfume, flower arrangements, party food
Avoid: Shopping in budget retailers or in a run-down area
Timely advice: Book a table for a romantic dinner for two

THE MOON IN SCORPIO

Shopping tip: You will be sharp and shrewd – unlikely to be taken in by sales patter
Buy: Crime or murder mystery novels, rich wines, a pack of Tarot cards, exotic spices, sexy underwear, photographic equipment, perfumes or aftershave lotions, red roses for your lover, a last will and testament form, a new set of kitchen knives
Avoid: Deviating from your shopping list
Timely advice: Make an appointment for a de-stressing massage

THE MOON IN AQUARIUS

Shopping tip: You're drawn to the weird and wonderful, so choose to shop in unusual stores
Buy: Lighting, electrical appliances, scientific instruments, a book on meditation, the latest kitchen gadget, anything electric blue, a chandelier, aromatherapy oils, cards and gifts for your friends
Avoid: Shopping in a rush – you need time to browse
Timely advice: Join a club

THE MOON IN PISCES

Shopping tip: Plan to shop in short bursts, with several breaks for coffee or snacks – when the Moon is in Pisces, our feet can give us problems
Buy: Cosmetics, alcoholic drinks, music, shoes and hosiery, a book about dreams, artist's materials, paintings, crystal glasses, decanters or bowls, romantic fiction, bedding, swimwear
Avoid: Major purchases – you are too suggestible and easily swayed by slick sales talk
Timely advice: Treat yourself to a reflexology session

FROM THE FIRST QUARTER TO THE LAST QUARTER

A favorable time to firm up decisions and make your important purchases. However, avoid any major financial outlay on the day before, or the day of, the Full Moon – you may be more than usually prone to impulse-buying. An excellent period for shopping is from the day after the Full Moon to the Last Quarter – you will make well-thought-out decisions and are more likely to get value for money.

FROM THE LAST QUARTER TO THE NEW MOON

An unsatisfactory time for shopping because energies are flagging all around – your judgement may not be at its sharpest, shop assistants won't be at their most helpful, shopping generally will be difficult and goods unappealing. You might consider catalog- or Internet-shopping as less problematic options.

IN THE GARDEN

When it comes to your garden, it may seem difficult trying to abide by lunar lore, and yet the success of using planetary influences has been recognized for thousands of years, backed up by extensive trials throughout Europe and America. Once the principles are grasped, look forward to healthy plants that are large, beautiful and disease-free, without recourse to chemicals – truly organic gardening.

QUICK TIPS

ANNUALS

Begin planting the day after the New Moon and up to the day before the first Quarter, when the Moon is in a fertile or semi-fertile sign. This will help plants to make short, shallow-lying roots and to establish themselves speedily.

BIENNIALS AND PERENNIALS

Begin planting the day after Full Moon and end on the day before the Last Quarter, when the Moon is in a fertile or semi-fertile sign. This will help plants to establish themselves slowly and to develop long, strong roots.

WEEDING

Weeding and hoeing are best done between the Last Quarter and the New Moon, when the Moon is in a barren sign. Avoid times when the Moon is in a fruitful sign – your weeding efforts won't last for very long.

SOIL CULTIVATION

Digging, plowing or tilling the soil should be carried out with the decreasing Moon and when the Moon is in a barren sign, or the weeds will spring up again all too quickly.

TRANSPLANTING

Always transplant when the Moon is increasing, between the New and Full Moons and during a fertile Moon sign.

GRAFTING

Grafts take best when the sap is rising and therefore when the Moon is waxing (from New to Full).

MOWING

Mow with the Waxing Moon to produce thick, lush regrowth. To slow growth, mow during the decreasing Moon.

COLLECTING SEED

Gathering seed is best done at Full Moon and preferably when the Moon is in the Fire or Air signs of Aries, Leo, Sagittarius, Gemini or Aquarius.

HARVESTING

Harvest fruit and vegetables during the waning period of the Moon, from Full Moon to New Moon, and preferably during the barren or semi-barren Fire or Air signs of Aries, Leo, Sagittarius, Gemini or Aquarius.

THE NATURE OF THE SIGNS

The 12 signs are grouped according to their fruitfulness. The barren or semi-barren signs are not good for growth, but are positively advantageous when it comes to weeding, pruning, destroying pests and other jobs concerned with soil management, control and elimination. Note that references to the fertility or barrenness of a sign apply strictly to agricultural procedures – not to individuals born under those signs.

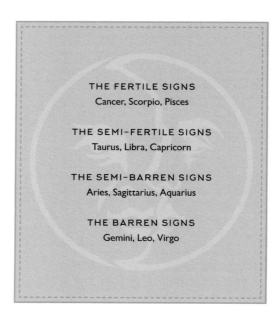

THE FERTILE SIGNS
Cancer, Scorpio, Pisces

THE SEMI-FERTILE SIGNS
Taurus, Libra, Capricorn

THE SEMI-BARREN SIGNS
Aries, Sagittarius, Aquarius

THE BARREN SIGNS
Gemini, Leo, Virgo

1. Always plant or sow at the right season for the plant concerned (e.g. annuals are planted in the spring of the year in which they will flower or fruit).

2. Pay attention to the situation preferred by each plant (free-draining soil, shady site, etc.).

3. Sow plants that crop above the ground during the Waxing Moon.

4. Sow plants that grow under the ground (such as roots and tubers) during the Waning Moon.

5. Sow annuals during the Waxing Moon. Annuals need to establish roots quickly but these need only be shallow, spreading just below the surface. Planting at this time encourages this type of root growth and shallow-rooted annuals will also be easier to pull out in the autumn once they have finished flowering.

6. Plant biennials during the Waning Moon. Biennials and perennials, such as shrubs and trees, need to concentrate their energies in producing a sturdy, wide-spreading root system, so they do better during the Waning Moon period, giving them a long, "quiet" period in which to establish themselves.

7. Never undertake any sowing or transplanting on New Moon, Full Moon and Quarter Moon days.

8. Coordinate the Lunar Phases with the Astrological Signs through which the Moon is passing at the time (see pp.110–11).

CHOOSING THE RIGHT SIGN/MOON PHASE

WHEN THE MOON IS IN ARIES
Nature: semi-barren
- Excellent time to weed when the Moon is in this sign and in a decreasing phase
- Plant pungent-flavored vegetables such as garlic just before the Moon leaves this sign
- Cultivate the soil
- Mow

WHEN THE MOON IS IN TAURUS
Nature: semi-fertile
- Best time for planting and sowing plants that crop under the ground, when the Moon is decreasing. Begin the day after Full Moon until the day before the Last Quarter
- Sow annuals, leafy vegetables and pastel-colored flowering plants when the Moon is in this sign and in a waxing phase
- Do not plant ivies and other vines

WHEN THE MOON IS IN GEMINI
Nature: barren
- Good time to weed, prune and destroy pests and diseases when the Moon is in this sign and between the Last Quarter and New Moon
- Cultivate the land
- Do not plant, sow or transplant

WHEN THE MOON IS IN CANCER
Nature: fertile
- Sow plants and flowers for hardiness and abundance when the Moon is in Cancer and during a waxing phase, from the day after New Moon to the day before Full Moon
- Best time to plant watery vegetables and fruits, such as melons and cucumbers, under this sign and during the increasing Moon
- Plant all mosses
- Water the garden well

WHEN THE MOON IS IN LEO
Nature: barren
- Do not plant, sow or transplant under this sign
- Excellent for digging up weeds, using systemic weed-killers and destroying pests and diseases, especially during decreasing Moon phases
- Prune

WHEN THE MOON IS IN VIRGO
Nature: barren
- Not recommended for sowing, planting or transplanting
- Prune and destroy weeds, pests and diseases
- Cultivate the soil

WHEN THE MOON IS IN LIBRA
Nature: semi-fertile
- Plant flowers for fragrance, beauty and rich colors when the Moon is in Libra and in a waxing phase, from the day after the New Moon to the day before the Full Moon
- Do not plant vegetables under this lunar sign
- Plant vines, climbers and creepers

WHEN THE MOON IS IN SCORPIO
Nature: fertile
- Excellent sign for sowing, planting and transplanting fruit, flowers and vegetables that crop above the ground, during the Moon's increasing phases between the day after New Moon up to the day before Full Moon
- Plants grown under this sign will be healthy, robust and long-stemmed, producing a mass of offshoots and seedlings
- Plant vines, climbers and creepers

WHEN THE MOON IS IN SAGITTARIUS
Nature: semi-barren
- Plant only pungent-tasting fruit or vegetables during a waxing period and just before the Moon leaves this sign
- Cultivate the soil
- Mow

WHEN THE MOON IS IN CAPRICORN
Nature: semi-fertile
- Useful sign, although not the best, for general sowing and planting. Beneficial for producing hardiness and resistance to drought conditions
- Desirable for plants that crop under the ground
- Do not weed under this Moon sign

WHEN THE MOON IS IN AQUARIUS
Nature: semi-barren
- Cultivate the land
- Do not plant, sow, transplant or weed
- Mow

WHEN THE MOON IS IN PISCES
Nature: fertile
- Excellent for promoting good root growth and for all general planting during the increasing phase, between the day after the New Moon until the day before Full Moon
- Sow compact, low-growing plants with pastel-colored flowers
- Not recommended for ivies or vines

MAKE YOUR OWN MOON GARDEN

According to ancient astrological lore, each plant comes under the dominion of one of the planets and it is the Moon that takes rulership over all white-flowering plants and silver-colored foliage. Try creating your own homage to the White Goddess, either by designing a whole Moon garden, or by planting up a small corner, a tiny terrace or even a window box in her honor.

To create your own Moon garden, choose only white or creamy white flowering plants – many of these, such as Madonna lilies, jasmine, nicotiana and stocks, have a glorious scent. Emphasize the whiteness by interspersing or edging with the soft grey-green and silver foliage of, for example, artemesia or quilted-leaved hostas. And don't forget to introduce water, for not only will this add an extra dimension to your garden and provide an environment for water lilies, which are also lunar-ruled, but it too is governed by the Moon.

THE CHANGING SEASONS

With a little care and imagination, your Moon garden will flower prolifically, giving changing interest from one season into the next, and providing you with an abundance of frothy blossom that will fill the air with fragrance. Moreover you will create for yourself a place of peace and tranquility, a haven that will reflect on Earth the beauty of the Goddess herself.

MOON GARDEN MAGIC

Here are some ideas for plants, herbs and vegetables, including annuals and perennials, to choose for your Moon garden.

FLOWERS
Water lilies, white poppies, daisies, snowdrops, Madonna lilies, white phlox, lily of the valley, all-white roses, lotus, nicotiana, white night-scented stocks, white saxifrage, lunaria

CLIMBING PLANTS
Convolvulus (often called the Moon flower – sacred to the Moon and bringing luck to its owner), honeysuckle, summer jasmine, passion flower

SHRUBS
Deutzia, white hydrangea, hebe (white), lilac (white), buddleia (white), philadelphus

TREES
Weeping willow, ash, aspens, olive, palm, maple, magnolia, elder

FRUITS AND VEGETABLES
Melons, cucumbers, squashes, watermelon, onions, watercress, lettuce

HERBS
Hyssop, rosemary (dew of the sea), lemon balm, chamomile, thyme

SILVER-LEAVED PLANTS
Artemesia, hostas, senecio, stachys, lychnis, sedum

CHAPTER 10

MOON LORE

The Moon has been woven into the myths and folk traditions of every
civilization through the ages. Superstitions abound, many of which are still
practiced to this day – often despite our better reasoning, but still observed as
if by compulsion. For the most part these beliefs involve little rituals that are
thought to transform our luck – or at least prevent misfortune descending on us.

NEW MOON SUPERSTITIONS

The energies of the New Moon are felt especially potently, so more superstitions are based around this phase than any other. For example, children were taught never to point to the New Moon as this was considered discourteous and guaranteed bad luck for the whole of the month to come. Nor was it deemed propitious to look at the New Moon through glass, or, even worse, reflected in the mirror, for the first glimpse of the new crescent should be made outside, in the open air. More bad luck was believed to descend on those who fell asleep with the Moon shining on their faces, for this was thought to cause nightmares or even induce madness.

However, to bow or curtsy to the New Moon was highly recommended, and ensured that a wish would be granted. In some countries, bowing several times was strongly advised. So, too, was turning a silver coin over in one's pocket at the sight of the New Moon – said to increase one's wealth.

CHILDREN AND CHILDBIRTH

Much of the folklore involving the Moon revolves around the knowledge of cosmic movements and planetary patterns and the effects that these have on all living things, both physically and behaviorally. Since conception and birth were seen as being linked to the phases of the Moon, it is not surprising that a good many old wives' tales involving children and childbirth have lunar knowledge at their core.

One such piece of wisdom advises expectant mothers in labor to drink raspberry leaf tea to reduce the pain of giving birth. This is a proven tip that many midwives find works well as the chemical constituents of the leaf help to relax the muscles during labor. However, a word of caution here – **raspberry leaf tea must not be taken until toward the very end of the pregnancy** as, in some cases, it can induce abortion. What is interesting about this ancient knowledge is, of course, that raspberries are traditionally ruled by the Moon.

Another piece of ancient lore is that a child develops certain characteristics according to the day on which they are born. The logic underlying this is that each day is said to be ruled by a particular planet, and the planet of the day stamps its own attributes upon those born under its sway. These characteristics have been captured in a famous rhyme:

Monday's child is fair of face
Tuesday's child is full of grace
Wednesday's child is full of woe
Thursday's child has far to go
Friday's child is loving and giving
Saturday's child works hard for a living
But the child that is born on the Sabbath Day
Is bonny and blithe, good and gay.

THE FACE OF THE MOON

Traditionally, it is the Moon that has rulership over Monday – *Lundi* in French and *Lunedi* in Italian take their root from *Luna*, the Latin word for Moon. Astrologically, the Moon has been said to confer upon all her subjects a round face or a fairer complexion, and it is this that is referred to in the first line of the verse shown above. It is interesting to note that another version substitutes

"Monday's child is full in the face" for the first line, thus capturing the other characteristic of roundness that is associated with the Moon's influence on facial features.

Another physiological characteristic associated with the Moon may be found on the hand. The Mount of Luna, located at the base of the palm, lies just above the wrist and in a direct line below the little finger. This area of the hand is associated with imagination, racial memories, sensitivity and psychic talents. When underdeveloped, imaginative potential is lacking and the person's nature may be cold and unresponsive. When overdeveloped, moodiness, oversensitivity and sometimes even mental instability may be marked in the personality, as may dreaminess and a flighty, inconstant disposition, just like the ever-changing faces of the Moon.

SPELLS AND INVOCATIONS

Moon lore also plays a role in all kinds of magical practices, with specific rituals and invocation assigned to the different phases of the Moon. Candles are frequently used in these practices, chants or rhymes are recited and the Moon goddesses are invoked in order to grant a wish or to answer a prayer.

Herbs are said to increase their potency if picked at appropriate times during the Moon's cycle, while any potions are more effective if taken at the right time. Talismans made when the Moon is New bring good fortune when it waxes to fullness, and any visualization exercises performed at New Moon can produce profound changes in both our conscious minds and our lives in general.

WISHING ON THE MOON

Try this on the night of the New Moon. Sit in a quiet room, light a white candle and visualize something that you long to happen. It might be an improvement in your health, an ambition you want to realize, the return of a lost lover, a windfall or a lucky break. Hold the thought in your mind as you write it down on a sheet of white paper.

Now, fold the paper and slip it underneath a bowl of white flowers, which you have placed by a windowsill, where it will pick up the rays of the Moon. Alternatively, if you hope to increase your wealth, slip a coin or a bank note under the bowl on the night of the Full Moon. If the wish is to be granted, you should see signs of it materializing before the month is out. But remember, only use magic in a positive way and only for good. Negative wishes that are harmful to others may have serious and unexpected repercussions on the person who makes them. Such are the laws that pertain to the magic of the Moon.

A PARTING THOUGHT
THE DARK OF THE MOON

As you gaze upon the Moon, consider this: had you been born and lived your entire life on the far side of the Moon, the fact that your world has such a profound influence on the lives of those who live on the Earth would not concern you one bit. Nor, as you stood in contemplation, looking at the face of the Sun, would you wonder about the nature of the planet around which your own life revolves. From your hot, arid wasteland, you could not imagine the blue skies that envelop our world, the lush vegetation that clothes our land, the sparkling waters that fill our great oceans. You would know nothing of these things for the simple reason that, from your vantage point, you could not see the Earth, and therefore could not even know that we exist.

As you gaze upon the Moon, ask yourself this: how much is there that we cannot fathom because, as yet, we do not recognize the existence of those things we cannot see?

TABLE 1: MOON CHARTS

LUNAR PHASE TABLES FOR THE YEARS 1950-2050

Listing in order: Year Month Day Hour Minute

Key: FM = Full Moon LQ = Last Quarter NM = New Moon FQ = First Quarter

All times given are GMT and individual adjustments must be made for different time zones.

1950	1	4	7:49.6	FM
1950	1	11	10:32.2	LQ
1950	1	18	8: 1.4	NM
1950	1	26	4:39.3	FQ
1950	2	2	22:17.8	FM
1950	2	9	18:33.5	LQ
1950	2	16	22:54.8	NM
1950	2	25	1:52.2	FQ
1950	3	4	10:35.1	FM
1950	3	11	2:39.7	LQ
1950	3	18	15:21.7	NM
1950	3	26	20: 9.7	FQ
1950	4	2	20:49.5	FM
1950	4	9	11:43.5	LQ
1950	4	17	8:26.5	NM
1950	4	25	10:39.6	FQ
1950	5	2	5:19.3	FM
1950	5	8	22:32.3	LQ
1950	5	17	0:55.2	NM
1950	5	24	21:27.7	FQ
1950	5	31	12:42.2	FM
1950	6	7	11:35.5	LQ
1950	6	15	15:52.9	NM
1950	6	23	5:12.4	FQ
1950	6	29	19:57.3	FM
1950	7	7	2:53.2	LQ
1950	7	15	5: 4.9	NM
1950	7	22	10:50.8	FQ
1950	7	29	4:16.7	FM
1950	8	5	19:55.5	LQ
1950	8	13	16:47.2	NM
1950	8	20	15:36.1	FQ
1950	8	27	14:49.9	FM
1950	9	4	13:53.6	LQ
1950	9	12	3:27.7	NM
1950	9	18	20:55.0	FQ
1950	9	26	4:21.1	FM
1950	10	4	7:53.9	LQ
1950	10	11	13:32.5	NM
1950	10	18	4:18.6	FQ
1950	10	25	20:47.2	FM
1950	11	3	1: 2.1	LQ
1950	11	9	23:25.1	NM
1950	11	16	15: 6.4	FQ
1950	11	24	15:15.5	FM
1950	12	2	16:23.4	LQ
1950	12	9	9:29.4	NM
1950	12	16	5:56.8	FQ
1950	12	24	10:24.6	FM
1951	1	1	5:12.4	LQ
1951	1	7	20:12.0	NM
1951	1	15	0:22.6	FQ
1951	1	23	4:48.8	FM
1951	1	30	15:14.7	LQ
1951	2	6	7:56.5	NM
1951	2	13	20:55.3	FQ
1951	2	21	21:14.2	FM
1951	2	28	23: 0.6	LQ
1951	3	7	20:53.3	NM
1951	3	15	17:40.6	FQ
1951	3	23	10:51.8	FM
1951	3	30	5:35.8	LQ
1951	4	6	10:53.9	NM
1951	4	14	12:56.6	FQ
1951	4	21	21:31.3	FM
1951	4	28	12:18.3	LQ
1951	5	6	1:37.1	NM
1951	5	14	5:32.4	FQ
1951	5	21	5:45.2	FM
1951	5	27	20:17.0	LQ
1951	6	4	16:41.0	NM
1951	6	12	18:52.1	FQ
1951	6	19	12:36.0	FM
1951	6	26	6:21.3	LQ
1951	7	4	7:47.7	NM
1951	7	12	4:56.4	FQ
1951	7	18	19:17.2	FM
1951	7	25	18:59.3	LQ
1951	8	2	22:38.3	NM
1951	8	10	12:22.5	FQ
1951	8	17	2:58.9	FM
1951	8	24	10:20.5	LQ
1951	9	1	12:48.3	NM
1951	9	8	18:16.2	FQ
1951	9	15	12:37.5	FM
1951	9	23	4:14.2	LQ

1951	10	1	1:55.2	NM
1951	10	8	0: 0.2	FQ
1951	10	15	0:50.1	FM
1951	10	22	23:57.0	LQ
1951	10	30	13:53.2	NM
1951	11	6	6:59.0	FQ
1951	11	13	15:51.8	FM
1951	11	21	20: 2.6	LQ
1951	11	29	0:59.6	NM
1951	12	5	16:21.0	FQ
1951	12	13	9:30.7	FM
1951	12	21	14:38.2	LQ
1951	12	28	11:43.7	NM
1952	1	4	4:42.3	FQ
1952	1	12	4:55.4	FM
1952	1	20	6: 9.7	LQ
1952	1	26	22:27.6	NM
1952	2	2	20: 1.3	FQ
1952	2	11	0:28.6	FM
1952	2	18	18: 1.2	LQ
1952	2	25	9:17.7	NM
1952	3	3	13:43.8	FQ
1952	3	11	18:15.3	FM
1952	3	19	2:39.5	LQ
1952	3	25	20:14.5	NM
1952	4	2	8:49.4	FQ
1952	4	10	8:55.2	FM
1952	4	17	9: 7.6	LQ
1952	4	24	7:29.2	NM
1952	5	2	3:58.3	FQ
1952	5	9	20:17.5	FM
1952	5	16	14:39.6	LQ
1952	5	23	19:29.2	NM
1952	5	31	21:46.6	FQ
1952	6	8	5: 8.2	FM
1952	6	14	20:28.6	LQ
1952	6	22	8:45.9	NM
1952	6	30	13:11.6	FQ
1952	7	7	12:34.8	FM
1952	7	14	3:43.6	LQ
1952	7	21	23:31.1	NM
1952	7	30	1:51.2	FQ
1952	8	5	19:41.0	FM
1952	8	12	13:28.4	LQ
1952	8	20	15:20.5	NM
1952	8	28	12: 3.6	FQ
1952	9	4	3:19.6	FM
1952	9	11	2:37.0	LQ
1952	9	19	7:21.6	NM
1952	9	26	20:31.0	FQ
1952	10	3	12:15.1	FM
1952	10	10	19:33.8	LQ
1952	10	18	22:41.8	NM
1952	10	26	4: 4.4	FQ
1952	11	1	23: 9.3	FM
1952	11	9	15:43.7	LQ
1952	11	17	12:55.1	NM
1952	11	24	11:34.9	FQ
1952	12	1	12:40.9	FM
1952	12	9	13:22.1	LQ
1952	12	17	2: 2.0	NM
1952	12	23	19:52.4	FQ
1952	12	31	5: 5.6	FM
1953	1	8	10: 9.6	LQ
1953	1	15	14: 8.4	NM
1953	1	22	5:43.7	FQ
1953	1	29	23:44.3	FM
1953	2	7	4:10.3	LQ
1953	2	14	1:11.0	NM
1953	2	20	17:45.4	FQ
1953	2	28	18:59.0	FM
1953	3	8	18:27.1	LQ
1953	3	15	11: 6.4	NM
1953	3	22	8:11.5	FQ
1953	3	30	12:56.2	FM
1953	4	7	4:59.0	LQ
1953	4	13	20:10.7	NM
1953	4	21	0:41.0	FQ
1953	4	29	4:22.4	FM
1953	5	6	12:21.7	LQ
1953	5	13	5: 7.7	NM
1953	5	20	18:19.8	FQ
1953	5	28	17: 4.8	FM
1953	6	4	17:36.8	LQ
1953	6	11	14:56.4	NM
1953	6	19	12: 0.6	FQ

1953	6	27	3:31.0	FM
1953	7	3	22: 4.9	LQ
1953	7	11	2:29.3	NM
1953	7	19	4:47.6	FQ
1953	7	26	12:22.1	FM
1953	8	2	3:17.8	LQ
1953	8	9	16:10.7	NM
1953	8	17	20: 8.7	FQ
1953	8	24	20:21.7	FM
1953	8	31	10:47.5	LQ
1953	9	8	7:47.8	NM
1953	9	16	9:49.9	FQ
1953	9	23	4:16.1	FM
1953	9	29	21:51.8	LQ
1953	10	8	0:40.3	NM
1953	10	15	21:44.3	FQ
1953	10	22	12:55.8	FM
1953	10	29	13: 9.3	LQ
1953	11	6	17:57.2	NM
1953	11	14	7:52.0	FQ
1953	11	20	23:11.9	FM
1953	11	28	8:15.6	LQ
1953	12	6	10:47.3	NM
1953	12	13	16:30.2	FQ
1953	12	20	11:43.2	FM
1953	12	28	5:43.5	LQ
1954	1	5	2:20.9	NM
1954	1	12	0:22.3	FQ
1954	1	19	2:36.6	FM
1954	1	27	3:29.5	LQ
1954	2	3	15:55.6	NM
1954	2	10	8:30.0	FQ
1954	2	17	19:17.2	FM
1954	2	25	23:31.1	LQ
1954	3	5	3:12.2	NM
1954	3	11	17:52.5	FQ
1954	3	19	12:42.7	FM
1954	3	27	16:15.9	LQ
1954	4	3	12:26.4	NM
1954	4	10	5: 5.9	FQ
1954	4	18	5:49.1	FM
1954	4	26	4:58.9	LQ
1954	5	2	20:24.0	NM
1954	5	9	18:17.1	FQ
1954	5	17	21:47.9	FM
1954	5	25	13:50.2	LQ
1954	6	1	4: 4.5	NM
1954	6	8	9:13.2	FQ
1954	6	16	12: 6.9	FM
1954	6	23	19:46.7	LQ
1954	6	30	12:26.9	NM
1954	7	8	1:33.3	FQ
1954	7	16	0:30.3	FM
1954	7	23	0:14.7	LQ
1954	7	29	22:20.5	NM
1954	8	6	18:51.3	FQ
1954	8	14	11: 4.3	FM
1954	8	21	4:51.8	LQ
1954	8	28	10:21.0	NM
1954	9	5	12:29.0	FQ
1954	9	12	20:20.5	FM
1954	9	19	11:12.0	LQ
1954	9	27	0:50.0	NM
1954	10	5	5:30.9	FQ
1954	10	12	5:10.8	FM
1954	10	18	20:31.2	LQ
1954	10	26	17:46.8	NM
1954	11	3	20:54.5	FQ
1954	11	10	14:30.0	FM
1954	11	17	9:33.4	LQ
1954	11	25	12:30.5	NM
1954	12	3	9:55.6	FQ
1954	12	10	0:57.2	FM
1954	12	17	2:22.0	LQ
1954	12	25	7:33.2	NM
1955	1	1	20:28.3	FQ
1955	1	8	12:44.1	FM
1955	1	15	22:14.9	LQ
1955	1	24	1: 7.0	NM
1955	1	31	5: 5.2	FQ
1955	2	7	1:42.4	FM
1955	2	14	19:41.7	LQ
1955	2	22	15:55.2	NM
1955	3	1	12:40.4	FQ
1955	3	8	15:40.7	FM
1955	3	16	16:37.6	LQ

1955	3	24	3:43.3	NM
1955	3	30	20:10.0	FQ
1955	4	7	6:34.3	FM
1955	4	15	11: 1.9	LQ
1955	4	22	13: 6.9	NM
1955	4	29	4:22.7	FQ
1955	5	6	22:13.6	FM
1955	5	15	1:43.0	LQ
1955	5	21	20:59.1	NM
1955	5	28	14: 1.1	FQ
1955	6	5	14: 8.3	FM
1955	6	13	12:37.1	LQ
1955	6	20	4:12.1	NM
1955	6	27	1:43.6	FQ
1955	7	5	5:28.9	FM
1955	7	12	20:30.7	LQ
1955	7	19	11:34.7	NM
1955	7	26	15:59.3	FQ
1955	8	3	19:31.0	FM
1955	8	11	2:33.3	LQ
1955	8	17	19:58.0	NM
1955	8	25	8:51.4	FQ
1955	9	2	8: 0.4	FM
1955	9	9	8: 0.2	LQ
1955	9	16	6:18.6	NM
1955	9	24	3:39.8	FQ
1955	10	1	19:18.7	FM
1955	10	8	14: 5.4	LQ
1955	10	15	19:31.7	NM
1955	10	23	23: 3.9	FQ
1955	10	31	6: 5.2	FM
1955	11	6	21:57.9	LQ
1955	11	14	12: 1.9	NM
1955	11	22	17:28.8	FQ
1955	11	29	16:50.9	FM
1955	12	6	8:37.2	LQ
1955	12	14	7: 7.9	NM
1955	12	22	9:39.7	FQ
1955	12	29	3:44.4	FM
1956	1	4	22:42.2	LQ
1956	1	13	3: 1.7	NM
1956	1	20	22:58.1	FQ
1956	1	27	14:40.3	FM
1956	2	3	16: 9.2	LQ
1956	2	11	21:38.7	NM
1956	2	19	9:20.8	FQ
1956	2	26	1:41.4	FM
1956	3	4	11:54.0	LQ
1956	3	12	13:37.9	NM
1956	3	19	17:13.6	FQ
1956	3	26	13:10.9	FM
1956	4	3	8: 6.5	LQ
1956	4	11	2:39.8	NM
1956	4	17	23:28.3	FQ
1956	4	25	1:40.3	FM
1956	5	3	2:56.2	LQ
1956	5	10	13: 5.1	NM
1956	5	17	5:15.8	FQ
1956	5	24	15:25.9	FM
1956	6	1	19:14.3	LQ
1956	6	8	21:29.7	NM
1956	6	15	11:56.4	FQ
1956	6	23	6:14.1	FM
1956	7	1	8:42.1	LQ
1956	7	8	4:38.0	NM
1956	7	14	20:46.8	FQ
1956	7	22	21:30.1	FM
1956	7	30	19:32.6	LQ
1956	8	6	11:25.4	NM
1956	8	13	8:44.6	FQ
1956	8	21	12:39.0	FM
1956	8	29	4:14.0	LQ
1956	9	4	18:57.3	NM
1956	9	12	0:11.8	FQ
1956	9	20	3:20.6	FM
1956	9	27	11:26.1	LQ
1956	10	4	4:24.0	NM
1956	10	11	18:42.8	FQ
1956	10	19	17:25.7	FM
1956	10	26	18: 3.1	LQ
1956	11	2	16:43.2	NM
1956	11	10	15: 8.4	FQ
1956	11	18	6:45.3	FM
1956	11	25	1:13.6	LQ
1956	12	2	8:12.7	NM
1956	12	10	11:51.4	FQ

1956	12	17	19: 6.5	FM
1956	12	24	10:10.7	LQ
1957	1	1	2:14.0	NM
1957	1	9	7: 6.7	FQ
1957	1	16	6:21.4	FM
1957	1	22	21:48.8	LQ
1957	1	30	21:25.0	NM
1957	2	7	23:23.3	FQ
1957	2	14	16:37.8	FM
1957	2	21	12:19.0	LQ
1957	3	1	16:12.8	NM
1957	3	9	11:49.9	FQ
1957	3	16	2:21.9	FM
1957	3	23	5: 4.4	LQ
1957	3	31	9:19.8	NM
1957	4	7	20:32.4	FQ
1957	4	14	12: 9.3	FM
1957	4	21	23: 0.9	LQ
1957	4	29	23:54.8	NM
1957	5	7	2:29.4	FQ
1957	5	13	22:34.2	FM
1957	5	21	17: 4.7	LQ
1957	5	29	11:39.9	NM
1957	6	5	7:10.0	FQ
1957	6	12	10: 2.1	FM
1957	6	20	10:24.7	LQ
1957	6	27	20:54.1	NM
1957	7	4	12: 9.8	FQ
1957	7	11	22:50.4	FM
1957	7	20	2:19.9	LQ
1957	7	27	4:28.7	NM
1957	8	2	18:55.7	FQ
1957	8	10	13: 9.2	FM
1957	8	18	16:18.0	LQ
1957	8	25	11:33.2	NM
1957	9	1	4:35.1	FQ
1957	9	9	4:56.3	FM
1957	9	17	4: 3.0	LQ
1957	9	23	19:18.8	NM
1957	9	30	17:49.0	FQ
1957	10	8	21:43.5	FM
1957	10	16	13:44.4	LQ
1957	10	23	4:43.5	NM
1957	10	30	10:47.3	FQ
1957	11	7	14:33.0	FM
1957	11	14	21:59.8	LQ
1957	11	21	16:19.5	NM
1957	11	29	6:57.9	FQ
1957	12	7	6:16.7	FM
1957	12	14	5:45.6	LQ
1957	12	21	6:12.4	NM
1957	12	29	4:52.9	FQ
1958	1	5	20: 9.6	FM
1958	1	12	14: 1.8	LQ
1958	1	19	22: 8.6	NM
1958	1	28	2:16.5	FQ
1958	2	4	8: 6.3	FM
1958	2	10	23:34.7	LQ
1958	2	18	15:39.1	NM
1958	2	26	20:51.8	FQ
1958	3	5	18:28.7	FM
1958	3	12	10:48.5	LQ
1958	3	20	9:50.6	NM
1958	3	28	11:18.3	FQ
1958	4	4	3:45.0	FM
1958	4	10	23:50.5	LQ
1958	4	19	3:24.1	NM
1958	4	26	21:34.8	FQ
1958	5	3	12:22.6	FM
1958	5	10	14:38.5	LQ
1958	5	18	19: 0.9	NM
1958	5	26	4:37.0	FQ
1958	6	1	20:54.1	FM
1958	6	9	6:59.9	LQ
1958	6	17	7:59.7	NM
1958	6	24	9:44.1	FQ
1958	7	1	6: 3.6	FM
1958	7	9	0:21.8	LQ
1958	7	16	18:33.0	NM
1958	7	23	14:19.8	FQ
1958	7	30	16:46.0	FM
1958	8	7	17:50.1	LQ
1958	8	15	3:32.8	NM
1958	8	21	19:45.7	FQ
1958	8	29	5:52.9	FM
1958	9	6	10:24.5	LQ

1958	9	13	12: 1.8	NM
1958	9	20	3:18.6	FQ
1958	9	27	21:44.2	FM
1958	10	6	1:20.5	LQ
1958	10	12	20:51.6	NM
1958	10	19	14: 7.2	FQ
1958	10	27	15:42.1	FM
1958	11	4	14:19.8	LQ
1958	11	11	6:33.8	NM
1958	11	18	4:59.5	FQ
1958	11	26	10:17.9	FM
1958	12	4	1:24.7	LQ
1958	12	10	17:23.8	NM
1958	12	17	23:52.5	FQ
1958	12	26	3:55.4	FM
1959	1	2	10:51.2	LQ
1959	1	9	5:35.2	NM
1959	1	16	21:26.4	FQ
1959	1	24	19:34.1	FM
1959	1	31	19: 7.5	LQ
1959	2	7	19:23.9	NM
1959	2	15	19:19.6	FQ
1959	2	23	8:55.4	FM
1959	3	2	2:55.5	LQ
1959	3	9	10:53.1	NM
1959	3	17	15:10.3	FQ
1959	3	24	20: 3.7	FM
1959	3	31	11: 7.9	LQ
1959	4	8	3:30.7	NM
1959	4	16	7:32.9	FQ
1959	4	23	5:13.8	FM
1959	4	29	20:39.4	LQ
1959	5	7	20:12.6	NM
1959	5	15	20: 8.6	FQ
1959	5	22	12:55.4	FM
1959	5	29	8:14.1	LQ
1959	6	6	11:53.9	NM
1959	6	14	5:22.4	FQ
1959	6	20	19:59.1	FM
1959	6	27	22:12.1	LQ
1959	7	6	2: 0.2	NM
1959	7	13	12: 1.7	FQ
1959	7	20	3:32.6	FM
1959	7	27	14:21.6	LQ
1959	8	4	14:33.2	NM
1959	8	11	17:10.6	FQ
1959	8	18	12:49.7	FM
1959	8	26	8: 3.2	LQ
1959	9	3	1:54.8	NM
1959	9	9	22: 8.2	FQ
1959	9	17	0:51.1	FM
1959	9	25	2:23.2	LQ
1959	10	2	12:30.1	NM
1959	10	9	4:23.7	FQ
1959	10	16	15:59.0	FM
1959	10	24	20:23.7	LQ
1959	10	31	22:40.4	NM
1959	11	7	13:24.3	FQ
1959	11	15	9:42.8	FM
1959	11	23	13: 4.6	LQ
1959	11	30	8:46.0	NM
1959	12	7	2:11.7	FQ
1959	12	15	4:49.7	FM
1959	12	23	3:28.9	LQ
1959	12	29	19: 9.7	NM
1960	1	5	18:52.0	FQ
1960	1	13	23:51.3	FM
1960	1	21	15: 0.9	LQ
1960	1	28	6:16.6	NM
1960	2	4	14:24.5	FQ
1960	2	12	17:24.7	FM
1960	2	19	23:47.6	LQ
1960	2	26	18:25.3	NM
1960	3	5	11: 4.9	FQ
1960	3	13	8:27.1	FM
1960	3	20	6:40.7	LQ
1960	3	27	7:39.2	NM
1960	4	4	7: 5.0	FQ
1960	4	11	20:28.7	FM
1960	4	18	12:57.1	LQ
1960	4	25	21:45.9	NM
1960	5	4	1: 1.2	FQ
1960	5	11	5:43.3	FM
1960	5	17	19:54.5	LQ
1960	5	25	12:27.4	NM
1960	6	2	16: 1.9	FQ
1960	6	9	13: 2.4	FM
1960	6	16	4:35.8	LQ
1960	6	24	3:27.5	NM
1960	7	2	3:48.8	FQ
1960	7	8	19:37.2	FM
1960	7	15	15:43.0	LQ
1960	7	23	18:30.7	NM
1960	7	31	12:39.1	FQ
1960	8	7	2:41.2	FM
1960	8	14	5:37.2	LQ
1960	8	22	9:14.8	NM
1960	8	29	19:22.8	FQ
1960	9	5	11:18.6	FM
1960	9	12	22:20.5	LQ
1960	9	20	23:11.8	NM
1960	9	28	1:13.5	FQ

1960	10	4	22:15.9	FM
1960	10	12	17:27.2	LQ
1960	10	20	12: 1.5	NM
1960	10	27	7:34.5	FQ
1960	11	3	11:57.6	FM
1960	11	11	13:49.7	LQ
1960	11	18	23:45.7	NM
1960	11	25	15:42.6	FQ
1960	12	3	4:24.7	FM
1960	12	11	9:39.7	LQ
1960	12	18	10:46.8	NM
1960	12	25	2:30.0	FQ
1961	1	1	23: 6.3	FM
1961	1	10	3: 3.0	LQ
1961	1	16	21:30.8	NM
1961	1	23	16:13.2	FQ
1961	1	31	18:46.8	FM
1961	2	8	16:49.5	LQ
1961	2	15	8:11.7	NM
1961	2	22	8:34.3	FQ
1961	3	2	13:35.2	FM
1961	3	10	2:57.0	LQ
1961	3	16	18:52.3	NM
1961	3	24	2:48.6	FQ
1961	4	1	5:48.9	FM
1961	4	8	10:15.7	LQ
1961	4	15	5:39.4	NM
1961	4	22	21:50.1	FQ
1961	4	30	18:42.7	FM
1961	5	7	15:58.0	LQ
1961	5	14	16:56.1	NM
1961	5	22	16:19.2	FQ
1961	5	30	4:39.0	FM
1961	6	5	21:19.6	LQ
1961	6	13	5:17.7	NM
1961	6	21	9: 1.9	FQ
1961	6	28	12:39.4	FM
1961	7	5	3:33.8	LQ
1961	7	12	19:12.0	NM
1961	7	20	23:13.9	FQ
1961	7	27	19:51.6	FM
1961	8	3	11:48.8	LQ
1961	8	11	10:36.1	NM
1961	8	19	10:51.4	FQ
1961	8	26	3:13.9	FM
1961	9	1	23: 6.4	LQ
1961	9	10	2:49.3	NM
1961	9	17	20:23.5	FQ
1961	9	24	11:33.2	FM
1961	10	1	14:10.6	LQ
1961	10	9	18:51.9	NM
1961	10	17	4:34.6	FQ
1961	10	23	21:30.1	FM
1961	10	31	8:59.3	LQ
1961	11	8	9:57.8	NM
1961	11	15	12:12.9	FQ
1961	11	22	9:43.2	FM
1961	11	30	6:19.0	LQ
1961	12	7	23:51.4	NM
1961	12	14	20: 6.4	FQ
1961	12	22	0:41.8	FM
1961	12	30	3:57.5	LQ
1962	1	6	12:35.5	NM
1962	1	13	5: 2.4	FQ
1962	1	20	18:16.7	FM
1962	1	28	23:37.7	LQ
1962	2	5	0:10.7	NM
1962	2	11	15:43.8	FQ
1962	2	19	13:18.2	FM
1962	2	27	15:51.0	LQ
1962	3	6	10:32.1	NM
1962	3	13	4:39.6	FQ
1962	3	21	7:56.2	FM
1962	3	29	4:11.4	LQ
1962	4	4	19:46.3	NM
1962	4	11	19:50.8	FQ
1962	4	20	0:34.9	FM
1962	4	27	12:59.8	LQ
1962	5	4	4:26.5	NM
1962	5	11	12:44.1	FQ
1962	5	19	14:33.7	FM
1962	5	26	19: 6.6	LQ
1962	6	2	13:28.6	NM
1962	6	10	6:20.7	FQ
1962	6	18	2: 4.1	FM
1962	6	24	23:44.1	LQ
1962	7	1	23:53.8	NM
1962	7	9	23:39.4	FQ
1962	7	17	11:42.6	FM
1962	7	24	4:20.0	LQ
1962	7	31	12:24.9	NM
1962	8	8	15:55.8	FQ
1962	8	15	20:10.9	FM
1962	8	22	10:28.2	LQ
1962	8	30	3: 9.7	NM
1962	9	7	6:45.6	FQ
1962	9	14	4:12.4	FM
1962	9	20	19:36.8	LQ
1962	9	28	19:39.8	NM
1962	10	6	19:55.0	FQ
1962	10	13	12:33.6	FM
1962	10	20	8:47.8	LQ

1962	10	28	13: 5.0	NM
1962	11	5	7:15.0	FQ
1962	11	11	22: 4.0	FM
1962	11	19	2: 9.6	LQ
1962	11	27	6:29.8	NM
1962	12	4	16:48.4	FQ
1962	12	11	9:28.0	FM
1962	12	18	22:42.7	LQ
1962	12	26	22:59.2	NM
1963	1	3	1: 2.5	FQ
1963	1	9	23: 8.8	FM
1963	1	17	20:35.7	LQ
1963	1	25	13:42.6	NM
1963	2	1	8:51.0	FQ
1963	2	8	14:52.0	FM
1963	2	16	17:41.0	LQ
1963	2	24	2: 6.6	NM
1963	3	2	17:17.9	FQ
1963	3	10	7:48.6	FM
1963	3	18	12: 9.7	LQ
1963	3	25	12:10.6	NM
1963	4	1	3:14.9	FQ
1963	4	9	0:56.6	FM
1963	4	17	2:53.7	LQ
1963	4	23	20:29.5	NM
1963	4	30	15: 6.9	FQ
1963	5	8	17:23.1	FM
1963	5	16	13:36.6	LQ
1963	5	23	4: 0.6	NM
1963	5	30	4:54.0	FQ
1963	6	7	8:30.9	FM
1963	6	14	20:53.5	LQ
1963	6	21	11:46.6	NM
1963	6	28	20:22.7	FQ
1963	7	6	21:56.3	FM
1963	7	14	1:57.6	LQ
1963	7	20	20:43.5	NM
1963	7	28	13:13.0	FQ
1963	8	5	9:32.2	FM
1963	8	12	6:22.0	LQ
1963	8	19	7:35.2	NM
1963	8	27	6:54.9	FQ
1963	9	3	19:35.1	FM
1963	9	10	11:43.6	LQ
1963	9	17	20:51.1	NM
1963	9	26	0:39.4	FQ
1963	10	3	4:45.5	FM
1963	10	9	19:28.8	LQ
1963	10	17	12:43.2	NM
1963	10	25	17:20.6	FQ
1963	11	1	13:56.8	FM
1963	11	8	6:38.3	LQ
1963	11	16	6:51.2	NM
1963	11	24	7:56.1	FQ
1963	11	30	23:55.5	FM
1963	12	7	21:35.2	LQ
1963	12	16	2: 7.2	NM
1963	12	23	19:54.7	FQ
1963	12	30	11: 5.0	FM
1964	1	6	15:59.6	LQ
1964	1	14	20:44.6	NM
1964	1	22	5:29.0	FQ
1964	1	28	23:23.5	FM
1964	2	5	12:45.0	LQ
1964	2	13	13: 3.0	NM
1964	2	20	13:24.7	FQ
1964	2	27	12:39.7	FM
1964	3	6	10: 2.6	LQ
1964	3	14	2:15.7	NM
1964	3	20	20:39.9	FQ
1964	3	28	2:48.7	FM
1964	4	5	5:47.3	LQ
1964	4	12	12:38.9	NM
1964	4	19	4: 9.7	FQ
1964	4	26	17:49.8	FM
1964	5	4	22:21.4	LQ
1964	5	11	21: 2.8	NM
1964	5	18	12:42.4	FQ
1964	5	26	9:29.1	FM
1964	6	3	11: 8.2	LQ
1964	6	10	4:23.3	NM
1964	6	16	23: 2.0	FQ
1964	6	25	1: 8.8	FM
1964	7	2	20:31.4	LQ
1964	7	9	11:31.5	NM
1964	7	16	11:47.3	FQ
1964	7	24	15:59.1	FM
1964	8	1	3:30.2	LQ
1964	8	7	19:17.5	NM
1964	8	15	3:19.7	FQ
1964	8	23	5:26.7	FM
1964	8	30	9:16.3	LQ
1964	9	6	4:34.4	NM
1964	9	13	21:23.9	FQ
1964	9	21	17:32.6	FM
1964	9	28	15: 3.1	LQ
1964	10	5	16:19.5	NM
1964	10	13	16:56.2	FQ
1964	10	21	4:46.8	FM
1964	10	27	22: 0.7	LQ
1964	11	4	7:16.5	NM
1964	11	12	12:20.0	FQ

1964	11	19	15:44.3	FM
1964	11	26	7:12.6	LQ
1964	12	4	1:19.2	NM
1964	12	12	6: 1.7	FQ
1964	12	19	2:42.1	FM
1964	12	25	19:28.5	LQ
1965	1	2	21: 7.8	NM
1965	1	10	20:59.8	FQ
1965	1	17	13:37.7	FM
1965	1	24	11: 8.7	LQ
1965	2	1	16:36.8	NM
1965	2	9	8:52.8	FQ
1965	2	16	0:27.0	FM
1965	2	23	5:41.1	LQ
1965	3	3	9:57.8	NM
1965	3	10	17:52.9	FQ
1965	3	17	11:24.5	FM
1965	3	25	1:38.3	LQ
1965	4	2	0:22.8	NM
1965	4	9	0:40.9	FQ
1965	4	15	23: 3.0	FM
1965	4	23	21: 8.4	LQ
1965	5	1	11:57.6	NM
1965	5	8	6:21.0	FQ
1965	5	15	11:53.0	FM
1965	5	23	14:42.3	LQ
1965	5	30	21:14.1	NM
1965	6	6	12:12.4	FQ
1965	6	14	2: 0.7	FM
1965	6	22	5:38.4	LQ
1965	6	29	4:53.5	NM
1965	7	5	19:37.3	FQ
1965	7	13	17: 3.0	FM
1965	7	21	17:55.2	LQ
1965	7	28	11:45.8	NM
1965	8	4	5:47.5	FQ
1965	8	12	8:24.0	FM
1965	8	20	3:52.1	LQ
1965	8	26	18:51.3	NM
1965	9	2	19:27.4	FQ
1965	9	10	23:33.8	FM
1965	9	18	11:59.7	LQ
1965	9	25	3:18.1	NM
1965	10	2	12:36.7	FQ
1965	10	10	14:15.5	FM
1965	10	17	19: 1.1	LQ
1965	10	24	14:11.6	NM
1965	11	1	8:25.6	FQ
1965	11	9	4:16.9	FM
1965	11	16	1:55.4	LQ
1965	11	23	4:10.9	NM
1965	12	1	5:25.2	FQ
1965	12	8	17:22.5	FM
1965	12	15	9:53.7	LQ
1965	12	22	21: 4.3	NM
1965	12	31	1:47.8	FQ
1966	1	7	5:17.0	FM
1966	1	13	20: 1.6	LQ
1966	1	21	15:47.7	NM
1966	1	29	19:49.5	FQ
1966	2	5	15:58.7	FM
1966	2	12	8:54.3	LQ
1966	2	20	10:50.5	NM
1966	2	28	10:15.8	FQ
1966	3	7	1:46.2	FM
1966	3	14	0:20.1	LQ
1966	3	22	4:47.8	NM
1966	3	29	20:43.8	FQ
1966	4	5	11:13.9	FM
1966	4	12	17:29.3	LQ
1966	4	20	20:36.7	NM
1966	4	28	3:49.4	FQ
1966	5	4	21: 1.0	FM
1966	5	12	11:20.4	LQ
1966	5	20	9:43.6	NM
1966	5	27	8:50.5	FQ
1966	6	3	7:40.5	FM
1966	6	11	5: 0.1	LQ
1966	6	18	20: 9.5	NM
1966	6	25	13:22.8	FQ
1966	7	2	19:36.7	FM
1966	7	10	21:45.1	LQ
1966	7	18	4:30.4	NM
1966	7	24	19: 0.1	FQ
1966	8	1	9: 5.7	FM
1966	8	9	12:57.2	LQ
1966	8	16	11:47.9	NM
1966	8	23	3: 2.0	FQ
1966	8	31	0:14.2	FM
1966	9	8	2: 7.9	LQ
1966	9	14	19:13.4	NM
1966	9	21	14:24.6	FQ
1966	9	29	16:48.4	FM
1966	10	7	13: 8.6	LQ
1966	10	14	3:51.9	NM
1966	10	21	5:34.2	FQ
1966	10	29	10: 1.5	FM
1966	11	5	22:18.6	LQ
1966	11	12	14:27.2	NM
1966	11	20	0:20.6	FQ
1966	11	28	2:42.0	FM
1966	12	5	6:23.1	LQ

1966	12	12	3:14.8	NM
1966	12	19	21:42.6	FQ
1966	12	27	17:44.9	FM
1967	1	3	14:20.4	LQ
1967	1	10	18: 7.8	NM
1967	1	18	19:43.0	FQ
1967	1	26	6:42.1	FM
1967	2	1	23: 4.6	LQ
1967	2	9	10:45.8	NM
1967	2	17	15:57.3	FQ
1967	2	24	17:44.8	FM
1967	3	3	9:11.9	LQ
1967	3	11	4:31.5	NM
1967	3	19	8:31.8	FQ
1967	3	26	3:22.0	FM
1967	4	1	20:59.7	LQ
1967	4	9	22:21.6	NM
1967	4	17	20:47.6	FQ
1967	4	24	12: 3.9	FM
1967	5	1	10:34.0	LQ
1967	5	9	14:56.7	NM
1967	5	17	5:17.1	FQ
1967	5	23	20:22.1	FM
1967	5	31	1:53.5	LQ
1967	6	8	5:14.6	NM
1967	6	15	11:11.6	FQ
1967	6	22	4:56.6	FM
1967	6	29	18:41.2	LQ
1967	7	7	17: 0.5	NM
1967	7	14	15:53.4	FQ
1967	7	21	14:39.0	FM
1967	7	29	12:15.4	LQ
1967	8	6	2:48.3	NM
1967	8	12	20:45.4	FQ
1967	8	20	2:26.4	FM
1967	8	28	5:35.8	LQ
1967	9	4	11:36.9	NM
1967	9	11	3: 7.3	FQ
1967	9	18	16:59.8	FM
1967	9	26	21:44.5	LQ
1967	10	3	20:23.8	NM
1967	10	10	12:12.1	FQ
1967	10	18	10:12.1	FM
1967	10	26	12: 4.6	LQ
1967	11	2	5:48.5	NM
1967	11	9	1: 0.2	FQ
1967	11	17	4:54.2	FM
1967	11	25	0:23.9	LQ
1967	12	1	16:10.5	NM
1967	12	8	17:57.6	FQ
1967	12	16	23:23.0	FM
1967	12	24	10:48.8	LQ
1967	12	31	3:40.0	NM
1968	1	7	14:23.0	FQ
1968	1	15	16:13.0	FM
1968	1	22	19:38.9	LQ
1968	1	29	16:31.2	NM
1968	2	6	12:20.1	FQ
1968	2	14	6:44.6	FM
1968	2	21	3:29.1	LQ
1968	2	28	6:57.7	NM
1968	3	7	9:20.3	FQ
1968	3	14	18:53.8	FM
1968	3	21	11: 9.0	LQ
1968	3	28	22:50.0	NM
1968	4	6	3:28.0	FQ
1968	4	13	4:52.8	FM
1968	4	19	19:36.3	LQ
1968	4	27	15:22.8	NM
1968	5	5	17:54.4	FQ
1968	5	12	13: 5.2	FM
1968	5	19	5:45.6	LQ
1968	5	27	7:31.2	NM
1968	6	4	4:47.0	FQ
1968	6	10	20:13.2	FM
1968	6	17	18:14.7	LQ
1968	6	25	22:25.4	NM
1968	7	3	12:42.5	FQ
1968	7	10	3:17.9	FM
1968	7	17	9:12.3	LQ
1968	7	25	11:49.7	NM
1968	8	1	18:35.4	FQ
1968	8	8	11:32.3	FM
1968	8	16	2:14.1	LQ
1968	8	23	23:56.4	NM
1968	8	30	23:36.1	FQ
1968	9	6	22: 7.0	FM
1968	9	14	20:32.1	LQ
1968	9	22	11: 7.6	NM
1968	9	29	5: 8.2	FQ
1968	10	6	11:46.4	FM
1968	10	14	15: 7.0	LQ
1968	10	21	21:43.6	NM
1968	10	28	12:40.8	FQ
1968	11	5	4:25.6	FM
1968	11	13	8:55.1	LQ
1968	11	20	8: 1.3	NM
1968	11	26	23:31.0	FQ
1968	12	4	23: 8.5	FM
1968	12	13	0:50.8	LQ
1968	12	19	18:19.3	NM
1968	12	26	14:14.4	FQ

1969	1	3	18:28.7	FM
1969	1	11	14: 1.2	LQ
1969	1	18	5: 0.4	NM
1969	1	25	8:22.6	FQ
1969	2	2	12:57.1	FM
1969	2	10	0: 9.0	LQ
1969	2	16	16:27.6	NM
1969	2	24	4:29.9	FQ
1969	3	4	5:18.9	FM
1969	3	11	7:45.4	LQ
1969	3	18	4:54.2	NM
1969	3	26	0:49.0	FQ
1969	4	2	18:47.2	FM
1969	4	9	13:59.3	LQ
1969	4	16	18:18.5	NM
1969	4	24	19:46.2	FQ
1969	5	2	5:15.4	FM
1969	5	8	20:12.9	LQ
1969	5	16	8:28.4	NM
1969	5	24	12:16.5	FQ
1969	5	31	13:19.7	FM
1969	6	7	3:40.6	LQ
1969	6	14	23:10.3	NM
1969	6	23	1:45.4	FQ
1969	6	29	20: 5.0	FM
1969	7	6	13:18.0	LQ
1969	7	14	14:12.1	NM
1969	7	22	12:10.5	FQ
1969	7	29	2:45.9	FM
1969	8	5	1:39.4	LQ
1969	8	13	5:16.3	NM
1969	8	20	20: 3.5	FQ
1969	8	27	10:32.5	FM
1969	9	3	16:58.6	LQ
1969	9	11	19:54.9	NM
1969	9	19	2:24.7	FQ
1969	9	25	20:20.2	FM
1969	10	3	11: 6.1	LQ
1969	10	11	9:37.7	NM
1969	10	18	8:31.8	FQ
1969	10	25	8:43.3	FM
1969	11	2	7:15.1	LQ
1969	11	9	22: 9.9	NM
1969	11	16	15:45.1	FQ
1969	11	23	23:53.1	FM
1969	12	2	3:51.3	LQ
1969	12	9	9:41.0	NM
1969	12	16	1: 9.3	FQ
1969	12	23	17:34.8	FM
1969	12	31	22:52.7	LQ
1970	1	7	20:35.7	NM
1970	1	14	13:18.2	FQ
1970	1	22	12:55.4	FM
1970	1	30	14:39.0	LQ
1970	2	6	7:14.2	NM
1970	2	13	4:10.5	FQ
1970	2	21	8:19.2	FM
1970	3	1	2:33.4	LQ
1970	3	7	17:44.5	NM
1970	3	14	21:16.5	FQ
1970	3	23	1:54.2	FM
1970	3	30	11: 4.7	LQ
1970	4	6	4:11.8	NM
1970	4	13	15:45.1	FQ
1970	4	21	16:24.0	FM
1970	4	28	17:18.9	LQ
1970	5	5	14:53.4	NM
1970	5	13	10:27.4	FQ
1970	5	21	3:40.0	FM
1970	5	27	22:32.8	LQ
1970	6	4	2:23.3	NM
1970	6	12	4: 7.3	FQ
1970	6	19	12:29.5	FM
1970	6	26	4: 3.0	LQ
1970	7	3	15:19.3	NM
1970	7	11	19:43.8	FQ
1970	7	18	20: 0.5	FM
1970	7	25	11: 1.7	LQ
1970	8	2	5:59.1	NM
1970	8	10	8:50.6	FQ
1970	8	17	3:16.8	FM
1970	8	23	20:36.3	LQ
1970	8	31	22: 1.6	NM
1970	9	8	19:38.7	FQ
1970	9	15	11: 9.9	FM
1970	9	22	9:43.3	LQ
1970	9	30	14:31.3	NM
1970	10	8	4:43.0	FQ
1970	10	14	20:21.1	FM
1970	10	22	2:48.2	LQ
1970	10	30	6:27.3	NM
1970	11	6	12:47.0	FQ
1970	11	13	7:27.4	FM
1970	11	20	23:13.6	LQ
1970	11	28	21:13.4	NM
1970	12	5	20:35.9	FQ
1970	12	12	21: 2.7	FM
1970	12	20	21: 8.8	LQ
1970	12	28	10:42.0	NM
1971	1	4	4:55.5	FQ
1971	1	11	13:19.9	FM
1971	1	19	18: 8.5	LQ
1971	1	26	22:54.9	NM
1971	2	2	14:31.1	FQ
1971	2	10	7:40.8	FM
1971	2	18	12:14.2	LQ
1971	2	25	9:48.9	NM
1971	3	4	2: 1.4	FQ
1971	3	12	2:33.1	FM
1971	3	20	2:30.0	LQ
1971	3	26	19:24.2	NM
1971	4	2	15:46.0	FQ
1971	4	10	20:10.4	FM
1971	4	18	12:57.7	LQ
1971	4	25	4: 2.7	NM
1971	5	2	7:33.5	FQ
1971	5	10	11:24.5	FM
1971	5	17	20:15.2	LQ
1971	5	24	12:32.9	NM
1971	6	1	0:41.2	FQ
1971	6	9	0: 4.7	FM
1971	6	16	1:25.0	LQ
1971	6	22	21:58.4	NM
1971	6	30	18:10.2	FQ
1971	7	8	10:38.0	FM
1971	7	15	5:48.2	LQ
1971	7	22	9:16.0	NM
1971	7	30	11: 7.4	FQ
1971	8	6	19:44.1	FM
1971	8	13	10:57.1	LQ
1971	8	20	22:54.4	NM
1971	8	29	2:57.3	FQ
1971	9	5	4: 4.0	FM
1971	9	11	18:25.1	LQ
1971	9	19	14:43.3	NM
1971	9	27	17:18.6	FQ
1971	10	4	12:20.8	FM
1971	10	11	5:30.7	LQ
1971	10	19	7:59.8	NM
1971	10	27	5:55.1	FQ
1971	11	2	21:20.4	FM
1971	11	9	20:52.2	LQ
1971	11	18	1:46.3	NM
1971	11	25	16:37.2	FQ
1971	12	2	7:48.8	FM
1971	12	9	16: 2.6	LQ
1971	12	17	19: 2.9	NM
1971	12	25	1:35.2	FQ
1971	12	31	20:19.8	FM
1972	1	8	13:31.1	LQ
1972	1	16	10:52.3	NM
1972	1	23	9:29.1	FQ
1972	1	30	10:58.0	FM
1972	2	7	11:12.8	LQ
1972	2	15	0:28.9	NM
1972	2	21	17:20.7	FQ
1972	2	29	3:11.3	FM
1972	3	8	7: 7.1	LQ
1972	3	15	11:35.2	NM
1972	3	22	2:11.9	FQ
1972	3	29	20: 4.9	FM
1972	4	6	23:45.6	LQ
1972	4	13	20:31.5	NM
1972	4	20	12:44.8	FQ
1972	4	28	12:44.2	FM
1972	5	6	12:27.1	LQ
1972	5	13	4: 8.8	NM
1972	5	20	1:15.3	FQ
1972	5	28	4:27.7	FM
1972	6	4	21:22.1	LQ
1972	6	11	11:30.9	NM
1972	6	18	15:40.1	FQ
1972	6	26	18:46.9	FM
1972	7	4	3:26.1	LQ
1972	7	10	19:39.7	NM
1972	7	18	7:45.7	FQ
1972	7	26	7:24.8	FM
1972	8	2	8: 3.2	LQ
1972	8	9	5:26.6	NM
1972	8	17	1:10.1	FQ
1972	8	24	18:23.2	FM
1972	8	31	12:49.4	LQ
1972	9	7	17:28.9	NM
1972	9	15	19:14.1	FQ
1972	9	23	4: 8.4	FM
1972	9	29	19:17.7	LQ
1972	10	7	8: 8.3	NM
1972	10	15	12:55.4	FQ
1972	10	22	13:26.6	FM
1972	10	29	4:42.5	LQ
1972	11	6	1:21.8	NM
1972	11	14	5: 0.8	FQ
1972	11	20	23: 7.8	FM
1972	11	27	17:45.7	LQ
1972	12	5	20:24.5	NM
1972	12	13	18:35.3	FQ
1972	12	20	9:45.7	FM
1972	12	27	10:28.0	LQ
1973	1	4	15:42.4	NM
1973	1	12	5:26.4	FQ
1973	1	18	21:28.2	FM
1973	1	26	6: 5.9	LQ
1973	2	3	9:23.1	NM
1973	2	10	14: 4.7	FQ
1973	2	17	10: 6.3	FM
1973	2	25	3:11.9	LQ
1973	3	5	0: 8.3	NM
1973	3	11	21:25.5	FQ
1973	3	18	23:32.7	FM
1973	3	26	23:47.6	LQ
1973	4	3	11:45.9	NM
1973	4	10	4:28.0	FQ
1973	4	17	13:50.0	FM
1973	4	25	17:59.8	LQ
1973	5	2	20:55.7	NM
1973	5	9	12: 6.8	FQ
1973	5	17	4:57.9	FM
1973	5	25	8:40.8	LQ
1973	6	1	4:35.1	NM
1973	6	7	21:11.0	FQ
1973	6	15	20:35.0	FM
1973	6	23	19:46.0	LQ
1973	6	30	11:39.5	NM
1973	7	7	8:25.9	FQ
1973	7	15	11:56.8	FM
1973	7	23	3:58.2	LQ
1973	7	29	18:59.4	NM
1973	8	5	22:27.0	FQ
1973	8	14	2:17.9	FM
1973	8	21	10:23.1	LQ
1973	8	28	3:25.7	NM
1973	9	4	15:22.1	FQ
1973	9	12	15:17.9	FM
1973	9	19	16:11.8	LQ
1973	9	26	13:53.7	NM
1973	10	4	10:31.6	FQ
1973	10	12	3:10.6	FM
1973	10	18	22:34.6	LQ
1973	10	26	3:16.4	NM
1973	11	3	6:28.9	FQ
1973	11	10	14:28.4	FM
1973	11	17	6:36.7	LQ
1973	11	24	19:56.0	NM
1973	12	3	1:28.9	FQ
1973	12	10	1:36.0	FM
1973	12	16	17:14.7	LQ
1973	12	24	15: 8.2	NM
1974	1	1	18: 6.9	FQ
1974	1	8	12:37.0	FM
1974	1	15	7: 5.4	LQ
1974	1	23	11: 2.9	NM
1974	1	31	7:39.3	FQ
1974	2	6	23:24.4	FM
1974	2	14	0: 5.4	LQ
1974	2	22	5:35.2	NM
1974	3	1	18: 2.4	FQ
1974	3	8	10: 2.9	FM
1974	3	15	19:16.3	LQ
1974	3	23	21:25.5	NM
1974	3	31	1:44.2	FQ
1974	4	6	21: 0.1	FM
1974	4	14	14:57.9	LQ
1974	4	22	10:17.4	NM
1974	4	29	7:39.5	FQ
1974	5	6	8:54.2	FM
1974	5	14	9:29.1	LQ
1974	5	21	20:34.7	NM
1974	5	28	13: 3.5	FQ
1974	6	4	22: 9.4	FM
1974	6	13	1:46.0	LQ
1974	6	20	4:55.7	NM
1974	6	26	19:20.1	FQ
1974	7	4	12:40.4	FM
1974	7	12	15:29.0	LQ
1974	7	19	12: 6.3	NM
1974	7	26	3:50.6	FQ
1974	8	3	3:57.5	FM
1974	8	11	2:46.8	LQ
1974	8	17	19: 1.4	NM
1974	8	24	15:37.5	FQ
1974	9	1	19:25.6	FM
1974	9	9	12: 1.6	LQ
1974	9	16	2:45.0	NM
1974	9	23	7: 6.4	FQ
1974	10	1	10:39.0	FM
1974	10	8	19:46.3	LQ
1974	10	15	12:24.5	NM
1974	10	23	1:51.8	FQ
1974	10	31	1:20.3	FM
1974	11	7	2:48.4	LQ
1974	11	14	0:53.6	NM
1974	11	21	22:39.5	FQ
1974	11	29	15:11.5	FM
1974	12	6	10:11.8	LQ
1974	12	13	16:26.2	NM
1974	12	21	19:44.9	FQ
1974	12	29	3:52.2	FM
1975	1	4	19: 6.2	LQ
1975	1	12	10:21.4	NM
1975	1	20	15:16.2	FQ
1975	1	27	15:10.6	FM
1975	2	3	6:24.7	LQ
1975	2	11	5:18.5	NM
1975	2	19	7:39.6	FQ
1975	2	26	1:15.4	FM
1975	3	4	20:21.0	LQ
1975	3	12	23:48.8	NM
1975	3	20	20: 5.0	FQ
1975	3	27	10:36.5	FM
1975	4	3	12:25.2	LQ
1975	4	11	16:40.0	NM
1975	4	19	4:41.0	FQ
1975	4	25	19:54.7	FM
1975	5	3	5:43.8	LQ
1975	5	11	7: 5.4	NM
1975	5	18	10:28.5	FQ
1975	5	25	5:49.9	FM
1975	6	2	23:23.2	LQ
1975	6	9	18:49.1	NM
1975	6	16	14:57.9	FQ
1975	6	23	16:53.6	FM
1975	7	1	16:38.6	LQ
1975	7	9	4: 9.8	NM
1975	7	15	19:46.5	FQ
1975	7	23	5:28.2	FM
1975	7	31	8:50.0	LQ
1975	8	7	11:57.1	NM
1975	8	14	2:23.6	FQ
1975	8	21	19:47.8	FM
1975	8	29	23:20.8	LQ
1975	9	5	19:18.7	NM
1975	9	12	11:58.9	FQ
1975	9	20	11:51.2	FM
1975	9	28	11:46.5	LQ
1975	10	5	3:23.4	NM
1975	10	12	1:15.0	FQ
1975	10	20	5: 7.1	FM
1975	10	27	22: 7.3	LQ
1975	11	3	13: 5.2	NM
1975	11	10	18:20.5	FQ
1975	11	18	22:29.6	FM
1975	11	26	6:52.4	LQ
1975	12	3	0:50.9	NM
1975	12	10	14:39.9	FQ
1975	12	18	14:40.8	FM
1975	12	25	14:52.8	LQ
1976	1	1	14:41.4	NM
1976	1	9	12:41.0	FQ
1976	1	17	4:48.4	FM
1976	1	23	23: 5.6	LQ
1976	1	31	6:21.7	NM
1976	2	8	10: 5.9	FQ
1976	2	15	16:44.6	FM
1976	2	22	8:17.1	LQ
1976	2	29	23:26.3	NM
1976	3	9	4:38.6	FQ
1976	3	16	2:53.8	FM
1976	3	22	18:55.4	LQ
1976	3	30	17: 9.1	NM
1976	4	7	19: 1.8	FQ
1976	4	14	11:49.1	FM
1976	4	21	7:14.8	LQ
1976	4	29	10:20.3	NM
1976	5	7	5:16.5	FQ
1976	5	13	20: 3.5	FM
1976	5	20	21:22.9	LQ
1976	5	29	1:47.4	NM
1976	6	5	12:19.1	FQ
1976	6	12	4:14.1	FM
1976	6	19	13:16.5	LQ
1976	6	27	14:50.2	NM
1976	7	4	17:28.4	FQ
1976	7	11	13: 8.3	FM
1976	7	19	6:30.6	LQ
1976	7	27	1:38.6	NM
1976	8	2	22: 7.2	FQ
1976	8	9	23:43.0	FM
1976	8	18	0:13.5	LQ
1976	8	25	11: 0.5	NM
1976	9	1	3:36.9	FQ
1976	9	8	12:52.0	FM
1976	9	16	17:21.1	LQ
1976	9	23	19:55.0	NM
1976	9	30	11:13.9	FQ
1976	10	8	4:56.5	FM
1976	10	16	8:59.8	LQ
1976	10	23	5: 9.9	NM
1976	10	29	22: 6.1	FQ
1976	11	6	23:16.3	FM
1976	11	14	22:40.0	LQ
1976	11	21	15:11.3	NM
1976	11	28	12:59.4	FQ
1976	12	6	18:16.3	FM
1976	12	14	10:15.3	LQ
1976	12	21	2: 9.2	NM
1976	12	28	7:48.5	FQ
1977	1	5	12:12.3	FM
1977	1	12	19:56.1	LQ
1977	1	19	14:13.2	NM
1977	1	27	5:11.8	FQ
1977	2	4	3:58.5	FM
1977	2	11	4: 8.7	LQ
1977	2	18	3:39.5	NM
1977	2	26	2:50.5	FQ
1977	3	5	17:15.6	FM
1977	3	12	11:36.5	LQ
1977	3	19	18:35.5	NM
1977	3	27	22:27.9	FQ
1977	4	4	4:11.0	FM
1977	4	10	19:16.7	LQ
1977	4	18	10:38.1	NM
1977	4	26	14:43.4	FQ
1977	5	3	13: 4.8	FM
1977	5	10	4:10.0	LQ
1977	5	18	2:53.5	NM
1977	5	26	3:20.8	FQ
1977	6	1	20:31.3	FM
1977	6	8	15: 8.2	LQ
1977	6	16	18:23.9	NM
1977	6	24	12:44.3	FQ
1977	7	1	3:24.0	FM
1977	7	8	4:39.8	LQ
1977	7	16	8:36.7	NM
1977	7	23	19:38.9	FQ
1977	7	30	10:51.8	FM
1977	8	6	20:40.2	LQ
1977	8	14	21:30.3	NM
1977	8	22	1: 5.2	FQ
1977	8	28	20: 9.1	FM
1977	9	5	14:32.9	LQ
1977	9	13	9:21.7	NM
1977	9	20	6:18.9	FQ
1977	9	27	8:16.5	FM
1977	10	5	9:21.5	LQ
1977	10	12	20:29.5	NM
1977	10	19	12:46.6	FQ
1977	10	26	23:35.4	FM
1977	11	4	4: 0.0	LQ
1977	11	11	7: 8.5	NM
1977	11	17	21:53.1	FQ
1977	11	25	17:32.3	FM
1977	12	3	21:17.9	LQ
1977	12	10	17:32.9	NM
1977	12	17	10:37.1	FQ
1977	12	25	12:50.2	FM
1978	1	2	12: 8.6	LQ
1978	1	9	4: 1.2	NM
1978	1	16	3: 2.7	FQ
1978	1	24	7:57.0	FM
1978	1	31	23:52.2	LQ
1978	2	7	14:56.6	NM
1978	2	14	22:10.6	FQ
1978	2	23	1:28.5	FM
1978	3	2	8:35.4	LQ
1978	3	9	2:39.6	NM
1978	3	16	18:22.0	FQ
1978	3	24	16:22.9	FM
1978	3	31	15:12.4	LQ
1978	4	7	15:18.6	NM
1978	4	15	13:57.8	FQ
1978	4	23	4:14.0	FM
1978	4	29	21: 3.7	LQ
1978	5	7	4:49.9	NM
1978	5	15	7:41.9	FQ
1978	5	22	13:19.0	FM
1978	5	29	3:31.8	LQ
1978	6	5	19: 3.9	NM
1978	6	13	22:45.9	FQ
1978	6	20	20:32.2	FM
1978	6	27	11:45.2	LQ
1978	7	5	9:51.6	NM
1978	7	13	10:50.2	FQ
1978	7	20	3: 6.0	FM
1978	7	26	22:31.9	LQ
1978	8	4	1: 0.9	NM
1978	8	11	20: 7.1	FQ
1978	8	18	10:14.3	FM
1978	8	25	12:18.1	LQ
1978	9	2	16: 8.2	NM
1978	9	10	3:20.4	FQ
1978	9	16	19: 0.5	FM
1978	9	24	5: 8.2	LQ
1978	10	2	6:39.4	NM
1978	10	9	9:38.0	FQ
1978	10	16	6: 8.8	FM
1978	10	24	0:35.5	LQ
1978	10	31	20: 5.3	NM
1978	11	7	16:18.5	FQ
1978	11	14	19:59.8	FM
1978	11	22	21:26.2	LQ
1978	11	30	8:18.8	NM
1978	12	7	0:34.7	FQ
1978	12	14	12:30.9	FM
1978	12	22	17:43.1	LQ
1978	12	29	19:36.2	NM
1979	1	5	11:15.5	FQ
1979	1	13	7: 9.2	FM
1979	1	21	11:24.6	LQ
1979	1	28	6:20.9	NM
1979	2	4	0:36.7	FQ
1979	2	12	2:40.0	FM
1979	2	20	1:17.9	LQ
1979	2	26	16:47.2	NM
1979	3	5	16:23.3	FQ
1979	3	13	21:15.5	FM
1979	3	21	11:22.3	LQ
1979	3	28	3: 1.7	NM
1979	4	4	9:58.5	FQ
1979	4	12	13:17.3	FM
1979	4	19	18:30.6	LQ

1979	4	26	13:17.0	NM
1979	5	4	4:26.8	FQ
1979	5	12	2: 3.5	FM
1979	5	18	23:57.7	LQ
1979	5	26	0: 2.6	NM
1979	6	2	22:38.6	FQ
1979	6	10	11:57.5	FM
1979	6	17	5: 2.4	LQ
1979	6	24	11:59.6	NM
1979	7	2	15:24.5	FQ
1979	7	9	20: 1.5	FM
1979	7	16	11: 0.7	LQ
1979	7	24	1:41.9	NM
1979	8	1	5:58.2	FQ
1979	8	8	3:23.1	FM
1979	8	14	19: 4.1	LQ
1979	8	22	17:11.2	NM
1979	8	30	18: 9.8	FQ
1979	9	6	10:59.7	FM
1979	9	13	6:17.0	LQ
1979	9	21	9:46.9	NM
1979	9	29	4:20.3	FQ
1979	10	5	19:35.7	FM
1979	10	12	21:25.1	LQ
1979	10	21	2:23.1	NM
1979	10	28	13: 6.4	FQ
1979	11	4	5:47.2	FM
1979	11	11	16:25.4	LQ
1979	11	19	18: 3.7	NM
1979	11	26	21: 9.4	FQ
1979	12	3	18: 7.8	FM
1979	12	11	13:60.0	LQ
1979	12	19	8:23.7	NM
1979	12	26	5:12.2	FQ
1980	1	2	9: 2.6	FM
1980	1	10	11:50.7	LQ
1980	1	17	21:20.1	NM
1980	1	24	13:59.6	FQ
1980	2	1	2:21.9	FM
1980	2	9	7:36.9	LQ
1980	2	16	8:52.1	NM
1980	2	23	0:15.4	FQ
1980	3	1	21: 0.3	FM
1980	3	9	23:50.2	LQ
1980	3	16	18:57.4	NM
1980	3	23	12:32.6	FQ
1980	3	31	15:15.0	FM
1980	4	8	12: 7.4	LQ
1980	4	15	3:48.0	NM
1980	4	22	3: 0.5	FQ
1980	4	30	7:37.3	FM
1980	5	7	20:51.8	LQ
1980	5	14	12: 2.3	NM
1980	5	21	19:16.5	FQ
1980	5	29	21:30.0	FM
1980	6	6	2:55.0	LQ
1980	6	12	20:40.6	NM
1980	6	20	12:32.2	FQ
1980	6	28	9: 4.7	FM
1980	7	5	7:29.5	LQ
1980	7	12	6:47.8	NM
1980	7	20	5:51.6	FQ
1980	7	27	18:56.5	FM
1980	8	3	12: 3.1	LQ
1980	8	10	19:11.2	NM
1980	8	18	22:29.6	FQ
1980	8	26	3:44.6	FM
1980	9	1	18:10.1	LQ
1980	9	9	10: 1.7	NM
1980	9	17	13:56.0	FQ
1980	9	24	12: 9.3	FM
1980	10	1	3:19.7	LQ
1980	10	9	2:50.6	NM
1980	10	17	3:48.2	FQ
1980	10	23	20:52.9	FM
1980	10	30	16:33.8	LQ
1980	11	7	20:43.0	NM
1980	11	15	15:47.1	FQ
1980	11	22	6:39.5	FM
1980	11	29	9:58.8	LQ
1980	12	7	14:35.2	NM
1980	12	15	1:47.1	FQ
1980	12	21	18: 8.5	FM
1980	12	29	6:32.1	LQ
1981	1	6	7:24.3	NM
1981	1	13	10:10.5	FQ
1981	1	20	7:39.4	FM
1981	1	28	4:20.2	LQ
1981	2	4	22:14.6	NM
1981	2	11	17:50.1	FQ
1981	2	18	22:58.6	FM
1981	2	27	1:16.7	LQ
1981	3	6	10:32.4	NM
1981	3	13	1:51.8	FQ
1981	3	20	15:23.1	FM
1981	3	28	19:36.9	LQ
1981	4	4	20:21.2	NM
1981	4	11	11:11.7	FQ
1981	4	19	7:60.0	FM
1981	4	27	10:16.9	LQ
1981	5	4	4:21.1	NM
1981	5	10	22:22.5	FQ
1981	5	19	0: 5.1	FM
1981	5	26	21: 2.3	LQ
1981	6	2	11:33.9	NM
1981	6	9	11:33.8	FQ
1981	6	17	15: 6.5	FM
1981	6	25	4:27.1	LQ
1981	7	1	19: 5.4	NM
1981	7	9	2:40.4	FQ
1981	7	17	4:41.3	FM
1981	7	24	9:41.9	LQ
1981	7	31	3:54.1	NM
1981	8	7	19:28.0	FQ
1981	8	15	16:39.3	FM
1981	8	22	14:17.7	LQ
1981	8	29	14:45.0	NM
1981	9	6	13:27.7	FQ
1981	9	14	3:11.1	FM
1981	9	20	19:49.6	LQ
1981	9	28	4: 8.2	NM
1981	10	6	7:46.7	FQ
1981	10	13	12:51.4	FM
1981	10	20	3:42.6	LQ
1981	10	27	20:14.0	NM
1981	11	5	1: 9.5	FQ
1981	11	11	22:28.1	FM
1981	11	18	14:55.4	LQ
1981	11	26	14:39.2	NM
1981	12	4	16:22.4	FQ
1981	12	11	8:42.6	FM
1981	12	18	5:48.3	LQ
1981	12	26	10:10.7	NM
1982	1	3	4:45.5	FQ
1982	1	9	19:53.6	FM
1982	1	16	23:59.4	LQ
1982	1	25	4:56.9	NM
1982	2	1	14:27.9	FQ
1982	2	8	7:57.6	FM
1982	2	15	20:23.6	LQ
1982	2	23	21:15.1	NM
1982	3	2	22:15.7	FQ
1982	3	9	20:45.7	FM
1982	3	17	17:17.7	LQ
1982	3	25	10:19.8	NM
1982	4	1	5: 9.3	FQ
1982	4	8	10:19.0	FM
1982	4	16	12:44.9	LQ
1982	4	23	20:30.5	NM
1982	4	30	12: 8.4	FQ
1982	5	8	0:45.4	FM
1982	5	16	5:13.3	LQ
1982	5	23	4:41.9	NM
1982	5	29	20: 7.5	FQ
1982	6	6	16: 0.3	FM
1982	6	14	18: 7.4	LQ
1982	6	21	11:53.1	NM
1982	6	28	5:57.3	FQ
1982	7	6	7:32.9	FM
1982	7	14	3:48.0	LQ
1982	7	20	18:57.7	NM
1982	7	27	18:22.5	FQ
1982	8	4	22:35.5	FM
1982	8	12	11: 9.8	LQ
1982	8	19	2:45.9	NM
1982	8	26	9:50.1	FQ
1982	9	3	12:30.3	FM
1982	9	10	17:20.2	LQ
1982	9	17	12: 9.7	NM
1982	9	25	4: 7.5	FQ
1982	10	3	1:10.6	FM
1982	10	9	23:28.3	LQ
1982	10	17	0: 4.2	NM
1982	10	25	0: 7.8	FQ
1982	11	1	12:58.7	FM
1982	11	8	6:40.1	LQ
1982	11	15	15:10.6	NM
1982	11	23	20: 5.7	FQ
1982	12	1	0:22.5	FM
1982	12	7	15:55.6	LQ
1982	12	15	9:19.5	NM
1982	12	23	14:17.3	FQ
1982	12	30	11:33.8	FM
1983	1	6	4: 2.0	LQ
1983	1	14	5: 9.1	NM
1983	1	22	5:34.0	FQ
1983	1	28	22:26.9	FM
1983	2	4	19:18.9	LQ
1983	2	13	0:33.4	NM
1983	2	20	17:32.3	FQ
1983	2	27	8:58.7	FM
1983	3	6	13:17.8	LQ
1983	3	14	17:45.7	NM
1983	3	22	2:26.0	FQ
1983	3	28	19:27.3	FM
1983	4	5	8:39.9	LQ
1983	4	13	8: 0.4	NM
1983	4	20	8:58.8	FQ
1983	4	27	6:31.3	FM
1983	5	5	3:44.3	LQ
1983	5	12	19:26.7	NM
1983	5	19	14:18.3	FQ
1983	5	26	18:48.5	FM
1983	6	3	21: 9.2	LQ
1983	6	11	4:38.8	NM
1983	6	17	19:47.2	FQ
1983	6	25	8:33.0	FM
1983	7	3	12:14.2	LQ
1983	7	10	12:19.5	NM
1983	7	17	2:51.6	FQ
1983	7	24	23:28.6	FM
1983	8	2	0:54.7	LQ
1983	8	8	19:19.0	NM
1983	8	15	12:47.8	FQ
1983	8	23	15: 1.4	FM
1983	8	31	11:24.6	LQ
1983	9	7	2:36.1	NM
1983	9	14	2:24.1	FQ
1983	9	22	6:38.6	FM
1983	9	29	20: 7.2	LQ
1983	10	6	11:16.7	NM
1983	10	13	19:42.2	FQ
1983	10	21	21:55.7	FM
1983	10	29	3:38.7	LQ
1983	11	4	22:22.1	NM
1983	11	12	15:49.3	FQ
1983	11	20	12:31.5	FM
1983	11	27	10:52.0	LQ
1983	12	4	12:27.2	NM
1983	12	12	13:10.0	FQ
1983	12	20	2: 1.7	FM
1983	12	26	18:54.2	LQ
1984	1	3	5:17.1	NM
1984	1	11	9:49.6	FQ
1984	1	18	14: 5.8	FM
1984	1	25	4:49.3	LQ
1984	2	1	23:47.4	NM
1984	2	10	4: 0.4	FQ
1984	2	17	0:41.4	FM
1984	2	23	17:12.9	LQ
1984	3	2	18:31.7	NM
1984	3	10	18:27.7	FQ
1984	3	17	10: 9.9	FM
1984	3	24	7:58.7	LQ
1984	4	1	12:10.5	NM
1984	4	9	4:51.5	FQ
1984	4	15	19:10.9	FM
1984	4	23	0:26.6	LQ
1984	5	1	3:46.4	NM
1984	5	8	11:49.8	FQ
1984	5	15	4:28.8	FM
1984	5	22	17:46.1	LQ
1984	5	30	16:49.0	NM
1984	6	6	16:42.1	FQ
1984	6	13	14:42.2	FM
1984	6	21	11:12.1	LQ
1984	6	29	3:19.4	NM
1984	7	5	21: 5.0	FQ
1984	7	13	2:20.7	FM
1984	7	21	4: 4.5	LQ
1984	7	28	11:52.2	NM
1984	8	4	2:34.2	FQ
1984	8	11	15:44.7	FM
1984	8	19	19:43.5	LQ
1984	8	26	19:26.7	NM
1984	9	2	10:31.3	FQ
1984	9	10	7: 3.1	FM
1984	9	18	9:33.2	LQ
1984	9	25	3:12.1	NM
1984	10	1	21:53.9	FQ
1984	10	10	0: 0.8	FM
1984	10	17	21:15.6	LQ
1984	10	24	12: 9.8	NM
1984	10	31	13: 8.5	FQ
1984	11	8	17:45.3	FM
1984	11	16	7: 0.7	LQ
1984	11	22	22:58.6	NM
1984	11	30	8: 1.9	FQ
1984	12	8	10:55.7	FM
1984	12	15	15:26.7	LQ
1984	12	22	11:48.6	NM
1984	12	30	5:29.3	FQ
1985	1	7	2:18.1	FM
1985	1	13	23:28.2	LQ
1985	1	21	2:30.2	NM
1985	1	29	3:30.5	FQ
1985	2	5	15:20.4	FM
1985	2	12	7:58.3	LQ
1985	2	19	18:44.3	NM
1985	2	27	23:41.5	FQ
1985	3	7	2:14.4	FM
1985	3	13	17:35.3	LQ
1985	3	21	12: 0.1	NM
1985	3	29	16:11.7	FQ
1985	4	5	11:33.3	FM
1985	4	12	4:42.6	LQ
1985	4	20	5:23.2	NM
1985	4	28	4:25.1	FQ
1985	5	4	19:53.1	FM
1985	5	11	17:35.0	LQ
1985	5	19	21:42.4	NM
1985	5	27	12:55.4	FQ
1985	6	3	3:50.3	FM
1985	6	10	8:20.8	LQ
1985	6	18	11:59.0	NM
1985	6	25	18:53.2	FQ
1985	7	2	12: 8.3	FM
1985	7	10	0:51.4	LQ
1985	7	17	23:56.9	NM
1985	7	24	23:39.9	FQ
1985	7	31	21:40.9	FM
1985	8	8	18:30.4	LQ
1985	8	16	10: 5.6	NM
1985	8	23	4:37.5	FQ
1985	8	30	9:27.0	FM
1985	9	7	12:16.8	LQ
1985	9	14	19:20.0	NM
1985	9	21	11: 4.9	FQ
1985	9	29	0: 9.1	FM
1985	10	7	5: 5.2	LQ
1985	10	14	4:33.6	NM
1985	10	20	20:14.4	FQ
1985	10	28	17:39.3	FM
1985	11	5	20: 8.0	LQ
1985	11	12	14:21.1	NM
1985	11	19	9: 4.7	FQ
1985	11	27	12:43.9	FM
1985	12	5	9: 2.8	LQ
1985	12	12	0:56.0	NM
1985	12	19	1:59.1	FQ
1985	12	27	7:32.6	FM
1986	1	3	19:48.7	LQ
1986	1	10	12:24.0	NM
1986	1	17	22:14.4	FQ
1986	1	26	0:33.6	FM
1986	2	2	4:42.4	LQ
1986	2	9	0:58.1	NM
1986	2	16	19:55.7	FQ
1986	2	24	15: 4.8	FM
1986	3	3	12:19.2	LQ
1986	3	10	14:54.5	NM
1986	3	18	16:39.4	FQ
1986	3	26	3: 4.0	FM
1986	4	1	19:31.8	LQ
1986	4	9	6:10.8	NM
1986	4	17	10:35.8	FQ
1986	4	24	12:48.0	FM
1986	5	1	3:23.6	LQ
1986	5	8	22:11.8	NM
1986	5	17	1: 0.4	FQ
1986	5	23	20:45.5	FM
1986	5	30	12:55.8	LQ
1986	6	7	14: 2.0	NM
1986	6	15	12: 0.4	FQ
1986	6	22	3:42.1	FM
1986	6	29	0:54.1	LQ
1986	7	7	4:55.7	NM
1986	7	14	20:10.9	FQ
1986	7	21	10:40.4	FM
1986	7	28	15:34.9	LQ
1986	8	5	18:35.8	NM
1986	8	13	2:22.7	FQ
1986	8	19	18:54.0	FM
1986	8	27	8:39.0	LQ
1986	9	4	7: 9.9	NM
1986	9	11	7:42.3	FQ
1986	9	18	5:33.3	FM
1986	9	26	3:18.3	LQ
1986	10	3	18:54.1	NM
1986	10	10	13:29.9	FQ
1986	10	17	19:21.9	FM
1986	10	25	22:27.5	LQ
1986	11	2	6: 1.7	NM
1986	11	8	21:12.1	FQ
1986	11	16	12:12.9	FM
1986	11	24	16:53.0	LQ
1986	12	1	16:43.0	NM
1986	12	8	8: 2.8	FQ
1986	12	16	7: 6.2	FM
1986	12	24	9:19.4	LQ
1986	12	31	3:11.3	NM
1987	1	6	22:35.3	FQ
1987	1	15	2:32.2	FM
1987	1	22	22:47.1	LQ
1987	1	29	13:47.0	NM
1987	2	5	16:20.9	FQ
1987	2	13	20:59.7	FM
1987	2	21	8:57.1	LQ
1987	2	28	0:53.6	NM
1987	3	7	11:58.2	FQ
1987	3	15	13:14.8	FM
1987	3	22	16:22.6	LQ
1987	3	29	12:48.3	NM
1987	4	6	7:48.3	FQ
1987	4	14	2:33.1	FM
1987	4	20	22:15.8	LQ
1987	4	28	1:36.6	NM
1987	5	6	2:26.6	FQ
1987	5	13	12:51.7	FM
1987	5	20	4: 2.9	LQ
1987	5	27	15:14.9	NM
1987	6	4	18:53.5	FQ
1987	6	11	20:49.7	FM
1987	6	18	11: 2.9	LQ
1987	6	26	5:37.7	NM
1987	7	4	8:34.9	FQ
1987	7	11	3:33.5	FM
1987	7	17	20:17.5	LQ
1987	7	25	20:37.7	NM
1987	8	2	19:24.7	FQ
1987	8	9	10:18.1	FM
1987	8	16	8:25.9	LQ
1987	8	24	11:58.4	NM
1987	9	1	3:48.3	FQ
1987	9	7	18:13.2	FM
1987	9	14	23:45.6	LQ
1987	9	23	3: 7.8	NM
1987	9	30	10:39.7	FQ
1987	10	7	4:12.3	FM
1987	10	14	18: 7.5	LQ
1987	10	22	17:27.3	NM
1987	10	29	17:11.1	FQ
1987	11	5	16:46.0	FM
1987	11	13	14:40.8	LQ
1987	11	21	6:32.6	NM
1987	11	28	0:38.2	FQ
1987	12	5	8: 1.5	FM
1987	12	13	11:43.6	LQ
1987	12	20	18:25.6	NM
1987	12	27	10: 2.0	FQ
1988	1	4	1:41.3	FM
1988	1	12	7: 5.7	LQ
1988	1	19	5:26.9	NM
1988	1	25	21:54.5	FQ
1988	2	2	20:52.4	FM
1988	2	10	23: 2.3	LQ
1988	2	17	15:56.3	NM
1988	2	24	12:15.9	FQ
1988	3	3	16: 2.1	FM
1988	3	11	10:57.0	LQ
1988	3	18	2: 4.6	NM
1988	3	25	4:42.6	FQ
1988	4	2	9:23.1	FM
1988	4	9	19:21.1	LQ
1988	4	16	12: 2.2	NM
1988	4	23	22:33.3	FQ
1988	5	1	23:43.2	FM
1988	5	9	1:23.2	LQ
1988	5	15	22:12.6	NM
1988	5	23	16:49.8	FQ
1988	5	31	10:55.6	FM
1988	6	7	6:22.5	LQ
1988	6	14	9:15.4	NM
1988	6	22	10:23.7	FQ
1988	6	29	19:47.7	FM
1988	7	6	11:37.9	LQ
1988	7	13	21:54.2	NM
1988	7	22	2:14.9	FQ
1988	7	29	3:27.3	FM
1988	8	4	18:24.6	LQ
1988	8	12	12:31.8	NM
1988	8	20	15:52.2	FQ
1988	8	27	10:57.4	FM
1988	9	3	3:52.4	LQ
1988	9	11	4:49.7	NM
1988	9	19	3:18.8	FQ
1988	9	25	19: 7.9	FM
1988	10	2	16:59.9	LQ
1988	10	10	21:48.9	NM
1988	10	18	13: 1.4	FQ
1988	10	25	4:35.9	FM
1988	11	1	10:12.8	LQ
1988	11	9	14:19.7	NM
1988	11	16	21:35.8	FQ
1988	11	23	15:53.1	FM
1988	12	1	6:50.4	LQ
1988	12	9	5:35.9	NM
1988	12	16	5:41.0	FQ
1988	12	23	5:28.9	FM
1988	12	31	4:57.1	LQ
1989	1	7	19:22.4	NM
1989	1	14	13:59.5	FQ
1989	1	21	21:33.8	FM
1989	1	30	2: 3.3	LQ
1989	2	6	7:37.8	NM
1989	2	12	23:16.1	FQ
1989	2	20	15:32.4	FM
1989	2	28	20: 9.7	LQ
1989	3	7	18:20.1	NM
1989	3	14	10:12.3	FQ
1989	3	22	9:58.8	FM
1989	3	30	10:22.8	LQ
1989	4	6	3:34.6	NM
1989	4	12	23:14.2	FQ
1989	4	21	3:15.1	FM
1989	4	28	20:47.1	LQ
1989	5	5	11:48.5	NM
1989	5	12	14:20.4	FQ
1989	5	20	18:18.5	FM
1989	5	28	4: 2.2	LQ
1989	6	3	19:54.9	NM
1989	6	11	6:59.0	FQ
1989	6	19	6:59.5	FM
1989	6	26	9:10.8	LQ
1989	7	3	5: 0.9	NM
1989	7	11	0:19.1	FQ
1989	7	18	17:43.9	FM
1989	7	25	13:33.5	LQ
1989	8	1	16: 6.9	NM
1989	8	9	17:29.4	FQ

1989	8	17	3: 8.8	FM
1989	8	23	18:42.6	LQ
1989	8	31	5:45.6	NM
1989	9	8	9:50.5	FQ
1989	9	15	11:52.2	FM
1989	9	22	2:11.8	LQ
1989	9	29	21:47.9	NM
1989	10	8	0:53.4	FQ
1989	10	14	20:33.1	FM
1989	10	21	13:20.2	LQ
1989	10	29	15:27.9	NM
1989	11	6	14:11.7	FQ
1989	11	13	5:52.5	FM
1989	11	20	4:44.5	LQ
1989	11	28	9:41.3	NM
1989	12	6	1:26.3	FQ
1989	12	12	16:30.8	FM
1989	12	19	23:55.0	LQ
1989	12	28	3:20.2	NM
1990	1	4	10:41.0	FQ
1990	1	11	4:57.7	FM
1990	1	18	21:18.3	LQ
1990	1	26	19:20.9	NM
1990	2	2	18:33.5	FQ
1990	2	9	19:16.4	FM
1990	2	17	18:50.0	LQ
1990	2	25	8:55.9	NM
1990	3	4	2: 6.3	FQ
1990	3	11	10:59.1	FM
1990	3	19	14:33.3	LQ
1990	3	26	19:50.0	NM
1990	4	2	10:25.2	FQ
1990	4	10	3:19.2	FM
1990	4	18	7: 4.9	LQ
1990	4	25	4:29.0	NM
1990	5	1	20:18.3	FQ
1990	5	9	19:31.5	FM
1990	5	17	19:46.6	LQ
1990	5	24	11:48.5	NM
1990	5	31	8:10.4	FQ
1990	6	8	11: 1.8	FM
1990	6	16	4:48.7	LQ
1990	6	22	18:55.7	NM
1990	6	29	22: 6.8	FQ
1990	7	8	1:24.2	FM
1990	7	15	11: 4.5	LQ
1990	7	22	2:54.9	NM
1990	7	29	14: 1.0	FQ
1990	8	6	14:20.3	FM
1990	8	13	15:55.1	LQ
1990	8	20	12:39.1	NM
1990	8	28	7:34.4	FQ
1990	9	5	1:46.6	FM
1990	9	11	20:54.1	LQ
1990	9	19	0:46.2	NM
1990	9	27	2: 6.2	FQ
1990	10	4	12: 2.9	FM
1990	10	11	3:32.7	LQ
1990	10	18	15:36.6	NM
1990	10	26	20:26.7	FQ
1990	11	2	21:49.6	FM
1990	11	9	13: 3.4	LQ
1990	11	17	9: 5.1	NM
1990	11	25	13:11.8	FQ
1990	12	2	7:51.2	FM
1990	12	9	2: 5.4	LQ
1990	12	17	4:22.7	NM
1990	12	25	3:16.2	FQ
1990	12	31	18:36.5	FM
1991	1	7	18:36.9	LQ
1991	1	15	23:50.7	NM
1991	1	23	14:21.8	FQ
1991	1	30	6:10.5	FM
1991	2	6	13:54.4	LQ
1991	2	14	17:33.4	NM
1991	2	21	22:58.6	FQ
1991	2	28	18:25.1	FM
1991	3	8	10:34.8	LQ
1991	3	16	8:12.8	NM
1991	3	23	6: 3.5	FQ
1991	3	30	7:17.8	FM
1991	4	7	6:47.9	LQ
1991	4	14	19:39.5	NM
1991	4	21	12:39.6	FQ
1991	4	28	20:58.9	FM
1991	5	7	0:48.2	LQ
1991	5	14	4:37.2	NM
1991	5	20	19:46.6	FQ
1991	5	28	11:37.1	FM
1991	6	5	15:31.5	LQ
1991	6	12	12: 7.1	NM
1991	6	19	4:20.0	FQ
1991	6	27	2:59.1	FM
1991	7	5	2:51.3	LQ
1991	7	11	19: 6.9	NM
1991	7	18	15:11.1	FQ
1991	7	26	18:25.3	FM
1991	8	3	11:26.3	LQ
1991	8	10	2:28.2	NM
1991	8	17	5: 0.9	FQ
1991	8	25	9: 8.4	FM
1991	9	1	18:17.2	LQ
1991	9	8	11: 1.0	NM
1991	9	15	22: 1.2	FQ
1991	9	23	22:41.4	FM
1991	10	1	0:30.7	LQ
1991	10	7	21:38.4	NM
1991	10	15	17:32.2	FQ
1991	10	23	11: 9.6	FM
1991	10	30	7:12.1	LQ
1991	11	6	11:10.7	NM
1991	11	14	14: 0.9	FQ
1991	11	21	22:57.8	FM
1991	11	28	15:23.0	LQ
1991	12	6	3:57.0	NM
1991	12	14	9:32.0	FQ
1991	12	21	10:24.3	FM
1991	12	28	1:56.8	LQ
1992	1	4	23:10.5	NM
1992	1	13	2:32.4	FQ
1992	1	19	21:28.9	FM
1992	1	26	15:28.7	LQ
1992	2	3	19: 0.5	NM
1992	2	11	16:14.7	FQ
1992	2	18	8: 4.2	FM
1992	2	25	7:57.4	LQ
1992	3	4	13:23.7	NM
1992	3	12	2:35.8	FQ
1992	3	18	18:17.9	FM
1992	3	26	2:31.2	LQ
1992	4	3	5: 3.3	NM
1992	4	10	10: 6.4	FQ
1992	4	17	4:42.6	FM
1992	4	24	21:40.8	LQ
1992	5	2	17:45.9	NM
1992	5	9	15:44.5	FQ
1992	5	16	16: 2.9	FM
1992	5	24	15:54.7	LQ
1992	6	1	3:57.8	NM
1992	6	7	20:48.1	FQ
1992	6	15	4:50.6	FM
1992	6	23	8:13.1	LQ
1992	6	30	12:19.1	NM
1992	7	7	2:44.8	FQ
1992	7	14	19: 7.7	FM
1992	7	22	22:14.7	LQ
1992	7	29	19:36.1	NM
1992	8	5	10:59.5	FQ
1992	8	13	10:28.9	FM
1992	8	21	10: 3.4	LQ
1992	8	28	2:42.7	NM
1992	9	3	22:38.9	FQ
1992	9	12	2:18.5	FM
1992	9	19	19:54.6	LQ
1992	9	26	10:40.7	NM
1992	10	3	14:11.3	FQ
1992	10	11	18: 4.8	FM
1992	10	19	4:13.3	LQ
1992	10	25	20:34.1	NM
1992	11	2	9:10.3	FQ
1992	11	10	9:21.7	FM
1992	11	17	11:40.3	LQ
1992	11	24	9:11.9	NM
1992	12	2	6:16.8	FQ
1992	12	9	23:42.0	FM
1992	12	16	19:14.5	LQ
1992	12	24	0:44.0	NM
1993	1	1	3:39.4	FQ
1993	1	8	12:38.2	FM
1993	1	15	4: 2.9	LQ
1993	1	22	18:28.2	NM
1993	1	30	23:21.2	FQ
1993	2	6	23:56.2	FM
1993	2	13	14:58.3	LQ
1993	2	21	13: 6.4	NM
1993	3	1	15:47.5	FQ
1993	3	8	9:46.6	FM
1993	3	15	4:17.7	LQ
1993	3	23	7:15.8	NM
1993	3	31	4:10.3	FQ
1993	4	6	18:43.9	FM
1993	4	13	19:39.3	LQ
1993	4	21	23:50.4	NM
1993	4	29	12:41.0	FQ
1993	5	6	3:34.1	FM
1993	5	13	12:20.6	LQ
1993	5	21	14: 7.8	NM
1993	5	28	18:21.9	FQ
1993	6	4	13: 2.5	FM
1993	6	12	5:37.6	LQ
1993	6	20	1:53.4	NM
1993	6	26	22:44.0	FQ
1993	7	3	23:45.5	FM
1993	7	11	22:51.2	LQ
1993	7	19	11:24.6	NM
1993	7	26	3:25.8	FQ
1993	8	2	12:10.2	FM
1993	8	10	15:21.8	LQ
1993	8	17	19:28.6	NM
1993	8	24	9:58.1	FQ
1993	9	1	2:33.6	FM
1993	9	9	6:27.9	LQ
1993	9	16	3:10.5	NM
1993	9	22	19:32.5	FQ
1993	9	30	18:54.7	FM
1993	10	8	19:36.0	LQ
1993	10	15	11:36.1	NM
1993	10	22	8:51.6	FQ
1993	10	30	12:38.7	FM
1993	11	7	6:36.1	LQ
1993	11	13	21:34.7	NM
1993	11	21	2: 2.7	FQ
1993	11	29	6:31.8	FM
1993	12	6	15:49.2	LQ
1993	12	13	9:27.7	NM
1993	12	20	22:26.5	FQ
1993	12	28	23: 6.6	FM
1994	1	5	0: 1.3	LQ
1994	1	11	23:11.7	NM
1994	1	19	20:27.8	FQ
1994	1	27	13:24.4	FM
1994	2	3	8: 7.4	LQ
1994	2	10	14:31.7	NM
1994	2	18	17:48.5	FQ
1994	2	26	1:16.8	FM
1994	3	4	16:54.9	LQ
1994	3	12	7: 6.6	NM
1994	3	20	12:15.5	FQ
1994	3	27	11:11.1	FM
1994	4	3	2:56.3	LQ
1994	4	11	0:18.9	NM
1994	4	19	2:35.0	FQ
1994	4	25	19:46.0	FM
1994	5	2	14:33.8	LQ
1994	5	10	17: 8.1	NM
1994	5	18	12:50.0	FQ
1994	5	25	3:39.6	FM
1994	6	1	4: 3.8	LQ
1994	6	9	8:27.6	NM
1994	6	16	19:56.6	FQ
1994	6	23	11:32.9	FM
1994	6	30	19:32.6	LQ
1994	7	8	21:38.0	NM
1994	7	16	1:12.2	FQ
1994	7	22	20:15.8	FM
1994	7	30	12:41.7	LQ
1994	8	7	8:45.4	NM
1994	8	14	5:58.5	FQ
1994	8	21	6:46.5	FM
1994	8	29	6:41.8	LQ
1994	9	5	18:32.8	NM
1994	9	12	11:35.6	FQ
1994	9	19	20: 0.4	FM
1994	9	28	0:24.2	LQ
1994	10	5	3:55.2	NM
1994	10	11	19:19.0	FQ
1994	10	19	12:18.7	FM
1994	10	27	16:45.3	LQ
1994	11	3	13:35.7	NM
1994	11	10	6:14.8	FQ
1994	11	18	6:58.5	FM
1994	11	26	7: 4.8	LQ
1994	12	2	23:54.6	NM
1994	12	9	21: 6.7	FQ
1994	12	18	2:18.4	FM
1994	12	25	19: 7.3	LQ
1995	1	1	10:56.8	NM
1995	1	8	15:46.8	FQ
1995	1	16	20:27.9	FM
1995	1	24	4:58.8	LQ
1995	1	30	22:49.6	NM
1995	2	7	12:53.9	FQ
1995	2	15	12:17.2	FM
1995	2	22	13: 4.8	LQ
1995	3	1	11:50.0	NM
1995	3	9	10:13.4	FQ
1995	3	17	1:27.5	FM
1995	3	23	20:11.1	LQ
1995	3	31	2:10.8	NM
1995	4	8	5:35.2	FQ
1995	4	15	12: 9.7	FM
1995	4	22	3:19.5	LQ
1995	4	29	17:38.2	NM
1995	5	7	21:44.3	FQ
1995	5	14	20:48.9	FM
1995	5	21	11:36.7	LQ
1995	5	29	9:28.5	NM
1995	6	6	10:26.0	FQ
1995	6	13	4: 3.6	FM
1995	6	19	22: 1.5	LQ
1995	6	28	0:50.8	NM
1995	7	5	20: 3.1	FQ
1995	7	12	10:49.4	FM
1995	7	19	11:10.2	LQ
1995	7	27	15:13.3	NM
1995	8	4	3:17.1	FQ
1995	8	10	18:15.6	FM
1995	8	18	3: 4.4	LQ
1995	8	26	4:30.9	NM
1995	9	2	9: 4.7	FQ
1995	9	9	3:36.5	FM
1995	9	16	21:10.3	LQ
1995	9	24	16:54.6	NM
1995	10	1	14:37.4	FQ
1995	10	8	15:52.0	FM
1995	10	16	16:27.7	LQ
1995	10	24	4:36.0	NM
1995	10	30	21:18.5	FQ
1995	11	7	7:21.5	FM
1995	11	15	11:42.5	LQ
1995	11	22	15:42.8	NM
1995	11	29	6:29.7	FQ
1995	12	7	1:28.3	FM
1995	12	15	5:33.6	LQ
1995	12	22	2:23.1	NM
1995	12	28	19: 7.2	FQ
1996	1	5	20:52.1	FM
1996	1	13	20:46.6	LQ
1996	1	20	12:52.0	NM
1996	1	27	11:13.4	FQ
1996	2	4	15:58.7	FM
1996	2	12	8:38.0	LQ
1996	2	18	23:32.4	NM
1996	2	26	5:51.7	FQ
1996	3	5	9:24.2	FM
1996	3	12	17:15.6	LQ
1996	3	19	10:47.3	NM
1996	3	27	1:31.0	FQ
1996	4	4	0: 9.1	FM
1996	4	10	23:36.5	LQ
1996	4	17	22:51.3	NM
1996	4	25	20:41.5	FQ
1996	5	3	11:50.5	FM
1996	5	10	5: 4.6	LQ
1996	5	17	11:48.6	NM
1996	5	25	14:14.7	FQ
1996	6	1	20:48.8	FM
1996	6	8	11: 6.6	LQ
1996	6	16	1:37.8	NM
1996	6	24	5:25.1	FQ
1996	7	1	3:59.9	FM
1996	7	7	18:56.1	LQ
1996	7	15	16:16.2	NM
1996	7	23	17:50.5	FQ
1996	7	30	10:36.8	FM
1996	8	6	5:26.2	LQ
1996	8	14	7:34.5	NM
1996	8	22	3:37.7	FQ
1996	8	28	17:53.2	FM
1996	9	4	19: 7.3	LQ
1996	9	12	23: 7.4	NM
1996	9	20	11:23.7	FQ
1996	9	27	2:51.2	FM
1996	10	4	12: 5.7	LQ
1996	10	12	14:14.2	NM
1996	10	19	18: 9.9	FQ
1996	10	26	14:11.3	FM
1996	11	3	7:52.6	LQ
1996	11	11	4:15.7	NM
1996	11	18	1: 9.8	FQ
1996	11	25	4:10.1	FM
1996	12	3	5: 8.1	LQ
1996	12	10	16:56.1	NM
1996	12	17	9:31.9	FQ
1996	12	24	20:41.3	FM
1997	1	2	1:46.8	LQ
1997	1	9	4:26.2	NM
1997	1	15	20: 2.6	FQ
1997	1	23	15:11.0	FM
1997	1	31	19:41.5	LQ
1997	2	7	15: 7.5	NM
1997	2	14	8:57.7	FQ
1997	2	22	10:27.0	FM
1997	3	2	9:38.3	LQ
1997	3	9	1:16.4	NM
1997	3	16	0: 6.7	FQ
1997	3	24	4:46.3	FM
1997	3	31	19:38.5	LQ
1997	4	7	11: 4.0	NM
1997	4	14	17: 1.1	FQ
1997	4	22	20:35.8	FM
1997	4	30	2:37.5	LQ
1997	5	6	20:48.9	NM
1997	5	14	10:56.6	FQ
1997	5	22	9:16.2	FM
1997	5	29	7:52.5	LQ
1997	6	5	7: 6.0	NM
1997	6	13	4:53.1	FQ
1997	6	20	19:11.6	FM
1997	6	27	12:44.2	LQ
1997	7	4	18:41.9	NM
1997	7	12	21:45.1	FQ
1997	7	20	3:23.2	FM
1997	7	26	18:30.9	LQ
1997	8	3	8:15.6	NM
1997	8	11	12:43.9	FQ
1997	8	18	10:58.1	FM
1997	8	25	2:26.5	LQ
1997	9	1	23:53.0	NM
1997	9	10	1:32.4	FQ
1997	9	16	18:52.2	FM
1997	9	23	13:37.4	LQ
1997	10	1	16:52.6	NM
1997	10	9	12:23.1	FQ
1997	10	16	3:46.7	FM
1997	10	23	4:50.2	LQ
1997	10	31	10: 1.8	NM
1997	11	7	21:44.5	FQ
1997	11	14	14:12.4	FM
1997	11	22	0: 0.1	LQ
1997	11	30	2:14.8	NM
1997	12	7	6:10.6	FQ
1997	12	14	2:37.9	FM
1997	12	21	21:44.8	LQ
1997	12	29	16:57.5	NM
1998	1	5	14:19.7	FQ
1998	1	12	17:24.7	FM
1998	1	20	19:41.8	LQ
1998	1	28	6: 2.2	NM
1998	2	3	22:55.2	FQ
1998	2	11	10:23.7	FM
1998	2	19	15:29.0	LQ
1998	2	26	17:27.5	NM
1998	3	5	8:42.6	FQ
1998	3	13	4:35.0	FM
1998	3	21	7:39.6	LQ
1998	3	28	3:15.2	NM
1998	4	3	20:19.7	FQ
1998	4	11	22:24.5	FM
1998	4	19	19:53.6	LQ
1998	4	26	11:42.9	NM
1998	5	3	10: 4.4	FQ
1998	5	11	14:30.9	FM
1998	5	19	4:36.2	LQ
1998	5	25	19:33.8	NM
1998	6	2	1:44.9	FQ
1998	6	10	4:20.0	FM
1998	6	17	10:39.4	LQ
1998	6	24	3:51.8	NM
1998	7	1	18:42.3	FQ
1998	7	9	16: 2.8	FM
1998	7	16	15:15.3	LQ
1998	7	23	13:45.0	NM
1998	7	31	12: 5.4	FQ
1998	8	8	2:11.8	FM
1998	8	14	19:50.8	LQ
1998	8	22	2: 4.2	NM
1998	8	30	5: 7.6	FQ
1998	9	6	11:23.3	FM
1998	9	13	2: 0.3	LQ
1998	9	20	17: 2.6	NM
1998	9	28	21:12.4	FQ
1998	10	5	20:13.5	FM
1998	10	12	11:12.9	LQ
1998	10	20	10:10.7	NM
1998	10	28	11:47.6	FQ
1998	11	4	5:19.7	FM
1998	11	11	0:29.8	LQ
1998	11	19	4:28.2	NM
1998	11	27	0:23.8	FQ
1998	12	3	15:20.9	FM
1998	12	10	17:55.0	LQ
1998	12	18	22:43.9	NM
1998	12	26	10:47.3	FQ
1999	1	2	2:51.4	FM
1999	1	9	14:23.2	LQ
1999	1	17	15:47.9	NM
1999	1	24	19:16.8	FQ
1999	1	31	16: 8.3	FM
1999	2	8	12: 0.5	LQ
1999	2	16	6:40.9	NM
1999	2	23	2:44.7	FQ
1999	3	2	6:59.9	FM
1999	3	10	8:43.8	LQ
1999	3	17	18:50.2	NM
1999	3	24	10:19.5	FQ
1999	3	31	22:50.0	FM
1999	4	9	2:53.7	LQ
1999	4	16	4:23.6	NM
1999	4	22	19: 2.6	FQ
1999	4	30	14:55.5	FM
1999	5	8	17:30.7	LQ
1999	5	15	12: 6.5	NM
1999	5	22	5:34.2	FQ
1999	5	30	6:40.7	FM
1999	6	7	4:21.4	LQ
1999	6	13	19: 4.3	NM
1999	6	20	18:12.6	FQ
1999	6	28	21:38.5	FM
1999	7	6	11:58.0	LQ
1999	7	13	2:25.3	NM
1999	7	20	9: 0.3	FQ
1999	7	28	11:26.4	FM
1999	8	4	17:28.0	LQ
1999	8	11	11: 9.7	NM
1999	8	19	1:47.9	FQ
1999	8	26	23:49.8	FM
1999	9	2	22:19.0	LQ
1999	9	9	22: 3.3	NM
1999	9	17	20: 7.5	FQ
1999	9	25	10:53.2	FM
1999	10	2	4: 4.1	LQ
1999	10	9	11:35.3	NM
1999	10	17	15: 1.3	FQ
1999	10	24	21: 4.4	FM
1999	10	31	12: 6.0	LQ
1999	11	8	3:54.1	NM
1999	11	16	9: 4.1	FQ
1999	11	23	7: 5.7	FM
1999	11	29	23:20.7	LQ

1999	12	7	22:33.1	NM
1999	12	16	0:51.0	FQ
1999	12	22	17:33.1	FM
1999	12	29	14: 6.0	LQ
2000	1	6	18:15.0	NM
2000	1	14	13:34.7	FQ
2000	1	21	4:41.8	FM
2000	1	28	7:58.7	LQ
2000	2	5	13: 4.9	NM
2000	2	12	23:21.8	FQ
2000	2	19	16:27.6	FM
2000	2	27	3:56.5	LQ
2000	3	6	5:19.2	NM
2000	3	13	6:59.6	FQ
2000	3	20	4:45.2	FM
2000	3	28	0:23.9	LQ
2000	4	4	18:14.6	NM
2000	4	11	13:31.5	FQ
2000	4	18	17:42.3	FM
2000	4	26	19:32.7	LQ
2000	5	4	4:14.0	NM
2000	5	10	20: 1.8	FQ
2000	5	18	7:35.3	FM
2000	5	26	11:57.2	LQ
2000	6	2	12:15.6	NM
2000	6	9	3:30.5	FQ
2000	6	16	22:28.3	FM
2000	6	25	1: 1.9	LQ
2000	7	1	19:21.5	NM
2000	7	8	12:54.1	FQ
2000	7	16	13:56.9	FM
2000	7	24	11: 3.7	LQ
2000	7	31	2:26.6	NM
2000	8	7	1: 2.9	FQ
2000	8	15	5:14.8	FM
2000	8	22	18:52.4	LQ
2000	8	29	10:20.7	NM
2000	9	5	16:28.6	FQ
2000	9	13	19:39.3	FM
2000	9	21	1:30.4	LQ
2000	9	27	19:54.1	NM
2000	10	5	11: 0.2	FQ
2000	10	13	8:55.6	FM
2000	10	20	8: 1.5	LQ
2000	10	27	7:58.9	NM
2000	11	4	7:27.4	FQ
2000	11	11	21:17.1	FM
2000	11	18	15:27.3	LQ
2000	11	25	23:12.7	NM
2000	12	4	3:56.0	FQ
2000	12	11	9: 5.0	FM
2000	12	18	0:44.1	LQ
2000	12	25	17:23.6	NM
2001	1	2	22:32.7	FQ
2001	1	9	20:26.0	FM
2001	1	16	12:37.2	LQ
2001	1	24	13: 8.7	NM
2001	2	1	14: 3.4	FQ
2001	2	8	7:12.8	FM
2001	2	15	3:26.3	LQ
2001	2	23	8:23.4	NM
2001	3	3	2: 4.0	FQ
2001	3	9	17:24.2	FM
2001	3	16	20:48.0	LQ
2001	3	25	1:24.0	NM
2001	4	1	10:50.5	FQ
2001	4	8	3:23.2	FM
2001	4	15	15:33.5	LQ
2001	4	23	15:28.4	NM
2001	4	30	17: 9.4	FQ
2001	5	7	13:53.9	FM
2001	5	15	10:12.7	LQ
2001	5	23	2:48.2	NM
2001	5	29	22:11.1	FQ
2001	6	6	1:40.8	FM
2001	6	14	3:30.6	LQ
2001	6	21	11:59.4	NM
2001	6	28	3:21.5	FQ
2001	7	5	15: 5.4	FM
2001	7	13	18:47.7	LQ
2001	7	20	19:45.6	NM
2001	7	27	10: 9.7	FQ
2001	8	4	5:57.5	FM
2001	8	12	7:55.6	LQ
2001	8	19	2:56.2	NM
2001	8	25	19:55.6	FQ
2001	9	2	21:44.9	FM
2001	9	10	19: 1.4	LQ
2001	9	17	10:28.2	NM
2001	9	24	9:30.9	FQ
2001	10	2	13:50.8	FM
2001	10	10	4:21.2	LQ
2001	10	16	19:24.1	NM
2001	10	24	2:57.9	FQ
2001	11	1	5:43.2	FM
2001	11	8	12:22.9	LQ
2001	11	15	6:41.2	NM
2001	11	22	23:20.8	FQ
2001	11	30	20:51.2	FM
2001	12	7	19:53.7	LQ
2001	12	14	20:49.3	NM
2001	12	22	20:57.8	FQ

2001	12	30	10:42.5	FM
2002	1	6	3:57.1	LQ
2002	1	13	13:30.9	NM
2002	1	21	17:48.8	FQ
2002	1	28	22:52.2	FM
2002	2	4	13:35.6	LQ
2002	2	12	7:43.3	NM
2002	2	20	12: 3.8	FQ
2002	2	27	9:18.3	FM
2002	3	6	1:27.0	LQ
2002	3	14	2: 4.9	NM
2002	3	22	2:29.9	FQ
2002	3	28	18:26.5	FM
2002	4	4	15:31.0	LQ
2002	4	12	19:23.5	NM
2002	4	20	12:49.7	FQ
2002	4	27	3: 1.3	FM
2002	5	4	7:17.7	LQ
2002	5	12	10:47.2	NM
2002	5	19	19:43.2	FQ
2002	5	26	11:52.3	FM
2002	6	3	0: 7.1	LQ
2002	6	10	23:48.1	NM
2002	6	18	0:30.4	FQ
2002	6	24	21:43.3	FM
2002	7	2	17:22.0	LQ
2002	7	10	10:27.0	NM
2002	7	17	4:48.3	FQ
2002	7	24	9: 7.9	FM
2002	8	1	10:24.9	LQ
2002	8	8	19:15.8	NM
2002	8	15	10:13.5	FQ
2002	8	22	22:30.1	FM
2002	8	31	2:33.4	LQ
2002	9	7	3:10.8	NM
2002	9	13	18: 9.2	FQ
2002	9	21	14: 0.4	FM
2002	9	29	17: 4.3	LQ
2002	10	6	11:18.3	NM
2002	10	13	5:33.8	FQ
2002	10	21	7:21.8	FM
2002	10	29	5:28.8	LQ
2002	11	4	20:35.7	NM
2002	11	11	20:52.6	FQ
2002	11	20	1:35.8	FM
2002	11	27	15:47.5	LQ
2002	12	4	7:36.2	NM
2002	12	11	15:49.7	FQ
2002	12	19	19:12.3	FM
2002	12	27	0:32.4	LQ
2003	1	2	20:25.1	NM
2003	1	10	13:16.8	FQ
2003	1	18	10:49.9	FM
2003	1	25	8:34.9	LQ
2003	2	1	10:50.8	NM
2003	2	9	11:13.0	FQ
2003	2	16	23:53.3	FM
2003	2	23	16:47.8	LQ
2003	3	3	2:37.2	NM
2003	3	11	7:16.5	FQ
2003	3	18	10:36.3	FM
2003	3	25	1:52.8	LQ
2003	4	1	19:20.6	NM
2003	4	9	23:41.1	FQ
2003	4	16	19:37.0	FM
2003	4	23	12:19.8	LQ
2003	5	1	12:16.3	NM
2003	5	9	11:53.4	FQ
2003	5	16	3:36.5	FM
2003	5	23	0:32.0	LQ
2003	5	31	4:21.0	NM
2003	6	7	20:27.6	FQ
2003	6	14	11:16.0	FM
2003	6	21	14:46.6	LQ
2003	6	29	18:39.6	NM
2003	7	7	2:32.8	FQ
2003	7	13	19:21.6	FM
2003	7	21	7: 3.2	LQ
2003	7	29	6:53.2	NM
2003	8	5	7:28.7	FQ
2003	8	12	4:48.3	FM
2003	8	20	0:49.9	LQ
2003	8	27	17:26.5	NM
2003	9	3	12:35.9	FQ
2003	9	10	16:36.2	FM
2003	9	18	19: 4.1	LQ
2003	9	26	3: 9.5	NM
2003	10	2	19:11.6	FQ
2003	10	10	7:28.3	FM
2003	10	18	12:32.6	LQ
2003	10	25	12:50.9	NM
2003	11	1	4:26.7	FQ
2003	11	9	1:15.4	FM
2003	11	17	4:16.7	LQ
2003	11	23	23: 0.1	NM
2003	11	30	17:17.6	FQ
2003	12	8	20:39.0	FM
2003	12	16	17:44.0	LQ
2003	12	23	9:44.9	NM
2003	12	30	10: 4.9	FQ
2004	1	7	15:42.6	FM
2004	1	15	4:47.4	LQ

2004	1	21	21: 7.6	NM
2004	1	29	6: 4.6	FQ
2004	2	6	8:49.7	FM
2004	2	13	13:41.4	LQ
2004	2	20	9:20.9	NM
2004	2	28	3:24.8	FQ
2004	3	6	23:17.1	FM
2004	3	13	21: 2.8	LQ
2004	3	20	22:44.6	NM
2004	3	28	23:48.8	FQ
2004	4	5	11: 5.3	FM
2004	4	12	3:48.2	LQ
2004	4	19	13:24.2	NM
2004	4	27	17:33.7	FQ
2004	5	4	20:35.5	FM
2004	5	11	11: 6.1	LQ
2004	5	19	4:54.5	NM
2004	5	27	7:58.3	FQ
2004	6	3	4:21.0	FM
2004	6	9	20: 4.2	LQ
2004	6	17	20:28.9	NM
2004	6	25	19: 9.3	FQ
2004	7	2	11:10.0	FM
2004	7	9	7:35.2	LQ
2004	7	17	11:25.1	NM
2004	7	25	3:38.8	FQ
2004	7	31	18: 6.1	FM
2004	8	7	22: 2.5	LQ
2004	8	16	1:24.4	NM
2004	8	23	10:13.5	FQ
2004	8	30	2:22.5	FM
2004	9	6	15:11.4	LQ
2004	9	14	14:28.9	NM
2004	9	21	15:55.2	FQ
2004	9	28	13: 9.1	FM
2004	10	6	10:12.8	LQ
2004	10	14	2:47.7	NM
2004	10	20	22: 0.3	FQ
2004	10	28	3: 7.6	FM
2004	11	5	5:55.2	LQ
2004	11	12	14:26.6	NM
2004	11	19	5:51.7	FQ
2004	11	26	20: 8.1	FM
2004	12	5	0:54.9	LQ
2004	12	12	1:29.0	NM
2004	12	18	16:40.5	FQ
2004	12	26	15: 7.3	FM
2005	1	3	17:47.5	LQ
2005	1	10	12: 3.9	NM
2005	1	17	6:57.9	FQ
2005	1	25	10:33.4	FM
2005	2	2	7:28.2	LQ
2005	2	8	22:30.3	NM
2005	2	16	0:16.0	FQ
2005	2	24	4:55.4	FM
2005	3	3	17:37.8	LQ
2005	3	10	9:13.5	NM
2005	3	17	19:19.4	FQ
2005	3	25	21: 1.0	FM
2005	4	2	0:51.8	LQ
2005	4	8	20:35.4	NM
2005	4	16	14:38.9	FQ
2005	4	24	10: 9.5	FM
2005	5	1	6:25.7	LQ
2005	5	8	8:48.7	NM
2005	5	16	8:58.8	FQ
2005	5	23	20:20.9	FM
2005	5	30	11:49.0	LQ
2005	6	6	21:58.1	NM
2005	6	15	1:24.7	FQ
2005	6	22	4:16.3	FM
2005	6	28	18:25.4	LQ
2005	7	6	12: 4.8	NM
2005	7	14	15:22.1	FQ
2005	7	21	11: 2.6	FM
2005	7	28	3:21.0	LQ
2005	8	5	3: 6.1	NM
2005	8	13	2:40.3	FQ
2005	8	19	17:54.8	FM
2005	8	26	15:19.9	LQ
2005	9	3	18:46.0	NM
2005	9	11	11:37.8	FQ
2005	9	18	2: 1.6	FM
2005	9	25	6:42.2	LQ
2005	10	3	10:27.7	NM
2005	10	10	19: 1.6	FQ
2005	10	17	12:13.8	FM
2005	10	25	1:18.4	LQ
2005	11	2	1:24.0	NM
2005	11	9	1:57.7	FQ
2005	11	16	0:57.5	FM
2005	11	23	22:13.5	LQ
2005	12	1	15: 0.4	NM
2005	12	8	9:37.1	FQ
2005	12	15	16:15.6	FM
2005	12	23	19:38.0	LQ
2005	12	31	3:11.8	NM
2006	1	6	18:57.4	FQ
2006	1	14	9:48.5	FM
2006	1	22	15:15.3	LQ
2006	1	29	14:15.7	NM
2006	2	5	6:29.6	FQ

2006	2	13	4:44.8	FM
2006	2	21	7:18.1	LQ
2006	2	28	0:32.8	NM
2006	3	6	20:16.6	FQ
2006	3	14	23:36.4	FM
2006	3	22	19:11.3	LQ
2006	3	29	10:17.6	NM
2006	4	5	12: 1.9	FQ
2006	4	13	16:42.1	FM
2006	4	21	3:28.7	LQ
2006	4	27	19:46.2	NM
2006	5	5	5:14.4	FQ
2006	5	13	6:53.6	FM
2006	5	20	9:21.2	LQ
2006	5	27	5:27.8	NM
2006	6	3	23: 6.9	FQ
2006	6	11	18: 5.4	FM
2006	6	18	14: 9.5	LQ
2006	6	25	16: 7.0	NM
2006	7	3	16:37.4	FQ
2006	7	11	3: 4.1	FM
2006	7	17	19:14.5	LQ
2006	7	25	4:32.0	NM
2006	8	2	8:46.4	FQ
2006	8	9	10:56.3	FM
2006	8	16	1:53.4	LQ
2006	8	23	19:10.6	NM
2006	8	31	22:57.2	FQ
2006	9	7	18:43.8	FM
2006	9	14	11:17.7	LQ
2006	9	22	11:45.8	NM
2006	9	30	11: 4.6	FQ
2006	10	7	3:13.8	FM
2006	10	14	0:27.2	LQ
2006	10	22	5:14.6	NM
2006	10	29	21:26.0	FQ
2006	11	5	12:58.9	FM
2006	11	12	17:47.0	LQ
2006	11	20	22:18.4	NM
2006	11	28	6:29.7	FQ
2006	12	5	0:25.3	FM
2006	12	12	14:33.1	LQ
2006	12	20	14: 1.2	NM
2006	12	27	14:48.8	FQ
2007	1	3	13:57.8	FM
2007	1	11	12:45.5	LQ
2007	1	19	4: 1.4	NM
2007	1	25	23: 2.8	FQ
2007	2	2	5:45.9	FM
2007	2	10	9:52.5	LQ
2007	2	17	16:15.4	NM
2007	2	24	7:57.3	FQ
2007	3	3	23:17.7	FM
2007	3	12	3:55.9	LQ
2007	3	19	2:44.1	NM
2007	3	25	18:17.5	FQ
2007	4	2	17:15.8	FM
2007	4	10	18: 5.4	LQ
2007	4	17	11:37.5	NM
2007	4	24	6:36.5	FQ
2007	5	2	10:10.7	FM
2007	5	10	4:27.9	LQ
2007	5	16	19:28.7	NM
2007	5	23	21: 2.8	FQ
2007	6	1	1: 5.3	FM
2007	6	8	11:43.8	LQ
2007	6	15	3:14.7	NM
2007	6	22	13:14.9	FQ
2007	6	30	13:50.4	FM
2007	7	7	16:55.3	LQ
2007	7	14	12: 5.1	NM
2007	7	22	6:28.9	FQ
2007	7	30	0:49.8	FM
2007	8	5	21:21.9	LQ
2007	8	12	23: 3.6	NM
2007	8	20	23:55.0	FQ
2007	8	28	10:37.3	FM
2007	9	4	2:35.0	LQ
2007	9	11	12:45.4	NM
2007	9	19	16:49.5	FQ
2007	9	26	19:47.1	FM
2007	10	3	10: 8.3	LQ
2007	10	11	5: 2.1	NM
2007	10	19	8:34.6	FQ
2007	10	26	4:53.1	FM
2007	11	1	21:20.1	LQ
2007	11	9	23: 4.3	NM
2007	11	17	22:33.6	FQ
2007	11	24	14:31.1	FM
2007	12	1	12:45.2	LQ
2007	12	9	17:41.2	NM
2007	12	17	10:18.0	FQ
2007	12	24	1:16.5	FM
2007	12	31	7:51.1	LQ
2008	1	8	11:37.6	NM
2008	1	15	19:46.0	FQ
2008	1	22	13:35.1	FM
2008	1	30	5: 3.3	LQ
2008	2	7	3:45.0	NM
2008	2	14	3:33.8	FQ
2008	2	21	3:30.5	FM
2008	2	29	2:19.9	LQ

2008	3	7	17:15.2	NM
2008	3	14	10:46.1	FQ
2008	3	21	18:39.9	FM
2008	3	29	21:49.4	LQ
2008	4	6	3:56.4	NM
2008	4	12	18:32.3	FQ
2008	4	20	10:25.6	FM
2008	4	28	14:14.1	LQ
2008	5	5	12:19.3	NM
2008	5	12	3:47.1	FQ
2008	5	20	2:11.9	FM
2008	5	28	2:58.2	LQ
2008	6	3	19:23.9	NM
2008	6	10	15: 3.5	FQ
2008	6	18	17:31.4	FM
2008	6	26	12:11.3	LQ
2008	7	3	2:20.0	NM
2008	7	10	4:34.9	FQ
2008	7	18	8: 0.5	FM
2008	7	25	18:43.0	LQ
2008	8	1	10:13.9	NM
2008	8	8	20:20.9	FQ
2008	8	16	21:18.3	FM
2008	8	23	23:51.1	LQ
2008	8	30	19:59.1	NM
2008	9	7	14: 5.5	FQ
2008	9	15	9:15.4	FM
2008	9	22	5: 6.2	LQ
2008	9	29	8:13.1	NM
2008	10	7	9: 5.9	FQ
2008	10	14	20: 4.5	FM
2008	10	21	11:56.9	LQ
2008	10	28	23:14.8	NM
2008	11	6	4: 4.6	FQ
2008	11	13	6:19.3	FM
2008	11	19	21:33.1	LQ
2008	11	27	16:55.9	NM
2008	12	5	21:26.3	FQ
2008	12	12	16:39.0	FM
2008	12	19	10:31.0	LQ
2008	12	27	12:23.6	NM
2009	1	4	11:56.6	FQ
2009	1	11	3:28.0	FM
2009	1	18	2:47.0	LQ
2009	1	26	7:56.1	NM
2009	2	2	23:13.0	FQ
2009	2	9	14:49.6	FM
2009	2	16	21:39.1	LQ
2009	2	25	1:36.5	NM
2009	3	4	7:45.7	FQ
2009	3	11	2:37.9	FM
2009	3	18	17:49.9	LQ
2009	3	26	16: 8.0	NM
2009	4	2	14:34.0	FQ
2009	4	9	14:56.0	FM
2009	4	17	13:38.7	LQ
2009	4	25	3:24.2	NM
2009	5	1	20:44.9	FQ
2009	5	9	4: 1.7	FM
2009	5	17	7:27.9	LQ
2009	5	24	12:12.3	NM
2009	5	31	3:23.1	FQ
2009	6	7	18:12.4	FM
2009	6	15	22:16.2	LQ
2009	6	22	19:36.2	NM
2009	6	29	11:29.4	FQ
2009	7	7	9:22.4	FM
2009	7	15	9:54.4	LQ
2009	7	22	2:35.5	NM
2009	7	28	22: 0.5	FQ
2009	8	6	0:56.0	FM
2009	8	13	18:56.1	LQ
2009	8	20	10: 2.1	NM
2009	8	27	11:42.2	FQ
2009	9	4	16: 3.9	FM
2009	9	12	2:16.6	LQ
2009	9	18	18:44.5	NM
2009	9	26	4:49.5	FQ
2009	10	4	6:11.6	FM
2009	10	11	8:56.9	LQ
2009	10	18	5:33.0	NM
2009	10	26	0:41.8	FQ
2009	11	2	19:15.5	FM
2009	11	9	15:57.6	LQ
2009	11	16	19:14.0	NM
2009	11	24	21:38.9	FQ
2009	12	2	7:32.2	FM
2009	12	9	0:15.6	LQ
2009	12	16	12: 3.5	NM
2009	12	24	17:36.6	FQ
2009	12	31	19:14.3	FM
2010	1	7	10:41.9	LQ
2010	1	15	7:13.1	NM
2010	1	23	10:54.4	FQ
2010	1	30	6:18.6	FM
2010	2	5	23:50.8	LQ
2010	2	14	2:53.0	NM
2010	2	22	0:42.9	FQ
2010	2	28	16:38.5	FM
2010	3	7	15:44.1	LQ
2010	3	15	21: 3.3	NM
2010	3	23	11: 0.4	FQ

2010	3	30	2:25.9	FM
2010	4	6	9:38.6	LQ
2010	4	14	12:31.1	NM
2010	4	21	18:20.5	FQ
2010	4	28	12:18.8	FM
2010	5	6	4:16.0	LQ
2010	5	14	1: 5.8	NM
2010	5	20	23:43.7	FQ
2010	5	27	23: 7.7	FM
2010	6	4	22:14.2	LQ
2010	6	12	11:15.5	NM
2010	6	19	4:30.8	FQ
2010	6	26	11:31.0	FM
2010	7	4	14:37.0	LQ
2010	7	11	19:41.1	NM
2010	7	18	10:11.8	FQ
2010	7	26	1:37.6	FM
2010	8	3	5: 0.6	LQ
2010	8	10	3: 8.6	NM
2010	8	16	18:14.7	FQ
2010	8	24	17: 5.9	FM
2010	9	1	17:23.5	LQ
2010	9	8	10:30.2	NM
2010	9	15	5:49.6	FQ
2010	9	23	9:18.7	FM
2010	10	1	3:53.4	LQ
2010	10	7	18:44.9	NM
2010	10	14	21:26.6	FQ
2010	10	23	1:38.2	FM
2010	10	30	12:47.0	LQ
2010	11	6	4:52.4	NM
2010	11	13	16:37.8	FQ
2010	11	21	17:29.2	FM
2010	11	28	20:37.9	LQ
2010	12	5	17:37.0	NM
2010	12	13	13:59.1	FQ
2010	12	21	8:15.2	FM
2010	12	28	4:20.3	LQ
2011	1	4	9: 4.6	NM
2011	1	12	11:33.1	FQ
2011	1	19	21:22.9	FM
2011	1	26	12:59.3	LQ
2011	2	3	2:32.6	NM
2011	2	11	7:20.1	FQ
2011	2	18	8:36.9	FM
2011	2	24	23:28.2	LQ
2011	3	4	20:47.6	NM
2011	3	12	23:46.0	FQ
2011	3	19	18:10.8	FM
2011	3	26	12: 8.4	LQ
2011	4	3	14:33.6	NM
2011	4	11	12: 5.7	FQ
2011	4	18	2:44.2	FM
2011	4	25	2:47.1	LQ
2011	5	3	6:51.4	NM
2011	5	10	20:32.8	FQ
2011	5	17	11: 8.3	FM
2011	5	24	18:52.3	LQ
2011	6	1	21: 2.9	NM
2011	6	9	2:10.5	FQ
2011	6	15	20:13.1	FM
2011	6	23	11:49.3	LQ
2011	7	1	8:53.9	NM
2011	7	8	6:29.6	FQ
2011	7	15	6:39.5	FM
2011	7	23	5: 4.0	LQ
2011	7	30	18:39.8	NM
2011	8	6	11: 9.0	FQ
2011	8	13	18:57.8	FM
2011	8	21	21:56.8	LQ
2011	8	29	3: 4.3	NM
2011	9	4	17:40.3	FQ
2011	9	12	9:27.5	FM
2011	9	20	13:40.3	LQ
2011	9	27	11: 9.2	NM
2011	10	4	3:16.1	FQ
2011	10	12	2: 7.3	FM
2011	10	20	3:31.7	LQ
2011	10	26	19:56.8	NM
2011	11	2	16:38.7	FQ
2011	11	10	20:18.2	FM
2011	11	18	15:10.2	LQ
2011	11	25	6:11.1	NM
2011	12	2	9:52.8	FQ
2011	12	10	14:38.4	FM
2011	12	18	0:48.8	LQ
2011	12	24	18: 8.4	NM
2012	1	1	6:16.1	FQ
2012	1	9	7:32.2	FM
2012	1	16	9: 9.4	LQ
2012	1	23	7:41.7	NM
2012	1	31	4:11.7	FQ
2012	2	7	21:56.2	FM
2012	2	14	17: 5.7	LQ
2012	2	21	22:37.2	NM
2012	3	1	1:23.3	FQ
2012	3	8	9:41.7	FM
2012	3	15	1:27.0	LQ
2012	3	22	14:39.5	NM
2012	3	30	19:42.1	FQ
2012	4	6	19:20.4	FM
2012	4	13	10:51.2	LQ
2012	4	21	7:20.3	NM
2012	4	29	9:58.3	FQ
2012	5	6	3:36.1	FM
2012	5	12	21:48.1	LQ
2012	5	20	23:48.4	NM
2012	5	28	20:16.1	FQ
2012	6	4	11:11.7	FM
2012	6	11	10:42.7	LQ
2012	6	19	15: 3.0	NM
2012	6	27	3:30.5	FQ
2012	7	3	18:51.8	FM
2012	7	11	1:49.6	LQ
2012	7	19	4:24.5	NM
2012	7	26	8:56.9	FQ
2012	8	2	3:27.4	FM
2012	8	9	18:56.7	LQ
2012	8	17	15:54.5	NM
2012	8	24	13:54.8	FQ
2012	8	31	13:57.8	FM
2012	9	8	13:16.2	LQ
2012	9	16	2:10.6	NM
2012	9	22	19:42.6	FQ
2012	9	30	3:18.5	FM
2012	10	8	7:34.2	LQ
2012	10	15	12: 2.6	NM
2012	10	22	3:33.8	FQ
2012	10	29	19:50.5	FM
2012	11	7	0:36.9	LQ
2012	11	13	22: 8.3	NM
2012	11	20	14:32.6	FQ
2012	11	28	14:47.5	FM
2012	12	6	15:32.8	LQ
2012	12	13	8:42.4	NM
2012	12	20	5:19.9	FQ
2012	12	28	10:22.7	FM
2013	1	5	3:58.9	LQ
2013	1	11	19:45.3	NM
2013	1	18	23:45.9	FQ
2013	1	27	4:40.5	FM
2013	2	3	13:57.6	LQ
2013	2	10	7:22.8	NM
2013	2	17	20:31.3	FQ
2013	2	25	20:28.9	FM
2013	3	4	21:54.7	LQ
2013	3	11	19:54.3	NM
2013	3	19	17:27.5	FQ
2013	3	27	9:30.3	FM
2013	4	3	4:38.9	LQ
2013	4	10	9:38.8	NM
2013	4	18	12:32.6	FQ
2013	4	25	19:60.0	FM
2013	5	2	11:16.6	LQ
2013	5	10	0:31.7	NM
2013	5	18	4:36.4	FQ
2013	5	25	4:27.1	FM
2013	5	31	19: 0.3	LQ
2013	6	8	15:59.0	NM
2013	6	16	17:25.4	FQ
2013	6	23	11:33.6	FM
2013	6	30	4:55.4	LQ
2013	7	8	7:16.1	NM
2013	7	16	3:20.0	FQ
2013	7	22	18:16.5	FM
2013	7	29	17:44.7	LQ
2013	8	6	21:51.5	NM
2013	8	14	10:57.6	FQ
2013	8	21	1:45.1	FM
2013	8	28	9:35.8	LQ
2013	9	5	11:36.2	NM
2013	9	12	17: 9.9	FQ
2013	9	19	11:12.6	FM
2013	9	27	3:56.2	LQ
2013	10	5	0:34.2	NM
2013	10	11	23: 3.9	FQ
2013	10	18	23:37.6	FM
2013	10	26	23:42.1	LQ
2013	11	3	12:49.5	NM
2013	11	10	5:58.8	FQ
2013	11	17	15:16.5	FM
2013	11	25	19:30.4	LQ
2013	12	3	0:22.3	NM
2013	12	9	15:13.2	FQ
2013	12	17	9:29.3	FM
2013	12	25	13:50.3	LQ
2014	1	1	11:15.0	NM
2014	1	8	3:40.3	FQ
2014	1	16	4:53.6	FM
2014	1	24	5:21.0	LQ
2014	1	30	21:40.6	NM
2014	2	6	19:22.6	FQ
2014	2	14	23:54.8	FM
2014	2	22	17:16.9	LQ
2014	3	1	8: 2.7	NM
2014	3	8	13:27.1	FQ
2014	3	16	17:10.8	FM
2014	3	24	1:47.6	LQ
2014	3	30	18:48.1	NM
2014	4	7	8:31.7	FQ
2014	4	15	7:45.3	FM
2014	4	22	7:53.1	LQ
2014	4	29	6:17.6	NM
2014	5	7	3:16.8	FQ
2014	5	14	19:18.8	FM
2014	5	21	13: 0.6	LQ
2014	5	28	18:43.1	NM
2014	6	5	20:41.0	FQ
2014	6	13	4:13.8	FM
2014	6	19	18:40.1	LQ
2014	6	27	8:10.6	NM
2014	7	5	12: 0.7	FQ
2014	7	12	11:26.8	FM
2014	7	19	2: 9.7	LQ
2014	7	26	22:42.9	NM
2014	8	4	0:50.9	FQ
2014	8	10	18:10.9	FM
2014	8	17	12:27.0	LQ
2014	8	25	14:13.0	NM
2014	9	2	11:11.9	FQ
2014	9	9	1:38.9	FM
2014	9	16	2: 5.8	LQ
2014	9	24	6:13.5	NM
2014	10	1	19:33.0	FQ
2014	10	8	10:50.7	FM
2014	10	15	19:13.3	LQ
2014	10	23	21:56.2	NM
2014	10	31	2:48.9	FQ
2014	11	6	22:22.9	FM
2014	11	14	15:17.9	LQ
2014	11	22	12:32.1	NM
2014	11	29	10: 7.4	FQ
2014	12	6	12:27.2	FM
2014	12	14	12:53.9	LQ
2014	12	22	1:36.3	NM
2014	12	28	18:32.8	FQ
2015	1	5	4:54.1	FM
2015	1	13	9:49.0	LQ
2015	1	20	13:14.9	NM
2015	1	27	4:49.7	FQ
2015	2	3	23:10.0	FM
2015	2	12	3:52.0	LQ
2015	2	18	23:49.3	NM
2015	2	25	17:15.1	FQ
2015	3	5	18: 6.6	FM
2015	3	13	17:49.5	LQ
2015	3	20	9:38.7	NM
2015	3	27	7:43.8	FQ
2015	4	4	12: 7.4	FM
2015	4	12	3:45.2	LQ
2015	4	18	18:59.3	NM
2015	4	25	23:56.8	FQ
2015	5	4	3:44.8	FM
2015	5	11	10:36.9	LQ
2015	5	18	4:15.7	NM
2015	5	25	17:20.7	FQ
2015	6	2	16:22.0	FM
2015	6	9	15:43.1	LQ
2015	6	16	14: 7.7	NM
2015	6	24	11: 4.1	FQ
2015	7	2	2:22.4	FM
2015	7	8	20:26.0	LQ
2015	7	16	1:26.2	NM
2015	7	24	4: 5.3	FQ
2015	7	31	10:45.8	FM
2015	8	7	2: 5.5	LQ
2015	8	14	14:54.8	NM
2015	8	22	19:32.2	FQ
2015	8	29	18:37.7	FM
2015	9	5	9:57.0	LQ
2015	9	13	6:42.5	NM
2015	9	21	9: 0.1	FQ
2015	9	28	2:52.1	FM
2015	10	4	21: 8.2	LQ
2015	10	13	0: 6.7	NM
2015	10	20	20:32.2	FQ
2015	10	27	12: 6.0	FM
2015	11	3	12:25.6	LQ
2015	11	11	17:47.8	NM
2015	11	19	6:28.1	FQ
2015	11	25	22:44.8	FM
2015	12	3	7:42.1	LQ
2015	12	11	10:30.0	NM
2015	12	18	15:15.2	FQ
2015	12	25	11:12.0	FM
2016	1	2	5:31.7	LQ
2016	1	10	1:31.3	NM
2016	1	16	23:27.5	FQ
2016	1	24	1:46.3	FM
2016	2	1	3:29.1	LQ
2016	2	8	14:40.0	NM
2016	2	15	7:47.9	FQ
2016	2	22	18:20.6	FM
2016	3	1	23:12.6	LQ
2016	3	9	1:56.0	NM
2016	3	15	17: 4.4	FQ
2016	3	23	12: 1.6	FM
2016	3	31	15:18.7	LQ
2016	4	7	11:25.3	NM
2016	4	14	4: 0.7	FQ
2016	4	22	5:25.0	FM
2016	4	30	3:30.1	LQ
2016	5	6	19:31.3	NM
2016	5	13	17: 3.3	FQ
2016	5	21	21:16.6	FM
2016	5	29	12:13.7	LQ
2016	6	5	3: 1.8	NM
2016	6	12	8:10.7	FQ
2016	6	20	11: 5.0	FM
2016	6	27	18:21.0	LQ
2016	7	4	11: 3.4	NM
2016	7	12	0:52.7	FQ
2016	7	19	22:59.6	FM
2016	7	26	23: 2.6	LQ
2016	8	2	20:46.7	NM
2016	8	10	18:22.3	FQ
2016	8	18	9:29.8	FM
2016	8	25	3:44.1	LQ
2016	9	1	9: 5.0	NM
2016	9	9	11:51.0	FQ
2016	9	16	19: 7.8	FM
2016	9	23	9:59.2	LQ
2016	10	1	0:13.2	NM
2016	10	9	4:35.2	FQ
2016	10	16	4:25.1	FM
2016	10	22	19:16.2	LQ
2016	10	30	17:39.9	NM
2016	11	7	19:52.8	FQ
2016	11	14	13:53.6	FM
2016	11	21	8:35.0	LQ
2016	11	29	12:19.6	NM
2016	12	7	9: 4.0	FQ
2016	12	14	0: 6.9	FM
2016	12	21	1:56.8	LQ
2016	12	29	6:54.3	NM
2017	1	5	19:47.7	FQ
2017	1	12	11:35.2	FM
2017	1	19	22:14.4	LQ
2017	1	28	0: 8.3	NM
2017	2	4	4:19.8	FQ
2017	2	11	0:34.0	FM
2017	2	18	19:35.2	LQ
2017	2	26	15: 0.3	NM
2017	3	5	11:33.6	FQ
2017	3	12	14:54.8	FM
2017	3	20	16: 1.5	LQ
2017	3	28	2:59.4	NM
2017	4	3	18:40.9	FQ
2017	4	11	6: 9.3	FM
2017	4	19	10: 0.1	LQ
2017	4	26	12:18.2	NM
2017	5	3	2:48.2	FQ
2017	5	10	21:43.9	FM
2017	5	19	0:35.6	LQ
2017	5	25	19:46.4	NM
2017	6	1	12:43.0	FQ
2017	6	9	13:11.3	FM
2017	6	17	11:35.0	LQ
2017	6	24	2:32.7	NM
2017	7	1	0:51.8	FQ
2017	7	9	4: 8.5	FM
2017	7	16	19:27.6	LQ
2017	7	23	9:47.4	NM
2017	7	30	15:24.0	FQ
2017	8	7	18:12.8	FM
2017	8	15	1:16.9	LQ
2017	8	21	18:31.6	NM
2017	8	29	8:14.3	FQ
2017	9	6	7: 4.9	FM
2017	9	13	6:26.7	LQ
2017	9	20	5:30.8	NM
2017	9	28	2:55.2	FQ
2017	10	5	18:41.9	FM
2017	10	12	12:27.3	LQ
2017	10	19	19:12.6	NM
2017	10	27	22:23.3	FQ
2017	11	4	5:24.5	FM
2017	11	10	20:38.4	LQ
2017	11	18	11:42.9	NM
2017	11	26	17: 3.5	FQ
2017	12	3	15:48.5	FM
2017	12	10	7:53.0	LQ
2017	12	18	6:31.5	NM
2017	12	26	9:20.4	FQ
2018	1	2	2:25.5	FM
2018	1	8	22:26.6	LQ
2018	1	17	2:18.3	NM
2018	1	24	22:20.6	FQ
2018	1	31	13:27.8	FM
2018	2	7	15:55.8	LQ
2018	2	15	21: 6.9	NM
2018	2	23	8: 9.4	FQ
2018	3	2	0:52.2	FM
2018	3	9	11:22.9	LQ
2018	3	17	13:14.3	NM
2018	3	24	15:35.9	FQ
2018	3	31	12:37.8	FM
2018	4	8	7:21.0	LQ
2018	4	16	1:59.9	NM
2018	4	22	21:46.8	FQ
2018	4	30	0:59.2	FM
2018	5	8	2:11.6	LQ
2018	5	15	11:49.8	NM
2018	5	22	3:50.7	FQ
2018	5	29	14:20.8	FM
2018	6	6	18:34.1	LQ
2018	6	13	19:45.1	NM
2018	6	20	10:52.6	FQ
2018	6	28	4:54.6	FM
2018	7	6	7:52.8	LQ
2018	7	13	2:49.6	NM
2018	7	19	19:54.0	FQ
2018	7	27	20:22.3	FM
2018	8	4	18:19.8	LQ
2018	8	11	9:59.1	NM
2018	8	18	7:49.9	FQ
2018	8	26	11:58.4	FM
2018	9	3	2:39.2	LQ
2018	9	9	18: 2.7	NM
2018	9	16	23:16.1	FQ
2018	9	25	2:54.8	FM
2018	10	2	9:47.3	LQ
2018	10	9	3:47.8	NM
2018	10	16	18: 2.5	FQ
2018	10	24	16:47.6	FM
2018	10	31	16:42.5	LQ
2018	11	7	16: 2.9	NM
2018	11	15	14:54.5	FQ
2018	11	23	5:41.4	FM
2018	11	30	0:21.3	LQ
2018	12	7	7:21.7	NM
2018	12	15	11:49.6	FQ
2018	12	22	17:50.5	FM
2018	12	29	9:36.7	LQ
2019	1	6	1:29.9	NM
2019	1	14	6:46.3	FQ
2019	1	21	5:17.2	FM
2019	1	27	21:12.4	LQ
2019	2	4	21: 4.9	NM
2019	2	12	22:26.6	FQ
2019	2	19	15:54.0	FM
2019	2	26	11:29.7	LQ
2019	3	6	16: 5.5	NM
2019	3	14	10:27.0	FQ
2019	3	21	1:43.0	FM
2019	3	28	4:11.5	LQ
2019	4	5	8:52.4	NM
2019	4	12	19: 6.1	FQ
2019	4	19	11:12.3	FM
2019	4	26	22:19.4	LQ
2019	5	4	22:47.0	NM
2019	5	12	1:13.0	FQ
2019	5	18	21:11.6	FM
2019	5	26	16:34.5	LQ
2019	6	3	10: 3.0	NM
2019	6	10	6: 0.6	FQ
2019	6	17	8:31.3	FM
2019	6	25	9:48.0	LQ
2019	7	2	19:17.2	NM
2019	7	9	10:56.5	FQ
2019	7	16	21:39.5	FM
2019	7	25	1:20.5	LQ
2019	8	1	3:12.9	NM
2019	8	7	17:32.7	FQ
2019	8	15	12:31.3	FM
2019	8	23	14:58.9	LQ
2019	8	30	10:38.3	NM
2019	9	6	3:11.8	FQ
2019	9	14	4:35.4	FM
2019	9	22	2:43.5	LQ
2019	9	28	18:27.9	NM
2019	10	5	16:48.1	FQ
2019	10	13	21:10.8	FM
2019	10	21	12:41.6	LQ
2019	10	28	3:40.3	NM
2019	11	4	10:23.6	FQ
2019	11	12	13:37.4	FM
2019	11	19	21:13.2	LQ
2019	11	26	15: 7.7	NM
2019	12	4	6:58.9	FQ
2019	12	12	5:14.9	FM
2019	12	19	4:59.3	LQ
2019	12	26	5:15.5	NM
2020	1	3	4:46.9	FQ
2020	1	10	19:23.2	FM
2020	1	17	13: 0.6	LQ
2020	1	24	21:44.2	NM
2020	2	2	1:43.5	FQ
2020	2	9	7:34.6	FM
2020	2	15	22:19.2	LQ
2020	2	23	15:33.7	NM
2020	3	2	19:58.6	FQ
2020	3	9	17:48.6	FM
2020	3	16	9:35.7	LQ
2020	3	24	9:29.6	NM
2020	4	1	10:21.9	FQ
2020	4	8	2:35.6	FM
2020	4	14	22:57.0	LQ
2020	4	23	2:27.0	NM
2020	4	30	20:38.7	FQ
2020	5	7	10:45.6	FM
2020	5	14	14: 3.3	LQ
2020	5	22	17:39.8	NM
2020	5	30	3:30.4	FQ
2020	6	5	19:12.7	FM
2020	6	13	6:25.0	LQ
2020	6	21	6:42.3	NM
2020	6	28	8:16.5	FQ
2020	7	5	4:45.0	FM
2020	7	12	23:31.5	LQ

2020	7	20	17:33.6	NM
2020	7	27	12:33.8	FQ
2020	8	3	15:59.6	FM
2020	8	11	16:47.8	LQ
2020	8	19	2:42.3	NM
2020	8	25	17:59.2	FQ
2020	9	2	5:23.2	FM
2020	9	10	9:28.3	LQ
2020	9	17	11: 1.0	NM
2020	9	24	1:56.6	FQ
2020	10	1	21: 6.9	FM
2020	10	10	0:41.4	LQ
2020	10	16	19:32.2	NM
2020	10	23	13:24.3	FQ
2020	10	31	14:51.5	FM
2020	11	8	13:47.6	LQ
2020	11	15	5: 8.9	NM
2020	11	22	4:45.9	FQ
2020	11	30	9:32.1	FM
2020	12	8	0:38.0	LQ
2020	12	14	16:18.8	NM
2020	12	21	23:42.5	FQ
2020	12	30	3:30.4	FM
2021	1	6	9:38.6	LQ
2021	1	13	5: 2.6	NM
2021	1	20	21: 3.6	FQ
2021	1	28	19:18.6	FM
2021	2	4	17:38.7	LQ
2021	2	11	19: 8.2	NM
2021	2	19	18:49.1	FQ
2021	2	27	8:19.6	FM
2021	3	6	1:32.0	LQ
2021	3	13	10:23.5	NM
2021	3	21	14:41.8	FQ
2021	3	28	18:50.1	FM
2021	4	4	10: 4.2	LQ
2021	4	12	2:32.9	NM
2021	4	20	7: 0.0	FQ
2021	4	27	3:33.1	FM
2021	5	3	19:51.7	LQ
2021	5	11	19: 1.6	NM
2021	5	19	19:13.2	FQ
2021	5	26	11:14.9	FM
2021	6	2	7:26.1	LQ
2021	6	10	10:54.1	NM
2021	6	18	3:54.7	FQ
2021	6	24	18:40.2	FM
2021	7	1	21:12.7	LQ
2021	7	10	1:17.7	NM
2021	7	17	10:11.6	FQ
2021	7	24	2:37.5	FM
2021	7	31	13:18.3	LQ
2021	8	8	13:50.8	NM
2021	8	15	15:21.1	FQ
2021	8	22	12: 2.3	FM
2021	8	30	7:15.0	LQ
2021	9	7	0:52.0	NM
2021	9	13	20:41.3	FQ
2021	9	20	23:54.7	FM
2021	9	29	1:58.4	LQ
2021	10	6	11: 5.7	NM
2021	10	13	3:27.6	FQ
2021	10	20	14:57.7	FM
2021	10	28	20: 6.7	LQ
2021	11	4	21:15.4	NM
2021	11	11	12:48.4	FQ
2021	11	19	8:59.7	FM
2021	11	27	12:29.9	LQ
2021	12	4	7:44.5	NM
2021	12	11	1:37.5	FQ
2021	12	19	4:38.0	FM
2021	12	27	2:26.0	LQ
2022	1	2	18:35.8	NM
2022	1	9	18:13.3	FQ
2022	1	17	23:51.2	FM
2022	1	25	13:43.0	LQ
2022	2	1	5:49.2	NM
2022	2	8	13:51.9	FQ
2022	2	16	16:59.7	FM
2022	2	23	22:34.5	LQ
2022	3	2	17:38.3	NM
2022	3	10	10:46.4	FQ
2022	3	18	7:20.6	FM
2022	3	25	5:39.4	LQ
2022	4	1	6:27.7	NM
2022	4	9	6:48.4	FQ
2022	4	16	18:57.5	FM
2022	4	23	11:58.2	LQ
2022	4	30	20:30.7	NM
2022	5	9	0:22.2	FQ
2022	5	16	4:15.9	FM
2022	5	22	18:44.6	LQ
2022	5	30	11:32.2	NM
2022	6	7	14:49.2	FQ
2022	6	14	11:52.6	FM
2022	6	21	3:11.9	LQ
2022	6	29	2:53.4	NM
2022	7	7	2:14.9	FQ
2022	7	13	18:38.1	FM
2022	7	20	14:19.4	LQ
2022	7	28	17:55.4	NM
2022	8	5	11: 7.5	FQ
2022	8	12	1:36.1	FM
2022	8	19	4:36.6	LQ
2022	8	27	8:16.9	NM
2022	9	3	18: 8.8	FQ
2022	9	10	9:58.9	FM
2022	9	17	21:52.3	LQ
2022	9	25	21:54.1	NM
2022	10	3	0:15.4	FQ
2022	10	9	20:54.7	FM
2022	10	17	17:16.1	LQ
2022	10	25	10:48.3	NM
2022	11	1	6:38.9	FQ
2022	11	8	11: 2.8	FM
2022	11	16	13:29.5	LQ
2022	11	23	22:57.4	NM
2022	11	30	14:38.5	FQ
2022	12	8	4: 9.8	FM
2022	12	16	8:59.5	LQ
2022	12	23	10:17.9	NM
2022	12	30	1:22.6	FQ
2023	1	6	23: 9.9	FM
2023	1	15	2:13.5	LQ
2023	1	21	20:55.5	NM
2023	1	28	15:20.4	FQ
2023	2	5	18:30.7	FM
2023	2	13	16: 3.3	LQ
2023	2	20	7: 9.1	NM
2023	2	27	8: 6.6	FQ
2023	3	7	12:42.8	FM
2023	3	15	2:10.3	LQ
2023	3	21	17:26.7	NM
2023	3	29	2:33.2	FQ
2023	4	6	4:37.3	FM
2023	4	13	9:12.9	LQ
2023	4	20	4:15.8	NM
2023	4	27	21:21.1	FQ
2023	5	5	17:36.8	FM
2023	5	12	14:29.4	LQ
2023	5	19	15:55.9	NM
2023	5	27	15:23.8	FQ
2023	6	4	3:43.9	FM
2023	6	10	19:32.4	LQ
2023	6	18	4:39.2	NM
2023	6	26	7:51.3	FQ
2023	7	3	11:40.5	FM
2023	7	10	1:49.1	LQ
2023	7	17	18:33.1	NM
2023	7	25	22: 8.2	FQ
2023	8	1	18:33.4	FM
2023	8	8	10:29.9	LQ
2023	8	16	9:38.8	NM
2023	8	24	9:58.4	FQ
2023	8	31	1:37.1	FM
2023	9	6	22:22.5	LQ
2023	9	15	1:40.1	NM
2023	9	22	19:32.7	FQ
2023	9	29	9:58.4	FM
2023	10	6	13:49.0	LQ
2023	10	14	17:55.1	NM
2023	10	22	3:30.2	FQ
2023	10	28	20:24.5	FM
2023	11	5	8:38.8	LQ
2023	11	13	9:27.3	NM
2023	11	20	10:50.8	FQ
2023	11	27	9:16.7	FM
2023	12	5	5:52.0	LQ
2023	12	12	23:32.1	NM
2023	12	19	18:40.5	FQ
2023	12	27	0:33.7	FM
2024	1	4	3:32.9	LQ
2024	1	11	11:58.1	NM
2024	1	18	3:53.9	FQ
2024	1	25	17:54.7	FM
2024	2	2	23:20.1	LQ
2024	2	9	23: 0.7	NM
2024	2	16	15: 2.1	FQ
2024	2	24	12:31.3	FM
2024	3	3	15:25.4	LQ
2024	3	10	9: 2.8	NM
2024	3	17	4:11.8	FQ
2024	3	25	7: 1.6	FM
2024	4	2	3:15.8	LQ
2024	4	8	18:23.4	NM
2024	4	15	19:14.5	FQ
2024	4	23	23:51.2	FM
2024	5	1	11:27.9	LQ
2024	5	8	3:24.3	NM
2024	5	15	11:49.6	FQ
2024	5	23	13:55.9	FM
2024	5	30	17:13.7	LQ
2024	6	6	12:40.0	NM
2024	6	14	5:19.9	FQ
2024	6	22	1:10.5	FM
2024	6	28	21:55.1	LQ
2024	7	5	22:59.3	NM
2024	7	13	22:49.9	FQ
2024	7	21	10:19.8	FM
2024	7	28	2:54.0	LQ
2024	8	4	11:14.4	NM
2024	8	12	15:19.8	FQ
2024	8	19	18:28.6	FM
2024	8	26	9:29.0	LQ
2024	9	3	1:56.8	NM
2024	9	11	6: 6.8	FQ
2024	9	18	2:36.7	FM
2024	9	24	18:52.6	LQ
2024	10	2	18:50.5	NM
2024	10	10	18:56.3	FQ
2024	10	17	11:27.9	FM
2024	10	24	8: 5.2	LQ
2024	11	1	12:48.2	NM
2024	11	9	5:56.6	FQ
2024	11	15	21:29.6	FM
2024	11	23	1:30.0	LQ
2024	12	1	6:22.4	NM
2024	12	8	15:27.7	FQ
2024	12	15	9: 2.6	FM
2024	12	22	22:19.9	LQ
2024	12	30	22:27.8	NM
2025	1	6	23:57.6	FQ
2025	1	13	22:27.7	FM
2025	1	21	20:32.2	LQ
2025	1	29	12:37.3	NM
2025	2	5	8: 3.8	FQ
2025	2	12	13:54.4	FM
2025	2	20	17:34.7	LQ
2025	2	28	0:46.7	NM
2025	3	6	16:33.7	FQ
2025	3	14	6:55.9	FM
2025	3	22	11:32.1	LQ
2025	3	29	11: 0.1	NM
2025	4	5	2:16.7	FQ
2025	4	13	0:23.9	FM
2025	4	21	1:37.7	LQ
2025	4	27	19:33.4	NM
2025	5	4	13:53.5	FQ
2025	5	12	16:58.1	FM
2025	5	20	12: 0.5	LQ
2025	5	27	3: 4.4	NM
2025	6	3	3:41.9	FQ
2025	6	11	7:46.1	FM
2025	6	18	19:21.0	LQ
2025	6	25	10:33.5	NM
2025	7	2	19:30.3	FQ
2025	7	10	20:38.9	FM
2025	7	18	0:39.7	LQ
2025	7	24	19:12.5	NM
2025	8	1	12:41.2	FQ
2025	8	9	7:57.1	FM
2025	8	16	5:14.4	LQ
2025	8	23	6: 7.1	NM
2025	8	31	6:25.5	FQ
2025	9	7	18:10.7	FM
2025	9	14	10:35.2	LQ
2025	9	21	19:54.6	NM
2025	9	29	23:54.8	FQ
2025	10	7	3:49.0	FM
2025	10	13	18:14.5	LQ
2025	10	21	12:26.0	NM
2025	10	29	16:22.0	FQ
2025	11	5	13:20.4	FM
2025	11	12	5:29.6	LQ
2025	11	20	6:48.3	NM
2025	11	28	6:59.8	FQ
2025	12	4	23:15.3	FM
2025	12	11	20:52.8	LQ
2025	12	20	1:44.4	NM
2025	12	27	19:10.6	FQ
2026	1	3	10: 4.3	FM
2026	1	10	15:49.2	LQ
2026	1	18	19:53.3	NM
2026	1	26	4:48.4	FQ
2026	2	1	22:10.6	FM
2026	2	9	12:44.7	LQ
2026	2	17	12: 3.1	NM
2026	2	24	12:29.0	FQ
2026	3	3	11:39.2	FM
2026	3	11	9:41.6	LQ
2026	3	19	1:26.0	NM
2026	3	25	19:19.4	FQ
2026	4	2	2:13.3	FM
2026	4	10	4:55.3	LQ
2026	4	17	11:54.3	NM
2026	4	24	2:33.4	FQ
2026	5	1	17:24.7	FM
2026	5	9	21:13.7	LQ
2026	5	16	20: 3.1	NM
2026	5	23	11:12.1	FQ
2026	5	31	8:46.8	FM
2026	6	8	10: 3.1	LQ
2026	6	15	2:56.0	NM
2026	6	21	21:56.0	FQ
2026	6	29	23:58.2	FM
2026	7	7	19:30.9	LQ
2026	7	14	9:45.1	NM
2026	7	21	11: 5.8	FQ
2026	7	29	14:37.2	FM
2026	8	6	2:22.9	LQ
2026	8	12	17:37.6	NM
2026	8	20	2:46.6	FQ
2026	8	28	4:20.0	FM
2026	9	4	7:52.4	LQ
2026	9	11	3:27.3	NM
2026	9	18	20:44.4	FQ
2026	9	26	16:50.4	FM
2026	10	3	13:26.3	LQ
2026	10	10	15:50.2	NM
2026	10	18	16:13.6	FQ
2026	10	26	4:13.1	FM
2026	11	1	20:30.0	LQ
2026	11	9	7: 2.5	NM
2026	11	17	11:48.5	FQ
2026	11	24	14:55.0	FM
2026	12	1	6:10.5	LQ
2026	12	9	0:52.8	NM
2026	12	17	5:43.2	FQ
2026	12	24	1:29.8	FM
2026	12	30	19: 1.0	LQ
2027	1	7	20:25.5	NM
2027	1	15	20:34.9	FQ
2027	1	22	12:18.5	FM
2027	1	29	10:56.8	LQ
2027	2	6	15:57.2	NM
2027	2	14	7:58.4	FQ
2027	2	20	23:24.2	FM
2027	2	28	5:18.5	LQ
2027	3	8	9:31.3	NM
2027	3	15	16:25.1	FQ
2027	3	22	10:44.0	FM
2027	3	30	0:56.6	LQ
2027	4	6	23:53.5	NM
2027	4	13	22:57.0	FQ
2027	4	20	22:27.4	FM
2027	4	28	20:20.3	LQ
2027	5	6	11: 0.4	NM
2027	5	13	4:44.7	FQ
2027	5	20	10:59.5	FM
2027	5	28	13:60.0	LQ
2027	6	4	19:41.7	NM
2027	6	11	10:57.3	FQ
2027	6	19	0:45.2	FM
2027	6	27	4:56.2	LQ
2027	7	4	3: 3.5	NM
2027	7	10	18:40.5	FQ
2027	7	18	15:46.3	FM
2027	7	26	16:56.6	LQ
2027	8	2	10: 6.4	NM
2027	8	9	4:55.3	FQ
2027	8	17	7:30.4	FM
2027	8	25	2:28.8	LQ
2027	8	31	17:42.0	NM
2027	9	7	18:32.0	FQ
2027	9	15	23: 5.4	FM
2027	9	23	10:21.8	LQ
2027	9	30	2:36.7	NM
2027	10	7	11:47.7	FQ
2027	10	15	13:48.9	FM
2027	10	22	17:30.6	LQ
2027	10	29	13:37.0	NM
2027	11	6	7:60.0	FQ
2027	11	14	3:27.8	FM
2027	11	21	0:50.1	LQ
2027	11	28	3:25.1	NM
2027	12	6	5:22.0	FQ
2027	12	13	16:10.6	FM
2027	12	20	9:13.1	LQ
2027	12	27	20:13.8	NM
2028	1	5	1:41.1	FQ
2028	1	12	4: 4.6	FM
2028	1	18	19:28.2	LQ
2028	1	26	15:14.1	NM
2028	2	3	19:11.4	FQ
2028	2	10	15: 4.6	FM
2028	2	17	8:10.1	LQ
2028	2	25	10:39.0	NM
2028	3	4	9: 2.7	FQ
2028	3	11	1: 6.5	FM
2028	3	17	23:25.0	LQ
2028	3	26	4:33.4	NM
2028	4	2	19:15.7	FQ
2028	4	9	10:27.0	FM
2028	4	16	16:38.6	LQ
2028	4	24	19:49.1	NM
2028	5	2	2:26.6	FQ
2028	5	8	19:49.4	FM
2028	5	16	10:44.4	LQ
2028	5	24	8:17.9	NM
2028	5	31	7:38.1	FQ
2028	6	7	6: 9.6	FM
2028	6	15	4:29.1	LQ
2028	6	22	18:28.9	NM
2028	6	29	12:12.6	FQ
2028	7	6	18:12.1	FM
2028	7	14	20:59.1	LQ
2028	7	22	3: 3.0	NM
2028	7	28	17:42.2	FQ
2028	8	5	8:11.6	FM
2028	8	13	11:48.2	LQ
2028	8	20	10:44.8	NM
2028	8	27	1:37.3	FQ
2028	9	3	23:49.6	FM
2028	9	12	0:48.1	LQ
2028	9	18	18:24.5	NM
2028	9	25	13:10.4	FQ
2028	10	3	16:26.9	FM
2028	10	11	11:58.3	LQ
2028	10	18	2:57.4	NM
2028	10	25	4:52.5	FQ
2028	11	2	9:19.0	FM
2028	11	9	21:26.8	LQ
2028	11	16	13:18.7	NM
2028	11	24	0:13.6	FQ
2028	12	2	1:41.7	FM
2028	12	9	5:39.9	LQ
2028	12	16	2: 7.4	NM
2028	12	23	21:44.7	FQ
2028	12	31	16:49.8	FM
2029	1	7	13:27.7	LQ
2029	1	14	17:26.1	NM
2029	1	22	19:24.3	FQ
2029	1	30	6: 4.8	FM
2029	2	5	21:53.9	LQ
2029	2	13	10:33.3	NM
2029	2	21	15:11.5	FQ
2029	2	28	17:11.5	FM
2029	3	7	7:53.4	LQ
2029	3	15	4:21.2	NM
2029	3	23	7:34.5	FQ
2029	3	30	2:27.5	FM
2029	4	5	19:53.1	LQ
2029	4	13	21:42.0	NM
2029	4	21	19:51.2	FQ
2029	4	28	10:37.7	FM
2029	5	5	9:49.2	LQ
2029	5	13	13:43.8	NM
2029	5	21	4:17.1	FQ
2029	5	27	18:38.3	FM
2029	6	4	1:20.2	LQ
2029	6	12	3:51.9	NM
2029	6	19	9:55.3	FQ
2029	6	26	3:23.1	FM
2029	7	3	17:59.9	LQ
2029	7	11	15:52.1	NM
2029	7	18	14:15.8	FQ
2029	7	25	13:36.7	FM
2029	8	2	11:18.6	LQ
2029	8	10	1:56.6	NM
2029	8	16	18:56.9	FQ
2029	8	24	1:52.3	FM
2029	9	1	4:36.1	LQ
2029	9	8	10:45.0	NM
2029	9	15	1:30.9	FQ
2029	9	22	16:30.4	FM
2029	9	30	20:58.8	LQ
2029	10	7	19:15.2	NM
2029	10	14	11:10.0	FQ
2029	10	22	9:29.1	FM
2029	10	30	11:33.4	LQ
2029	11	6	4:25.0	NM
2029	11	13	0:35.6	FQ
2029	11	21	4: 4.6	FM
2029	11	28	23:48.6	LQ
2029	12	5	14:53.4	NM
2029	12	12	17:49.6	FQ
2029	12	20	22:47.9	FM
2029	12	28	9:49.8	LQ
2030	1	4	2:51.2	NM
2030	1	11	14: 7.1	FQ
2030	1	19	15:56.2	FM
2030	1	26	18:15.4	LQ
2030	2	2	16: 9.7	NM
2030	2	10	11:51.1	FQ
2030	2	18	6:22.1	FM
2030	2	25	1:59.2	LQ
2030	3	4	6:37.1	NM
2030	3	12	8:49.1	FQ
2030	3	19	17:58.6	FM
2030	3	26	9:53.0	LQ
2030	4	2	22: 4.7	NM
2030	4	11	2:58.1	FQ
2030	4	18	3:21.7	FM
2030	4	24	18:40.4	LQ
2030	5	2	14:13.8	NM
2030	5	10	17:12.1	FQ
2030	5	17	11:20.1	FM
2030	5	24	4:58.6	LQ
2030	6	1	6:22.4	NM
2030	6	9	3:35.8	FQ
2030	6	15	18:41.1	FM
2030	6	22	17:20.8	LQ
2030	6	30	21:35.0	NM
2030	7	8	11: 2.1	FQ
2030	7	15	2:11.8	FM
2030	7	22	8: 9.0	LQ
2030	7	30	11:11.2	NM
2030	8	6	16:43.5	FQ
2030	8	13	10:44.3	FM
2030	8	21	1:17.0	LQ
2030	8	28	23: 7.3	NM
2030	9	4	21:56.9	FQ
2030	9	11	21:17.6	FM
2030	9	19	19:57.6	LQ
2030	9	27	9:54.6	NM
2030	10	4	3:58.0	FQ
2030	10	11	10:46.9	FM
2030	10	19	14:51.4	LQ
2030	10	26	20:17.3	NM
2030	11	2	11:58.1	FQ

2030	11	10	3:31.6	FM
2030	11	18	8:33.9	LQ
2030	11	25	6:47.1	NM
2030	12	1	22:58.4	FQ
2030	12	9	22:42.1	FM
2030	12	18	0: 2.9	LQ
2030	12	24	17:33.4	NM
2030	12	31	13:37.3	FQ
2031	1	8	18:27.4	FM
2031	1	16	12:48.6	LQ
2031	1	23	4:32.9	NM
2031	1	30	7:44.2	FQ
2031	2	7	12:48.3	FM
2031	2	14	22:51.1	LQ
2031	2	21	15:51.5	NM
2031	3	1	4: 2.8	FQ
2031	3	9	4:32.3	FM
2031	3	16	6:37.4	LQ
2031	3	23	3:52.0	NM
2031	3	31	0:32.6	FQ
2031	4	7	17:23.9	FM
2031	4	14	12:59.6	LQ
2031	4	21	16:59.9	NM
2031	4	29	19:20.3	FQ
2031	5	7	3:42.1	FM
2031	5	13	19: 8.7	LQ
2031	5	21	7:19.6	NM
2031	5	29	11:20.7	FQ
2031	6	5	12: 0.1	FM
2031	6	12	2:22.1	LQ
2031	6	19	22:26.5	NM
2031	6	28	0:20.2	FQ
2031	7	4	19: 2.4	FM
2031	7	11	11:51.1	LQ
2031	7	19	13:41.4	NM
2031	7	27	10:36.2	FQ
2031	8	3	1:46.5	FM
2031	8	10	0:24.8	LQ
2031	8	18	4:32.9	NM
2031	8	25	18:41.2	FQ
2031	9	1	9:21.1	FM
2031	9	8	16:15.3	LQ
2031	9	16	18:47.2	NM
2031	9	24	1:21.4	FQ
2031	9	30	18:58.0	FM
2031	10	8	10:51.3	LQ
2031	10	16	8:20.8	NM
2031	10	23	7:38.3	FQ
2031	10	30	7:33.1	FM
2031	11	7	7: 4.2	LQ
2031	11	14	21: 9.6	NM
2031	11	21	14:46.7	FQ
2031	11	28	23:19.4	FM
2031	12	7	3:22.4	LQ
2031	12	14	9: 5.8	NM
2031	12	21	0: 1.9	FQ
2031	12	28	17:33.9	FM
2032	1	5	22: 6.5	LQ
2032	1	12	20: 7.3	NM
2032	1	19	12:14.9	FQ
2032	1	27	12:53.0	FM
2032	2	4	13:50.3	LQ
2032	2	11	6:25.6	NM
2032	2	18	3:28.7	FQ
2032	2	26	7:43.9	FM
2032	3	5	1:47.9	LQ
2032	3	11	16:26.8	NM
2032	3	18	20:56.0	FQ
2032	3	27	0:47.7	FM
2032	4	3	10:11.0	LQ
2032	4	10	2:42.0	NM
2032	4	17	15:24.5	FQ
2032	4	25	15:11.8	FM
2032	5	2	16: 2.5	LQ
2032	5	9	13:38.3	NM
2032	5	17	9:44.7	FQ
2032	5	25	2:39.7	FM
2032	5	31	20:52.3	LQ
2032	6	8	1:34.6	NM
2032	6	16	3: 2.0	FQ
2032	6	23	11:34.9	FM
2032	6	30	2:13.4	LQ
2032	7	7	14:43.7	NM
2032	7	15	18:34.3	FQ
2032	7	22	18:54.0	FM
2032	7	29	9:27.4	LQ
2032	8	6	5:13.1	NM
2032	8	14	7:52.8	FQ
2032	8	21	1:49.2	FM
2032	8	27	19:35.5	LQ
2032	9	4	20:57.7	NM
2032	9	12	18:50.7	FQ
2032	9	19	9:32.0	FM
2032	9	26	9:14.3	LQ
2032	10	4	13:27.1	NM
2032	10	12	3:48.8	FQ
2032	10	18	18:59.2	FM
2032	10	26	2:30.9	LQ
2032	11	3	5:45.4	NM
2032	11	10	11:34.6	FQ
2032	11	17	6:42.9	FM
2032	11	24	22:50.8	LQ
2032	12	2	20:53.3	NM
2032	12	9	19:10.0	FQ
2032	12	16	20:49.7	FM
2032	12	24	20:42.3	LQ
2033	1	1	10:17.7	NM
2033	1	8	3:35.8	FQ
2033	1	15	13: 7.7	FM
2033	1	23	17:48.0	LQ
2033	1	30	22: 0.9	NM
2033	2	6	13:35.2	FQ
2033	2	14	7: 4.7	FM
2033	2	22	11:54.9	LQ
2033	3	1	8:25.2	NM
2033	3	8	1:27.7	FQ
2033	3	16	1:38.0	FM
2033	3	24	1:51.0	LQ
2033	3	30	17:53.6	NM
2033	4	6	15:14.6	FQ
2033	4	14	19:18.6	FM
2033	4	22	11:42.7	LQ
2033	4	29	2:48.1	NM
2033	5	6	6:46.4	FQ
2033	5	14	10:44.9	FM
2033	5	21	18:29.5	LQ
2033	5	28	11:38.5	NM
2033	6	4	23:40.3	FQ
2033	6	12	23:21.7	FM
2033	6	19	23:30.7	LQ
2033	6	26	21: 9.0	NM
2033	7	4	17:13.3	FQ
2033	7	12	9:31.1	FM
2033	7	19	4: 9.2	LQ
2033	7	26	8:13.9	NM
2033	8	3	10:26.5	FQ
2033	8	10	18:10.3	FM
2033	8	17	9:45.6	LQ
2033	8	24	21:40.6	NM
2033	9	2	2:24.4	FQ
2033	9	9	2:22.9	FM
2033	9	15	17:36.3	LQ
2033	9	23	13:40.7	NM
2033	10	1	16:33.6	FQ
2033	10	8	10:59.7	FM
2033	10	15	4:49.5	LQ
2033	10	23	7:29.4	NM
2033	10	31	4:47.3	FQ
2033	11	6	20:33.2	FM
2033	11	13	20:10.8	LQ
2033	11	22	1:40.2	NM
2033	11	29	15:16.4	FQ
2033	12	6	7:23.2	FM
2033	12	13	15:30.3	LQ
2033	12	21	18:47.9	NM
2033	12	29	0:21.5	FQ
2034	1	4	19:48.4	FM
2034	1	12	13:19.1	LQ
2034	1	20	10: 3.3	NM
2034	1	27	8:33.8	FQ
2034	2	3	10: 5.9	FM
2034	2	11	11:11.1	LQ
2034	2	18	23:12.3	NM
2034	2	25	16:36.2	FQ
2034	3	5	2:11.5	FM
2034	3	13	6:47.0	LQ
2034	3	20	10:16.7	NM
2034	3	27	1:20.4	FQ
2034	4	3	19:20.1	FM
2034	4	11	22:47.3	LQ
2034	4	18	19:27.7	NM
2034	4	25	11:36.1	FQ
2034	5	3	12:17.0	FM
2034	5	11	10:57.6	LQ
2034	5	18	3:14.1	NM
2034	5	24	23:58.3	FQ
2034	6	2	3:55.7	FM
2034	6	9	19:45.3	LQ
2034	6	16	10:27.4	NM
2034	6	23	14:35.2	FQ
2034	7	1	17:46.4	FM
2034	7	9	2: 0.8	LQ
2034	7	15	18:16.7	NM
2034	7	23	7: 4.9	FQ
2034	7	31	5:56.6	FM
2034	8	7	6:52.5	LQ
2034	8	14	3:54.0	NM
2034	8	22	0:43.6	FQ
2034	8	29	16:51.5	FM
2034	9	5	11:43.9	LQ
2034	9	12	16:14.6	NM
2034	9	20	18:40.6	FQ
2034	9	28	2:58.8	FM
2034	10	4	18: 7.2	LQ
2034	10	12	7:33.8	NM
2034	10	20	12: 4.7	FQ
2034	10	27	12:44.1	FM
2034	11	3	3:29.5	LQ
2034	11	11	1:17.8	NM
2034	11	19	4: 3.2	FQ
2034	11	25	22:33.8	FM
2034	12	2	16:48.3	LQ
2034	12	10	20:16.0	NM
2034	12	18	17:46.2	FQ
2034	12	25	8:56.2	FM
2035	1	1	10: 2.4	LQ
2035	1	9	15: 4.7	NM
2035	1	17	4:46.4	FQ
2035	1	23	20:18.2	FM
2035	1	31	6: 3.8	LQ
2035	2	8	8:23.9	NM
2035	2	15	13:18.1	FQ
2035	2	22	8:55.2	FM
2035	3	2	3: 3.2	LQ
2035	3	9	23:11.5	NM
2035	3	16	20:16.1	FQ
2035	3	23	22:42.9	FM
2035	3	31	23: 9.5	LQ
2035	4	8	10:59.7	NM
2035	4	15	2:55.8	FQ
2035	4	22	13:21.3	FM
2035	4	30	16:56.5	LQ
2035	5	7	20: 5.2	NM
2035	5	14	10:28.9	FQ
2035	5	22	4:26.3	FM
2035	5	30	7:32.6	LQ
2035	6	6	3:21.7	NM
2035	6	12	19:50.0	FQ
2035	6	20	19:38.2	FM
2035	6	28	18:44.3	LQ
2035	7	5	10: 0.5	NM
2035	7	12	7:32.8	FQ
2035	7	20	10:38.0	FM
2035	7	28	2:57.0	LQ
2035	8	3	17:13.0	NM
2035	8	10	21:52.8	FQ
2035	8	19	1: 2.0	FM
2035	8	26	9: 9.5	LQ
2035	9	2	2: 0.6	NM
2035	9	9	14:48.3	FQ
2035	9	17	14:25.6	FM
2035	9	24	14:41.4	LQ
2035	10	1	13: 7.8	NM
2035	10	9	9:51.2	FQ
2035	10	17	2:37.7	FM
2035	10	23	20:59.0	LQ
2035	10	31	2:59.9	NM
2035	11	8	5:52.3	FQ
2035	11	15	13:51.0	FM
2035	11	22	5:18.9	LQ
2035	11	29	19:39.2	NM
2035	12	8	1: 6.6	FQ
2035	12	15	0:35.4	FM
2035	12	21	16:30.9	LQ
2035	12	29	14:32.8	NM
2036	1	6	17:49.1	FQ
2036	1	13	11:18.1	FM
2036	1	20	6:48.4	LQ
2036	1	28	10:19.0	NM
2036	2	5	7: 1.6	FQ
2036	2	11	22:10.2	FM
2036	2	18	23:49.4	LQ
2036	2	27	5: 1.5	NM
2036	3	5	16:49.4	FQ
2036	3	12	9:10.6	FM
2036	3	19	18:42.0	LQ
2036	3	27	20:59.8	NM
2036	4	4	0: 4.1	FQ
2036	4	10	20:23.5	FM
2036	4	18	14: 9.3	LQ
2036	4	26	9:35.9	NM
2036	5	3	5:55.5	FQ
2036	5	10	8:10.5	FM
2036	5	18	8:42.2	LQ
2036	5	25	19:18.8	NM
2036	6	1	11:35.9	FQ
2036	6	8	21: 3.1	FM
2036	6	17	1: 5.5	LQ
2036	6	24	3:11.3	NM
2036	6	30	18:14.8	FQ
2036	7	8	11:20.8	FM
2036	7	16	14:41.6	LQ
2036	7	23	10:18.5	NM
2036	7	30	2:58.0	FQ
2036	8	7	2:50.7	FM
2036	8	15	1:37.6	LQ
2036	8	21	17:36.5	NM
2036	8	28	14:44.6	FQ
2036	9	5	18:47.6	FM
2036	9	13	10:30.8	LQ
2036	9	20	1:52.6	NM
2036	9	27	6:13.4	FQ
2036	10	5	10:17.3	FM
2036	10	12	18:11.0	LQ
2036	10	19	11:50.9	NM
2036	10	27	1:14.3	FQ
2036	11	4	0:46.5	FM
2036	11	11	1:30.6	LQ
2036	11	18	0:15.4	NM
2036	11	25	22:28.3	FQ
2036	12	3	14:10.7	FM
2036	12	10	9:20.8	LQ
2036	12	17	15:36.0	NM
2036	12	25	19:45.0	FQ
2037	1	2	2:37.2	FM
2037	1	8	18:31.7	LQ
2037	1	16	9:36.5	NM
2037	1	24	14:56.3	FQ
2037	1	31	14: 5.7	FM
2037	2	7	5:46.1	LQ
2037	2	15	4:56.2	NM
2037	2	23	6:42.1	FQ
2037	3	2	0:29.4	FM
2037	3	8	19:28.1	LQ
2037	3	16	23:38.9	NM
2037	3	24	18:40.5	FQ
2037	3	31	9:54.7	FM
2037	4	7	11:28.0	LQ
2037	4	15	16:10.8	NM
2037	4	23	3:12.8	FQ
2037	4	29	18:55.1	FM
2037	5	7	4:58.5	LQ
2037	5	15	5:56.9	NM
2037	5	22	9:10.4	FQ
2037	5	29	4:25.5	FM
2037	6	5	22:51.1	LQ
2037	6	13	17:12.2	NM
2037	6	20	13:47.6	FQ
2037	6	27	15:21.4	FM
2037	7	5	16: 2.9	LQ
2037	7	13	2:33.3	NM
2037	7	19	18:33.5	FQ
2037	7	27	4:16.9	FM
2037	8	4	7:53.9	LQ
2037	8	11	10:42.7	NM
2037	8	18	1: 1.7	FQ
2037	8	25	19:11.3	FM
2037	9	2	22: 6.0	LQ
2037	9	9	18:26.4	NM
2037	9	16	10:37.3	FQ
2037	9	24	11:33.9	FM
2037	10	2	10:31.4	LQ
2037	10	9	2:35.6	NM
2037	10	16	0:15.9	FQ
2037	10	24	4:38.9	FM
2037	10	31	21: 8.3	LQ
2037	11	7	12: 4.6	NM
2037	11	14	17:58.8	FQ
2037	11	22	21:37.7	FM
2037	11	30	6: 8.4	LQ
2037	12	6	23:40.5	NM
2037	12	14	14:42.5	FQ
2037	12	22	13:41.1	FM
2037	12	29	14: 7.2	LQ
2038	1	5	13:44.1	NM
2038	1	13	12:35.6	FQ
2038	1	21	4: 2.3	FM
2038	1	27	22: 3.1	LQ
2038	2	4	5:55.2	NM
2038	2	12	9:32.3	FQ
2038	2	19	16:11.6	FM
2038	2	26	6:58.7	LQ
2038	3	5	23:17.8	NM
2038	3	14	3:43.9	FQ
2038	3	21	2:11.5	FM
2038	3	27	17:38.5	LQ
2038	4	4	16:45.5	NM
2038	4	12	18: 3.6	FQ
2038	4	19	10:37.4	FM
2038	4	26	6:17.0	LQ
2038	5	4	9:21.6	NM
2038	5	12	4:19.2	FQ
2038	5	18	18:24.5	FM
2038	5	25	20:44.6	LQ
2038	6	3	0:25.5	NM
2038	6	10	11:12.3	FQ
2038	6	17	2:31.1	FM
2038	6	24	12:41.1	LQ
2038	7	2	13:32.8	NM
2038	7	9	16: 1.5	FQ
2038	7	16	11:48.7	FM
2038	7	24	5:42.1	LQ
2038	8	1	0:40.5	NM
2038	8	7	20:22.6	FQ
2038	8	14	22:57.2	FM
2038	8	22	23:14.5	LQ
2038	8	30	10:12.7	NM
2038	9	6	1:52.0	FQ
2038	9	13	12:24.9	FM
2038	9	21	16:29.0	LQ
2038	9	28	18:57.8	NM
2038	10	5	9:53.6	FQ
2038	10	13	4:23.0	FM
2038	10	21	8:24.9	LQ
2038	10	28	3:53.8	NM
2038	11	3	21:25.0	FQ
2038	11	11	22:29.3	FM
2038	11	19	22:11.5	LQ
2038	11	26	13:48.6	NM
2038	12	3	12:47.2	FQ
2038	12	11	17:32.9	FM
2038	12	19	9:30.7	LQ
2038	12	26	1: 4.7	NM
2039	1	2	7:38.7	FQ
2039	1	10	11:48.2	FM
2039	1	17	18:43.6	LQ
2039	1	24	13:39.4	NM
2039	2	1	4:47.9	FQ
2039	2	9	3:42.5	FM
2039	2	16	2:38.3	LQ
2039	2	23	3:21.0	NM
2039	3	3	2:17.7	FQ
2039	3	10	16:38.2	FM
2039	3	17	10:10.2	LQ
2039	3	24	18: 2.8	NM
2039	4	1	21:56.8	FQ
2039	4	9	2:55.4	FM
2039	4	15	18: 9.4	LQ
2039	4	23	9:37.5	NM
2039	5	1	14: 8.9	FQ
2039	5	8	11:22.1	FM
2039	5	15	3:19.1	LQ
2039	5	23	1:40.1	NM
2039	5	31	2:25.4	FQ
2039	6	6	18:49.0	FM
2039	6	13	14:18.4	LQ
2039	6	21	17:22.9	NM
2039	6	29	11:18.0	FQ
2039	7	6	2: 4.2	FM
2039	7	13	3:40.3	LQ
2039	7	21	7:55.0	NM
2039	7	28	17:50.8	FQ
2039	8	4	9:57.2	FM
2039	8	11	19:38.0	LQ
2039	8	19	20:50.9	NM
2039	8	26	23:17.8	FQ
2039	9	2	19:23.7	FM
2039	9	10	13:47.2	LQ
2039	9	18	8:23.0	NM
2039	9	25	4:54.4	FQ
2039	10	2	7:23.1	FM
2039	10	10	9: 0.4	LQ
2039	10	17	19: 9.1	NM
2039	10	24	11:52.8	FQ
2039	10	31	22:36.9	FM
2039	11	9	3:47.2	LQ
2039	11	16	5:46.6	NM
2039	11	22	21:18.6	FQ
2039	11	30	16:51.2	FM
2039	12	8	20:46.3	LQ
2039	12	15	16:33.1	NM
2039	12	22	10: 3.2	FQ
2039	12	30	12:39.4	FM
2040	1	7	11: 7.2	LQ
2040	1	14	3:27.1	NM
2040	1	21	2:22.7	FQ
2040	1	29	7:56.7	FM
2040	2	5	22:34.0	LQ
2040	2	12	14:27.3	NM
2040	2	19	21:35.0	FQ
2040	2	28	1: 2.3	FM
2040	3	6	7:20.7	LQ
2040	3	13	1:49.5	NM
2040	3	20	17:60.0	FQ
2040	3	28	15:14.8	FM
2040	4	4	14: 8.5	LQ
2040	4	11	14: 3.8	NM
2040	4	19	13:38.6	FQ
2040	4	27	2:40.9	FM
2040	5	3	20: 2.2	LQ
2040	5	11	3:31.3	NM
2040	5	19	7: 2.2	FQ
2040	5	26	11:49.8	FM
2040	6	2	2:19.9	LQ
2040	6	9	18: 6.2	NM
2040	6	17	21:34.4	FQ
2040	6	24	19:21.6	FM
2040	7	1	10:20.2	LQ
2040	7	9	9:17.3	NM
2040	7	17	9:18.5	FQ
2040	7	24	2: 7.6	FM
2040	7	30	21: 8.0	LQ
2040	8	8	0:28.1	NM
2040	8	15	18:38.2	FQ
2040	8	22	9:11.3	FM
2040	8	29	11:18.2	LQ
2040	9	6	15:14.5	NM
2040	9	14	2: 9.5	FQ
2040	9	20	17:43.5	FM
2040	9	28	4:42.5	LQ
2040	10	6	5:26.1	NM
2040	10	13	8:43.1	FQ
2040	10	20	4:50.1	FM
2040	10	28	0:28.1	LQ
2040	11	4	18:55.8	NM
2040	11	11	15:25.2	FQ
2040	11	18	19: 6.8	FM
2040	11	26	21: 9.6	LQ
2040	12	4	7:33.1	NM
2040	12	10	23:31.5	FQ
2040	12	18	12:16.7	FM
2040	12	26	17: 5.1	LQ
2041	1	2	19: 8.3	NM
2041	1	9	10: 7.3	FQ
2041	1	17	7:12.4	FM
2041	1	25	10:35.6	LQ
2041	2	1	5:44.6	NM
2041	2	7	23:41.3	FQ
2041	2	16	2:22.6	FM
2041	2	24	0:30.8	LQ

2041–2043	2043–2045	2045–2047	2047–2049	2049–2050
2041 3 2 15:42.2 NM	2043 3 25 14:26.6 FM	2045 4 17 7:29.2 NM	2047 5 9 18:25.0 FM	2049 5 31 14:3.2 NM
2041 3 9 15:51.9 FQ	2043 4 2 18:57.9 LQ	2045 4 24 7:12.5 FQ	2047 5 16 16:46.4 LQ	2049 6 8 17:58.2 FQ
2041 3 17 20:21.2 FM	2043 4 9 19:8.1 NM	2045 5 1 5:52.6 FM	2047 5 24 20:28.4 NM	2049 6 15 19:28.9 FM
2041 3 25 10:33.9 LQ	2043 4 16 10:10.0 FQ	2045 5 9 2:53.5 LQ	2047 6 1 11:54.8 FQ	2049 6 22 9:43.2 LQ
2041 4 1 1:33.0 NM	2043 4 24 7:23.7 FM	2045 5 16 18:28.6 NM	2047 6 8 2:4.9 FM	2049 6 30 4:52.5 NM
2041 4 8 9:39.4 FQ	2043 5 2 9:0.2 LQ	2045 5 23 12:39.5 FQ	2047 6 15 7:45.7 LQ	2049 7 8 7:11.7 FQ
2041 4 16 12:3.5 FM	2043 5 9 3:22.5 NM	2045 5 30 17:53.2 FM	2047 6 23 10:36.1 NM	2049 7 15 2:31.0 FM
2041 4 23 17:25.9 LQ	2043 5 15 21:5.8 FQ	2045 6 7 20:25.6 LQ	2047 6 30 17:37.4 FQ	2049 7 21 18:50.1 LQ
2041 4 30 11:49.9 NM	2043 5 23 23:38.2 FM	2045 6 15 3:6.5 NM	2047 7 7 10:33.7 FM	2049 7 29 20:8.4 NM
2041 5 8 3:55.8 FQ	2043 5 31 19:25.9 LQ	2045 6 21 18:30.2 FQ	2047 7 15 0:11.0 LQ	2049 8 6 17:53.0 FQ
2041 5 16 0:55.6 FM	2043 6 7 10:36.5 NM	2045 6 29 7:17.1 FM	2047 7 22 22:49.3 NM	2049 8 13 9:20.4 FM
2041 5 22 22:27.7 LQ	2043 6 14 10:19.0 FQ	2045 7 7 11:33.0 LQ	2047 7 29 22:3.6 FQ	2049 8 20 7:11.6 LQ
2041 5 29 22:59.3 NM	2043 6 22 14:22.4 FM	2045 7 14 10:30.1 NM	2047 8 5 20:38.6 FM	2049 8 28 11:18.8 NM
2041 6 6 21:43.0 FQ	2043 6 30 2:54.8 LQ	2045 7 21 1:54.4 FQ	2047 8 13 17:36.5 LQ	2049 9 5 2:29.1 FQ
2041 6 14 11:1.7 FM	2043 7 6 17:52.5 NM	2045 7 28 22:12.4 FM	2047 8 21 9:16.2 NM	2049 9 11 17:4.5 FM
2041 6 21 3:14.1 LQ	2043 7 14 1:46.8 FQ	2045 8 5 23:59.2 LQ	2047 8 28 2:50.7 FQ	2049 9 18 23:4.0 LQ
2041 6 28 11:19.7 NM	2043 7 22 3:26.3 FM	2045 8 12 17:40.7 NM	2047 9 4 8:54.7 FM	2049 9 27 2:4.6 NM
2041 7 6 14:15.0 FQ	2043 7 29 8:25.1 LQ	2045 8 19 11:56.9 FQ	2047 9 12 11:20.9 LQ	2049 10 4 9:39.7 FQ
2041 7 13 19:3.6 FM	2043 8 5 2:24.1 NM	2045 8 27 14:9.8 FM	2047 9 19 18:31.6 NM	2049 10 11 2:52.8 FM
2041 7 20 9:15.4 LQ	2043 8 12 18:57.5 FQ	2045 9 4 10:5.3 LQ	2047 9 26 9:30.3 FQ	2049 10 18 17:55.8 LQ
2041 7 28 1:4.2 NM	2043 8 20 15:1.7 FM	2045 9 11 1:28.8 NM	2047 10 3 23:43.0 FM	2049 10 26 16:14.5 NM
2041 8 5 4:54.7 FQ	2043 8 27 13:12.1 LQ	2045 9 18 1:31.1 FQ	2047 10 12 4:23.7 LQ	2049 11 2 16:20.3 FQ
2041 8 12 2:7.2 FM	2043 9 3 13:18.5 NM	2045 9 26 6:13.7 FM	2047 10 19 3:28.6 NM	2049 11 9 15:37.8 FM
2041 8 18 17:45.4 LQ	2043 9 11 13:2.2 FQ	2045 10 3 18:33.3 LQ	2047 10 25 19:14.2 FQ	2049 11 17 14:33.5 LQ
2041 8 26 16:17.1 NM	2043 9 19 1:49.8 FM	2045 10 10 10:37.8 NM	2047 11 2 16:59.9 FM	2049 11 25 5:35.3 NM
2041 9 3 17:20.1 FQ	2043 9 26 18:43.5 LQ	2045 10 17 18:56.0 FQ	2047 11 10 19:40.8 LQ	2049 12 1 23:41.2 FQ
2041 9 10 9:25.7 FM	2043 10 3 3:13.7 NM	2045 10 25 21:33.5 FM	2047 11 17 13:0.2 NM	2049 12 9 7:28.8 FM
2041 9 17 5:34.6 LQ	2043 10 11 7:7.0 FQ	2045 11 2 2:11.4 LQ	2047 11 24 8:41.5 FQ	2049 12 17 11:17.4 LQ
2041 9 25 8:41.6 NM	2043 10 18 11:58.1 FM	2045 11 8 21:49.9 NM	2047 12 2 11:57.1 FM	2049 12 24 17:52.0 NM
2041 10 3 3:33.4 FQ	2043 10 25 2:30.5 LQ	2045 11 16 15:26.3 FQ	2047 12 10 8:30.1 LQ	2049 12 31 8:54.4 FQ
2041 10 9 18:3.6 FM	2043 11 1 19:59.4 NM	2045 11 24 11:45.9 FM	2047 12 16 23:40.0 NM	2050 1 8 1:40.1 FM
2041 10 16 21:6.3 LQ	2043 11 10 0:15.4 FQ	2045 12 1 2:1.5 LQ	2047 12 24 1:51.6 FQ	2050 1 16 6:20.5 LQ
2041 10 25 1:30.1 NM	2043 11 16 21:54.5 FM	2045 12 8 11:42.8 NM	2048 1 1 6:58.1 FM	2050 1 23 4:58.1 NM
2041 11 1 12:5.5 FQ	2043 11 23 13:48.1 LQ	2045 12 16 13:8.9 FQ	2048 1 8 18:50.5 LQ	2050 1 29 20:49.2 FQ
2041 11 8 4:43.8 FM	2043 12 1 14:38.8 NM	2045 12 24 0:51.6 FM	2048 1 15 11:34.7 NM	2050 2 6 14:40.9 FM
2041 11 15 16:7.9 LQ	2043 12 9 15:29.1 FQ	2045 12 30 18:13.9 LQ	2048 1 22 21:57.7 FQ	2050 2 14 22:13.1 LQ
2041 11 23 17:36.4 NM	2043 12 16 8:3.7 FM	2046 1 6 4:26.3 NM	2048 1 30 0:16.5 FM	2050 2 21 15:5.8 NM
2041 11 30 19:49.4 FQ	2043 12 23 5:6.0 LQ	2046 1 13 9:43.8 FQ	2048 2 7 3:17.9 LQ	2050 3 8 11:30.5 FM
2041 12 7 17:42.4 FM	2043 12 31 9:49.4 NM	2046 1 21 12:53.3 FM	2048 2 14 0:34.2 NM	2050 3 16 10:9.9 LQ
2041 12 15 13:35.0 LQ	2044 1 8 4:2.8 FQ	2046 1 29 4:14.1 LQ	2048 2 21 19:24.6 FQ	2050 3 23 0:44.0 NM
2041 12 23 8:6.4 NM	2044 1 14 18:52.5 FM	2046 2 5 23:12.0 NM	2048 2 28 14:40.9 FM	2050 3 30 4:18.0 FQ
2041 12 30 3:46.7 FQ	2044 1 21 23:47.7 LQ	2046 2 13 3:21.8 FQ	2048 3 7 10:46.8 LQ	2050 4 7 8:14.5 FM
2042 1 6 8:54.2 FM	2044 1 30 4:5.6 NM	2046 2 20 23:45.6 FM	2048 3 14 14:30.6 NM	2050 4 14 18:25.5 LQ
2042 1 14 11:26.7 LQ	2044 2 6 13:46.8 FQ	2046 2 27 16:25.5 LQ	2048 3 22 16:5.4 FQ	2050 4 21 10:29.1 NM
2042 1 21 20:42.8 NM	2044 2 13 6:42.6 FM	2046 3 7 18:17.4 NM	2048 3 30 2:6.9 FM	2050 4 29 22:9.6 FQ
2042 1 28 12:49.9 FQ	2044 2 20 20:21.1 LQ	2046 3 15 17:13.3 FQ	2048 4 5 18:12.5 LQ	2050 5 6 22:29.0 FM
2042 2 5 1:58.3 FM	2044 2 28 20:13.8 NM	2046 3 22 9:27.5 FM	2048 4 13 5:22.4 NM	2050 5 14 0:5.3 LQ
2042 2 13 7:18.5 LQ	2044 3 6 21:17.8 FQ	2046 3 29 6:59.5 LQ	2048 4 21 10:3.7 FQ	2050 5 20 20:54.2 NM
2042 2 20 7:40.6 NM	2044 3 13 19:41.6 FM	2046 4 6 11:53.8 NM	2048 4 28 11:15.0 FM	2050 5 28 16:6.1 FQ
2042 2 26 23:30.7 FQ	2044 3 21 16:54.5 LQ	2046 4 14 3:21.6 FQ	2048 5 5 2:24.2 LQ	2050 6 5 9:54.0 FM
2042 3 6 20:10.9 FM	2044 3 29 9:27.8 NM	2046 4 20 18:21.2 FM	2048 5 12 21:0.4 NM	2050 6 12 4:40.9 LQ
2042 3 14 23:23.2 LQ	2044 4 5 3:45.8 FQ	2046 4 27 23:31.8 LQ	2048 5 20 0:17.3 FQ	2050 6 19 8:24.5 NM
2042 3 21 17:25.5 NM	2044 4 12 9:39.6 FM	2046 5 6 2:57.7 NM	2048 5 27 18:58.7 FM	2050 6 27 9:19.1 FQ
2042 3 28 12:1.1 FQ	2044 4 20 11:51.2 LQ	2046 5 13 10:25.2 FQ	2048 6 3 12:6.4 LQ	2050 7 4 18:53.4 FM
2042 4 5 14:17.4 FM	2044 4 27 19:43.8 NM	2046 5 20 3:15.2 FM	2048 6 11 12:51.5 NM	2050 7 11 9:47.6 LQ
2042 4 13 11:10.5 LQ	2044 5 4 10:28.9 FQ	2046 5 27 17:7.2 LQ	2048 6 19 10:50.2 FQ	2050 7 18 21:18.7 NM
2042 4 20 2:22.0 NM	2044 5 12 0:17.5 FM	2046 6 4 15:23.2 NM	2048 6 26 2:8.8 FM	2050 7 27 1:7.2 FQ
2042 4 27 2:20.9 FQ	2044 5 20 4:4.6 LQ	2046 6 11 15:28.5 FQ	2048 7 2 23:59.6 LQ	2050 8 3 2:22.7 FM
2042 5 5 6:50.9 FM	2044 5 27 3:41.1 NM	2046 6 18 13:10.0 FM	2048 7 11 4:5.2 NM	2050 8 9 16:50.1 LQ
2042 5 12 19:19.0 LQ	2044 6 2 18:34.2 FQ	2046 6 26 10:40.8 LQ	2048 7 18 18:32.4 FQ	2050 8 17 11:48.4 NM
2042 5 19 10:57.4 NM	2044 6 10 15:17.3 FM	2046 7 4 1:39.3 NM	2048 7 25 9:34.3 FM	2050 8 25 14:57.4 FQ
2042 5 26 18:19.8 FQ	2044 6 18 17:2.3 LQ	2046 7 10 19:54.7 FQ	2048 8 1 14:32.5 LQ	2050 9 1 9:32.6 FM
2042 6 3 20:51.1 FM	2044 6 25 10:26.0 NM	2046 7 18 0:55.4 FM	2048 8 9 17:59.5 NM	2050 9 8 2:52.6 LQ
2042 6 11 1:1.6 LQ	2044 7 2 4:49.1 FQ	2046 7 26 3:21.1 LQ	2048 8 17 0:33.0 FQ	2050 9 16 3:49.6 NM
2042 6 17 19:50.6 NM	2044 7 10 6:23.6 FM	2046 8 2 10:25.8 NM	2048 8 23 18:7.5 FM	2050 9 24 2:34.6 FQ
2042 6 25 11:30.4 FQ	2044 7 18 2:48.9 LQ	2046 8 9 1:17.2 FQ	2048 8 31 7:43.8 LQ	2050 9 30 17:32.8 FM
2042 7 3 8:12.2 FM	2044 7 24 17:12.2 NM	2046 8 16 14:51.2 FM	2048 9 8 6:24.8 NM	2050 10 7 16:13.0 LQ
2042 7 10 5:40.3 LQ	2044 7 31 17:41.0 FQ	2046 8 24 18:38.5 LQ	2048 9 15 6:5.5 FQ	2050 10 15 20:48.6 NM
2042 7 17 5:53.8 NM	2044 8 8 21:15.8 FM	2046 8 31 18:25.8 NM	2048 9 22 4:46.5 FM	2050 10 23 12:11.0 FQ
2042 7 25 5:2.8 FQ	2044 8 16 10:5.2 LQ	2046 9 7 9:41.1 FQ	2048 9 30 2:46.9 LQ	2050 10 30 3:16.4 FM
2042 8 1 17:36.2 FM	2044 8 23 1:7.3 NM	2046 9 15 6:41.1 FM	2048 10 7 17:45.4 NM	2050 11 6 9:58.4 LQ
2042 8 8 10:37.6 LQ	2044 8 30 9:19.4 FQ	2046 9 23 8:17.9 LQ	2048 10 14 12:22.2 FQ	2050 11 14 13:41.3 NM
2042 8 15 18:2.5 NM	2044 9 7 11:26.4 FM	2046 9 30 2:26.2 NM	2048 10 21 18:25.3 FM	2050 11 21 20:26.0 FQ
2042 8 23 21:56.4 FQ	2044 9 14 15:59.4 LQ	2046 10 6 20:41.6 FQ	2048 10 29 22:15.8 LQ	2050 11 28 15:10.2 FM
2042 8 31 2:5.2 FM	2044 9 21 11:4.4 NM	2046 10 14 23:43.4 FM	2048 11 6 4:38.9 NM	2050 12 6 6:30.0 LQ
2042 9 6 17:12.3 LQ	2044 9 29 3:31.9 FQ	2046 10 22 20:9.5 LQ	2048 11 13 0:31.1 FQ	2050 12 14 5:18.3 NM
2042 9 14 8:51.3 NM	2044 10 7 0:32.0 FM	2046 10 29 11:18.2 NM	2048 11 20 11:21.1 FM	2050 12 21 4:16.2 FQ
2042 9 22 13:21.7 FQ	2044 10 13 21:54.3 LQ	2046 11 5 12:28.7 FQ	2048 11 28 16:35.4 LQ	2050 12 28 5:16.0 FM
2042 9 29 10:36.6 FM	2044 10 20 23:37.3 NM	2046 11 13 17:6.9 FM	2048 12 5 15:31.0 NM	
2042 10 6 2:37.7 LQ	2044 10 28 23:29.3 FQ	2046 11 21 6:12.1 LQ	2048 12 12 7:30.9 FQ	
2042 10 14 2:4.4 NM	2044 11 5 12:28.6 FM	2046 11 27 21:51.9 NM	2048 12 20 6:41.0 FM	
2042 10 22 2:54.2 FQ	2044 11 12 5:11.5 LQ	2046 12 5 7:56.5 FQ	2048 12 28 8:33.5 LQ	
2042 10 28 19:49.9 FM	2044 11 19 14:58.8 NM	2046 12 13 9:58.0 FM	2049 1 4 2:25.9 NM	
2042 11 4 15:53.4 LQ	2044 11 27 19:37.6 FQ	2046 12 20 14:45.0 LQ	2049 1 10 21:57.4 FQ	
2042 11 12 20:29.4 NM	2044 12 4 23:35.7 FM	2046 12 27 2:14.6 NM	2049 1 19 2:30.8 FM	
2042 11 20 14:32.3 FQ	2044 12 11 14:54.4 LQ	2047 1 4 5:32.1 FQ	2049 1 26 21:34.6 LQ	
2042 11 26 7:0.0 FM	2044 12 19 8:54.5 NM	2047 1 11 1:23.9 FM	2049 2 2 13:18.1 NM	
2042 12 4 9:20.6 LQ	2044 12 27 14:0.8 FQ	2047 1 18 22:34.9 LQ	2049 2 9 15:39.9 FQ	
2042 12 12 14:30.5 NM	2045 1 3 10:22.1 FM	2047 1 26 1:46.8 NM	2049 2 17 20:50.0 FM	
2042 12 20 0:28.3 FQ	2045 1 10 3:33.7 LQ	2047 2 3 3:15.1 FQ	2049 2 25 7:37.9 LQ	
2042 12 26 17:43.4 FM	2045 1 18 4:26.7 NM	2047 2 10 14:42.2 FM	2049 3 4 0:14.7 NM	
2043 1 2 6:9.4 LQ	2045 1 26 5:9.4 FQ	2047 2 17 6:45.1 LQ	2049 3 11 11:27.5 FQ	
2043 1 11 6:54.0 NM	2045 2 1 21:6.6 FM	2047 2 24 18:28.8 NM	2049 3 19 12:26.5 FM	
2043 1 18 9:5.7 FQ	2045 2 9 19:4.6 LQ	2047 3 4 22:54.4 FQ	2049 3 26 15:12.3 LQ	
2043 1 25 6:57.0 FM	2045 2 16 23:52.3 NM	2047 3 12 1:39.0 FM	2049 4 2 11:42.9 NM	
2043 2 1 4:15.5 LQ	2045 2 24 16:36.9 FQ	2047 3 18 16:1.3 LQ	2049 4 10 7:28.6 FQ	
2043 2 9 21:8.6 NM	2045 3 3 7:53.1 FM	2047 3 26 11:46.7 NM	2049 4 18 1:7.9 FM	
2043 2 16 17:1.2 FQ	2045 3 11 13:46.7 LQ	2047 4 3 15:12.6 FQ	2049 4 24 21:13.5 LQ	
2043 2 23 21:58.3 FM	2045 3 18 16:13.6 NM	2047 4 10 10:36.5 FM	2049 5 2 0:14.6 NM	
2043 3 4 1:8.7 LQ	2045 3 26 4:41.6 FQ	2047 4 18 7:1.9 LQ	2049 5 10 1:59.1 FQ	
2043 3 11 9:10.6 NM	2045 4 2 0:14.6 FM	2047 4 25 4:41.6 NM	2049 5 17 11:16.6 FM	
2043 3 18 1:4.4 FQ	2045 4 9 7:55.0 LQ	2047 5 3 3:27.2 FQ	2049 5 24 2:56.4 LQ	

SOLAR ECLIPSES FOR THE YEARS 1950-2050

Date	Year	Time: GMT	Sign
18 Mar	1950	15:20	Pis
12 Sep	1950	03:29	Vir
7 Mar	1951	20:51	Pis
1 Sep	1951	12:50	Vir
25 Feb	1952	09:16	Pis
20 Aug	1952	16:20	Leo
14 Feb	1953	01:10	Aqu
11 July	1953	02:28	Can
5 Jan	1954	02:21	Cap
30 June	1954	12:26	Can
25 Dec	1954	07:33	Cap
20 June	1955	04:12	Gem
14 Dec	1955	07:07	Sag
8 June	1956	21:29	Gem
2 Dec	1956	08:13	Sag
29 Apr	1957	23:54	Tau
23 Oct	1957	04:43	Lib
19 Apr	1958	15:23	Ari
12 Oct	1958	20:52	Lib
8 Apr	1959	03:29	Ari
2 Oct	1959	12:31	Lib
27 Mar	1960	07:37	Ari
20 Sep	1960	23:12	Vir
13 Feb	1961	05:07	Cap
15 Feb	1961	08:10	Aqu
11 Aug	1961	10:36	Leo
5 Feb	1962	0:10	Aqu
31 July	1962	12:24	Leo
25 Jan	1963	13:42	Aqu
20 July	1963	20:43	Can
14 Jan	1964	20:43	Cap
10 June	1964	04:22	Gem
9 July	1964	11:31	Can
4 Dec	1964	01:18	Sag
30 May	1965	21:13	Gem
23 Nov	1965	04:10	Sag
20 May	1966	09:42	Tau
12 Nov	1966	14:26	Sco
9 May	1967	14:55	Tau
2 Nov	1967	5:48	Sco
28 Mar	1968	22:48	Ari
22 Sep	1968	11:08	Vir
18 Mar	1969	04:51	Pis
11 Sep	1969	19:56	Vir
7 Mar	1970	17:42	Pis
31 Aug	1970	22:01	Vir
25 Feb	1971	09:49	Pis
22 July	1971	09:15	Can
20 Aug	1971	22:53	Leo
16 Jan	1972	10:52	Cap
10 July	1972	19:39	Can
4 Jan	1973	15:42	Cap
30 June	1973	11:39	Can
24 Dec	1973	15:07	Cap
20 June	1974	04:56	Gem
13 Dec	1974	16:25	Sag
11 May	1975	07:05	Tau
3 Nov	1975	13:05	Sco
29 Apr	1976	10:29	Tau
23 Oct	1976	05:10	Lib
18 Apr	1977	10:35	Ari
12 Oct	1977	20:31	Lib
7 Apr	1978	15:15	Ari
2 Oct	1978	06:41	Lib
26 Feb	1979	16:45	Pis
22 Aug	1979	17:10	Leo
16 Feb	1980	08:51	Aqu
10 Aug	1980	19:09	Leo
4 Feb	1981	22:14	Aqu
31 July	1981	03:52	Leo
25 Jan	1982	04:56	Aqu
21 June	1982	11:52	Gem
20 July	1982	18:57	Can
15 Dec	1982	09:18	Sag
11 June	1983	04:38	Gem
4 Dec	1983	12:26	Sag
30 May	1984	16:48	Gem
22 Nov	1984	22:57	Sag
19 May	1985	21:41	Tau
12 Nov	1985	14:20	Sco
9 Apr	1986	06:08	Ari
3 Oct	1986	18:55	Lib
29 Mar	1987	12:46	Ari
23 Sep	1987	03:08	Vir
18 Mar	1988	02:02	Pis
11 Sep	1988	04:49	Vir
7 Mar	1989	18:19	Pis
31 Aug	1989	05:45	Vir
26 Jan	1990	19:20	Aqu
22 July	1990	02:54	Can
15 Jan	1991	23:50	Cap
11 July	1991	19:06	Can
4 Jan	1992	23:10	Cap
30 June	1992	12:18	Can
24 Dec	1992	00:43	Cap
21 May	1993	14:07	Gem
13 Nov	1993	21:34	Sco
10 May	1994	17:07	Tau
3 Nov	1994	13:35	Sco
29 Apr	1995	17:36	Tau
24 Oct	1995	04:36	Sco
17 Apr	1996	22:49	Ari
12 Oct	1996	14:14	Lib
8 Mar	1997	01:15	Pis
1 Sep	1997	23:52	Vir
26 Feb	1998	17:26	Pis
22 Aug	1998	02:03	Leo
16 Feb	1999	06:39	Aqu
11 Aug	1999	11:08	Leo
5 Feb	2000	13:03	Aqu
1 July	2000	3:20	Can
31 July	2000	02:25	Leo
25 Dec	2000	17:22	Cap
21 June	2001	12:04	Can
14 Dec	2001	20:53	Sag
10 June	2002	23:46	Gem
4 Dec	2002	07:34	Sag
31 May	2003	04:20	Gem
23 Nov	2003	22:59	Sag
19 Apr	2004	13:21	Ari
14 Oct	2004	02:48	Lib
8 Apr	2005	20:32	Ari
3 Oct	2005	10:28	Lib
29 Mar	2006	10:15	Ari
22 Sep	2006	11:45	Vir
19 Mar	2007	2:42	Pis
11 Sep	2007	12:44	Vir
7 Feb	2008	03:44	Aqu
1 Aug	2008	10:12	Leo
26 Jan	2009	07:55	Aqu
22 July	2009	02:34	Can
15 Jan	2010	07:11	Cap
11 July	2010	19:40	Can
4 Jan	2011	09:02	Cap
1 June	2011	21:02	Gem
1 July	2011	08:54	Can
25 Nov	2011	06:09	Sag
20 May	2012	23:47	Gem
13 Nov	2012	22:08	Sco
10 May	2013	00:28	Tau
3 Nov	2013	12:50	Sco
29 Apr	2014	06:14	Tau
23 Oct	2014	21:56	Sco
20 Mar	2015	09:46	Pis
13 Sep	2015	06:55	Vir
09 Mar	2016	01:58	Pis
01 Sep	2016	09:08	Vir
26 Feb	2017	14:54	Pis
21 Aug	2017	18:26	Leo
15 Feb	2018	20:52	Aqu
13 July	2018	03:02	Can
11 Aug	2018	09:47	Leo
06 Jan	2019	01:42	Cap
02 Jul	2019	19:24	Can
26 Dec	2019	05:18	Cap
21 Jun	2020	06:41	Can
14 Dec	2020	16:14	Sag
10 Jun	2021	10:43	Gem
04 Dec	2021	07:34	Sag
30 Apr	2022	20:42	Tau
25 Oct	2022	11:01	Sco
20 Apr	2023	04:17	Ari
14 Oct	2023	18:00	Lib
08 Apr	2024	18:18	Ari
02 Oct	2024	18:46	Lib
29 Mar	2025	10:48	Aqu
21 Sep	2025	19:43	Vir
17 Feb	2026	12:13	Aqu
12 Aug	2026	17:47	Leo
06 Feb	2027	16:00	Aqu
02 Aug	2027	10:07	Leo
26 Jan	2028	15:08	Aqu
22 Jul	2028	02:56	Can
14 Jan	2029	17:13	Cap
12 Jun	2029	04:06	Gem
11 Jul	2029	15:37	Can
05 Dec	2029	15:03	Sag
01 Jun	2030	06:29	Gem
25 Nov	2030	06:51	Sag
21 May	2031	07:16	Tau
14 Nov	2031	21:07	Sco
09 May	2032	13:26	Tau
03 Nov	2032	05:34	Sco
30 Mar	2033	18:02	Ari
23 Sep	2033	13:54	Lib
20 Mar	2034	10:18	Pis
12 Sep	2034	16:19	Vir
09 Mar	2035	23:05	Pis
02 Sep	2035	01:56	Vir
27 Feb	2036	04:46	Pis
23 Jul	2036	10:32	Leo
21 Aug	2036	17:25	Leo
16 Jan	2037	09:48	Cap
13 Jul	2037	02:40	Can
05 Jan	2038	13:47	Cap
02 Jul	2038	13:32	Can
26 Dec	2038	01:00	Cap
21 Jun	2039	17:12	Can
15 Dec	2039	16:23	Sag
11 May	2040	03:43	Tau
04 Nov	2040	19:09	Sco
30 Apr	2041	11:42	Tau
25 Oct	2041	01:36	Sco
20 Apr	2042	02:17	Tau
14 Oct	2042	02:00	Lib
09 Apr	2043	18:57	Ari
03 Oct	2043	03:01	Lib
28 Feb	2044	20:24	Pis
23 Aug	2044	01:17	Vir
16 Feb	2045	23:56	Aqu
12 Aug	2045	17:42	Leo
05 Feb	2046	23:06	Aqu
02 Aug	2046	10:21	Leo
26 Jan	2047	01:33	Aqu
23 Jun	2047	10:52	Can
22 Jul	2047	22:36	Can
16 Dec	2047	23:50	Sag
11 Jun	2048	12:58	Gem
05 Dec	2048	15:35	Sag
31 May	2049	13:59	Gem
25 Nov	2049	05:33	Sag
20 May	2050	20:42	Tau
14 Nov	2050	13:30	Sco

ECLIPSE TABLES

LUNAR ECLIPSES FOR THE YEARS 1950-2050

Date	Year	Time: GMT	Sign	Date	Year	Time	Sign	Date	Year	Time	Sign	Date	Year	Time	Sign
2 Apr	1950	20:49	Lib	06 Sep	1979	10:59	Pis	16 Aug	2008	21:16	Aqu	27 Jul	2037	04:09	Aqu
26 Sep	1950	4:21	Ari	01 Mar	1980	21:00	Vir	09 Feb	2009	14:49	Leo	21 Jan	2038	03:49	Leo
21 Feb	1951	21:12	Vir	27 July	1980	18:54	Aqu	07 July	2009	09:21	Cap	17 Jun	2038	02:45	Sag
23 Mar	1951	10:50	Lib	26 Aug	1980	03:42	Pis	06 Aug	2009	00:55	Aqu	16 Jul	2038	11:35	Cap
17 Aug	1951	02:59	Aqu	20 Jan	1981	07:39	Leo	31 Dec	2009	19:13	Can	11 Dec	2038	17:44	Gem
15 Sep	1951	12:38	Pis	17 July	1981	04:39	Cap	26 June	2010	11:30	Cap	06 Jun	2039	18:54	Sag
11 Feb	1952	00:28	Leo	09 Jan	1982	19:53	Can	21 Dec	2010	08:13	Gem	30 Nov	2039	16:56	Gem
05 Aug	1952	19:40	Aqu	06 July	1982	07:32	Cap	15 June	2011	20:13	Sag	26 May	2040	11:46	Sag
29 Jan	1953	23:44	Leo	30 Dec	1982	11:33	Can	10 Dec	2011	14:36	Gem	18 Nov	2040	19:04	Tau
26 July	1953	12:21	Aqu	25 June	1983	08:32	Cap	04 June	2012	11:11	Sag	16 May	2041	00:43	Sco
19 Jan	1954	02:37	Can	20 Dec	1983	02:00	Gem	28 Nov	2012	14:46	Gem	08 Nov	2041	04:35	Tau
16 July	1954	00:29	Cap	15 May	1984	04:29	Sco	25 Apr	2013	19:57	Sco	05 Apr	2042	14:30	Lib
08 Jan	1955	12:44	Can	13 June	1984	14:42	Sag	25 May	2013	04:25	Sag	29 Sep	2042	10:45	Ari
05 June	1955	14:08	Sag	08 Nov	1984	17:43	Tau	18 Oct	2013	23:37	Ari	25 Mar	2043	14:32	Lib
29 Nov	1955	16:50	Gem	04 May	1985	19:53	Sco	15 Apr	2014	07:42	Lib	19 Sep	2043	01:51	Pis
24 May	1956	15:26	Sag	28 Oct	1985	17:38	Tau	08 Oct	2014	10:50	Ari	13 Mar	2044	19:38	Vir
18 Nov	1956	06:45	Tau	24 Apr	1986	12:46	Sco	04 Apr	2015	12:01	Lib	07 Sep	2044	11:20	Pis
13 May	1957	22:34	Sco	17 Oct	1986	19:22	Ari	28 Sep	2015	02:48	Ari	03 Mar	2045	07:43	Vir
07 Nov	1957	14:32	Tau	14 Apr	1987	14:31	Lib	23 Mar	2016	11:48	Lib	27 Aug	2045	13:54	Pis
04 Apr	1958	03:45	Lib	07 Oct	1987	04:12	Ari	16 Sep	2016	18:55	Pis	22 Jan	2046	13:02	Leo
27 Oct	1958	15:41	Tau	03 Mar	1988	16:01	Vir	11 Feb	2017	00:45	Leo	18 Jul	2046	01:06	Cap
24 Mar	1959	20:02	Lib	27 Aug	1988	10:56	Pis	07 Aug	2017	18:21	Aqu	12 Jan	2047	01:26	Can
17 Sep	1959	00:52	Pis	20 Feb	1989	15:32	Vir	31 Jan	2018	13:31	Leo	07 Jul	2047	10:35	Cap
13 Mar	1960	08:26	Vir	17 Aug	1989	03:07	Aqu	27 Jul	2018	20:22	Aqu	01 Jan	2048	06:53	Can
05 Sep	1960	11:19	Pis	09 Feb	1990	19:16	Leo	21 Jan	2019	05:13	Leo	26 Jun	2048	02:02	Cap
02 Mar	1961	13:35	Vir	06 Aug	1990	14:19	Aqu	16 Jul	2019	21:31	Cap	20 Dec	2048	06:27	Gem
26 Aug	1961	03:13	Pis	30 Jan	1991	06:10	Leo	10 Jan	2020	19:11	Can	17 May	2049	11:26	Sco
19 Feb	1962	13:18	Vir	27 June	1991	02:58	Cap	05 Jun	2020	19:26	Sag	15 Jun	2049	19:14	Sag
17 July	1962	11:41	Cap	26 July	1991	18:24	Aqu	05 Jul	2020	04:31	Cap	09 Nov	2049	15:52	Tau
15 Aug	1962	20:09	Aqu	21 Dec	1991	10:23	Gem	30 Nov	2020	09:44	Gem	06 May	2050	22:32	Sco
09 Jan	1963	23:08	Can	15 June	1992	04:50	Sag	26 May	2021	11:19	Sag	30 Oct	2050	03:21	Tau
06 July	1963	21:55	Cap	09 Dec	1992	23:41	Gem	19 Nov	2021	09:04	Tau				
30 Dec	1963	11:04	Can	04 June	1993	13:02	Sag	16 May	2022	04:12	Sco				
25 June	1964	01:08	Cap	29 Nov	1993	06:31	Gem	08 Nov	2022	11:00	Tau				
19 Dec	1964	02:41	Gem	25 May	1994	03:39	Sag	05 May	2023	17:24	Sco				
14 June	1965	01:59	Sag	18 Nov	1994	06:57	Tau	28 Oct	2023	20:15	Tau				
08 Dec	1965	17:21	Gem	15 Apr	1995	12:08	Lib	25 Mar	2024	07:13	Lib				
04 May	1966	21:00	Sco	08 Oct	1995	15:52	Ari	18 Sep	2024	02:45	Pis				
29 Oct	1966	10:00	Tau	04 Apr	1996	00:07	Lib	14 Mar	2025	06:59	Vir				
24 Apr	1967	12:03	Sco	27 Sep	1996	02:51	Ari	07 Sep	2025	18:12	Pis				
18 Oct	1967	10:11	Ari	24 Mar	1997	04:45	Lib	03 Mar	2026	11:34	Vir				
13 Apr	1968	04:52	Lib	16 Sep	1997	18:50	Pis	28 Aug	2026	04:14	Pis				
06 Oct	1968	12:46	Ari	13 Mar	1998	04:34	Vir	20 Feb	2027	23:14	Vir				
02 Apr	1969	18:45	Lib	08 Aug	1998	02:10	Aqu	18 Jul	2027	16:04	Cap				
27 Aug	1969	10:32	Pis	06 Sep	1998	11:21	Pis	17 Aug	2027	07:14	Aqu				
25 Sep	1969	20:21	Ari	31 Jan	1999	16:06	Leo	12 Jan	2028	04:14	Can				
21 Feb	1970	08:19	Vir	28 July	1999	11:25	Aqu	06 Jul	2028	18:20	Cap				
17 Aug	1970	03:15	Aqu	21 Jan	2000	04:40	Leo	31 Dec	2028	16:53	Can				
10 Feb	1971	07:41	Leo	16 July	2000	13:55	Cap	26 Jun	2029	03:23	Cap				
06 Aug	1971	19:42	Aqu	09 Jan	2001	20:24	Can	20 Dec	2029	22:43	Gem				
30 Jan	1972	10:58	Leo	05 July	2001	15:04	Cap	15 Jun	2030	18:34	Sag				
26 July	1972	7:24	Aqu	30 Dec	2001	10:40	Can	09 Dec	2030	22:28	Gem				
18 Jan	1973	21:28	Can	26 May	2002	11:51	Sag	07 May	2031	03:52	Sco				
15 June	1973	20:35	Sag	24 June	2002	21:42	Cap	05 Jun	2031	11:45	Sag				
10 Dec	1973	1:35	Gem	19 Nov	2002	01:34	Tau	30 Oct	2031	07:46	Tau				
04 June	1974	22:10	Sag	16 May	2003	03:36	Sco	25 Apr	2032	15:14	Sco				
29 Nov	1974	15:10	Gem	09 Nov	2003	01:13	Tau	18 Oct	2032	19:03	Ari				
25 May	1975	5:51	Sag	04 May	2004	20:33	Sco	14 Apr	2033	19:13	Lib				
18 Nov	1975	22:28	Tau	28 Oct	2004	03:07	Tau	08 Oct	2033	10:56	Ari				
13 May	1976	20:04	Sco	24 Apr	2005	10:06	Sco	03 Apr	2034	19:06	Lib				
06 Nov	1976	23:15	Tau	17 Oct	2005	12:14	Ari	28 Sep	2034	02:47	Ari				
04 Apr	1977	04:09	Lib	14 Mar	2006	23:35	Vir	22 Feb	2035	09:06	Vir				
27 Sep	1977	08:17	Ari	07 Sep	2006	18:42	Pis	19 Aug	2035	01:12	Aqu				
24 Mar	1978	16:20	Lib	03 Mar	2007	23:17	Vir	11 Feb	2036	22:13	Leo				
16 Sep	1978	19:01	Pis	28 Aug	2007	10:35	Pis	07 Aug	2036	02:52	Aqu				
13 Mar	1979	21:14	Vir	21 Feb	2008	03:30	Vir	31 Jan	2037	14:01	Leo				

MOON SIGN TABLES FOR THE YEARS 1950–2050
TABLE 1

YEAR OF BIRTH						JAN	FEB	MAR	APR	MAY	JUN	JUL	AUG	SEP	OCT	NOV	DEC
1950	1969	1988	2007	2026	2045	TAU	CAN	CAN	VIR	LIB	SAG	CAP	PIS	ARI	GEM	CAN	LEO
1951	1970	1989	2008	2027	2046	LIB	SAG	SAG	AQU	PIS	TAU	GEM	CAN	VIR	LIB	SAG	CAP
1952	1971	1990	2009	2028	2047	PIS	ARI	TAU	GEM	CAN	VIR	LIB	SAG	CAP	AQU	ARI	TAU
1953	1972	1991	2010	2029	2048	CAN	VIR	VIR	LIB	SAG	CAP	PIS	ARI	GEM	CAN	VIR	LIB
1954	1973	1992	2011	2030	2049	SCO	CAP	CAP	PIS	ARI	GEM	CAN	VIR	SCO	SAG	CAP	AQU
1955	1974	1993	2012	2031	2050	ARI	TAU	GEM	LEO	VIR	LIB	SCO	CAP	PIS	ARI	TAU	CAN
1956	1975	1994	2013	2032		LEO	LIB	LIB	SAG	CAP	PIS	ARI	TAU	CAN	LEO	LIB	SCO
1957	1976	1995	2014	2033		CAP	AQU	PIS	ARI	TAU	CAN	LEO	LIB	SCO	CAP	AQU	ARI
1958	1977	1996	2015	2034		TAU	CAN	CAN	VIR	LIB	SAG	CAP	AQU	ARI	TAU	CAN	LEO
1959	1978	1997	2016	2035		LIB	SCO	SAG	CAP	GEM	ARI	TAU	CAN	LEO	VIR	SCO	SAG
1960	1979	1998	2017	2036		AQU	ARI	ARI	GEM	CAN	LEO	VIR	SCO	CAP	AQU	ARI	TAU
1961	1980	1999	2018	2037		GEM	LEO	LEO	LIB	SCO	CAP	AQU	ARI	TAU	GEM	LEO	VIR
1962	1981	2000	2019	2038		SCO	SAG	CAP	CAP	ARI	TAU	GEM	LEO	LIB	SCO	SAG	CAP
1963	1982	2001	2020	2039		PIS	TAU	TAU	CAN	LEO	LIB	SCO	SAG	AQU	PIS	TAU	GEM
1964	1983	2002	2021	2040		LEO	VIR	LIB	SCO	SAG	PIS	CAP	TAU	CAN	LEO	VIR	LIB
1965	1984	2003	2022	2041		SAG	CAP	AQU	PIS	TAU	GEM	LEO	VIR	SCO	SAG	AQU	PIS
1966	1985	2004	2023	2042		ARI	GEM	GEM	LEO	VIR	SAG	SAG	AQU	PIS	ARI	GEM	CAN
1967	1986	2005	2024	2043		VIR	SCO	SCO	CAP	AQU	PIS	TAU	GEM	LEO	VIR	LIB	SAG
1968	1987	2006	2025	2044		CAP	PIS	PIS	TAU	GEM	LEO	VIR	SCO	SAG	CAP	PIS	ARI

TABLE 2: NUMBER OF SIGNS TO BE ADDED FOR EACH DAY OF THE MONTH

DAY	ADD (SIGNS)	DAY	ADD (SIGNS)
1	0	16	7
2	1	17	7
3	1	18	8
4	1	19	8
5	2	20	9
6	2	21	9
7	3	22	10
8	3	23	10
9	4	24	10
10	4	25	11
11	5	26	11
12	5	27	12
13	5	28	12
14	6	29	1
15	6	30	1
		31	2

TABLE 3: SIGNS OF THE ZODIAC

1.	Aries (ARI)	7.	Libra (LIB)
2.	Taurus (TAU)	8.	Scorpio (SCO)
3.	Gemini (GEM)	9.	Sagittarius (SAG)
4.	Cancer (CAN)	10.	Capricorn (CAP)
5.	Leo (LEO)	11.	Aquarius (AQU)
6.	Virgo (VIR)	12.	Pisces (PIS)

Note: Count through the signs in a continuous loop, so number 1 follows on from number 12.

HOW TO FIND YOUR MOON SIGN USING THE TABLES ABOVE

The Moon takes about two-and-a-quarter days to pass through each sign of the Zodiac and completes one Zodiac circuit in about 27 days. It returns to the same position in the Zodiac on the same date every 19 years. This cycle means that tables can be drawn up, from which you can find your sign. To find your Moon sign, first, use Table 1 to reveal the sign occupied by the Moon on the first day of the month of your birth. Now turn to Table 2 and find the number of the day on which you were born and the number of signs you need to count on through the Zodiac (Table 3) to discover which sign the Moon occupied on your birthday. To find out which sign the Moon is in at any given time, simply apply this principle. This method is fairly accurate in most cases, but if you disagree with the characteristics of the sign you come up with, it may be because your birthday falls on a day when the Moon changes sign. So, turn to the preceding or following sign to see if either of these seems more fitting.

Example 1:

To find the Moon sign for a person born on 12 October 1975:

From Table 1: On 1 October 1975, the Moon was in Leo

From Table 2: 12 days means counting on five signs

From Table 3: Counting on five signs brings us to Capricorn – the person's Moon sign.

Example 2:

Here's someone you might recognize. The most famous Russian ballet dancer of all time was born on 17 March, 1938. To find his Moon sign, follow the above procedure to find that he is a Libra – the sign of perfect balance and beauty (the person in question is Rudolf Nureyev).

INDEX

A
aggression 34
Air signs 40, 99
alcohol, effects of 34, 98
annual planting 108, 109
annular eclipse 18, 19
Aquarius, Moon in 82–5, 94, 105, 107, 110
Aries, Moon in 42–5, 93, 105, 106, 110
Aristotle 28
astrological chart 20
astrological signs 18
Astromoon 38–89

B
Babylonian tradition 27
baking 104
Balsamic Moon 8, 14
Bardot, Brigitte 12
barren signs 108
biennial planting 108, 109
birth and rebirth 22
Birth Chart 41
birth phase 12
Blue Moon 10–11
boiling waters 28
brewing 104
business success 90–103

C
Cancer, Moon in 54–7, 93, 105, 107, 110
candles 113
Capricorn, Moon in 78–81, 94, 105, 106, 110
childbirth 28–33, 112, 113
children 112
company profiles 95
conception 29, 30, 32
contraception 30
Contracting Moon 8
cosmic calendars 11
Crescent Moon 8, 10, 24
crimes of passion 34

D
dark goddesses 22, 24, 27
Dark Moon 27
design 104
Developing Moon 8, 10
Dewan, Edmond 30
Diana, Princess of Wales 41
Disseminating Moon 8, 14
divorce 99
DIY 104
Dynamic Day ("D-Day") 92

E
earthquakes 16
11-day cycle 18

18-year cycle 16, 18
Earth Goddess 111
Earth signs 40, 99
Earth's shadow 19
Earthshine 19
eclipse effects 18, 20
eclipse tables 125–6
eclipses 18, 19, 21
Egyptian tradition 24
elements 40
emotional effects 18, 40, 96
entertaining 105
evil forces 34

F
feminine principles 32
fertile signs 108
fertility 28–33
fertility calendars 33
Fire signs 40, 99
First Crescent Moon 8, 10, 13
First Quarter Moon 8, 10, 13
Full Moon 8, 10, 14

G
gardening 108, 109, 111
Gemini, Moon in 50–3, 93, 105, 107, 110
George VI 41
Gibbous Moon 8, 14, 100–3
goal-setting 11
goddesses and gods 22–7, 111, 113
good and evil forces 34
good vibrations 98
gravitational pull 16
Greek tradition 22–7

H
health and wellbeing 96–111
Hebraic tradition 27
herbs 111, 113
Hindu tradition 22, 27
house-buying/-moving 104
human behavior 34

I
illness 98
imagination 113
intoxication 34, 98
invocations 113

J
Jonas, Eugen 30

K
Krakatoa eruption 11

L
Last Quarter Moon 8, 10, 14
Leo, Moon in 58–61, 93, 105,

106, 110
Libra, Moon in 66–9, 94, 105, 107, 110
light goddesses 22–4
lunar cycle:
    how to work with 12
    and illness 98
lunar eclipses 18, 19
lunar gardening, eight rules of success 109
lunar halo 16
lunar phases 8, 10, 11
lunar rhythms 28, 30

M
maiden goddesses 22–4, 23
marriage 98, 99
masculine principles 32
Menaker, Abraham 28
Menaker, Walter 28
menstrual cycle 30
mental health 98, 113
"Monday's child..." rhyme 112–13
month, definition of 11
Moon:
    dark of the 96, 114
    definition of 112–13
Moon charts 115–24
Moon cycle stages, length of 8
Moon faces 24, 112
Moon garden 111
Moon Goddess 22
Moon guidance 92
Moon-influenced crimes 34–7
Moon madness 98
Moon phases, choosing 110
Moon power 30
Moon signs 18, 41, 42–89
    how to find 39–40, 127
    Sun signs vs 38
    tables 1950–2050 127
    unique nature of 90
Moonquakes 16
Moon's shadow 19
mystical trinity 22

N
Natal Chart 40
Nature, cycles of 22
neap tides 16
New Moon 8, 22
    criminal activity during 37
    personality 13
New Moon Day 92
Norse tradition 22

O
ovulation 30

P
partial eclipse 18, 19
perennial planting 108, 109
perigee 37
personal relationships 98
personality 13
physiological characteristic 112–13
Pisces, Moon in 86–9, 94, 105, 107, 110
plants 108–9, 111
psychic talent 113
psychopathic tendencies 37
public view 95

Q
quiet period 109

R
racial tensions 37
rebirth 22
recommended activities, Moon-related 100–3
relationships 98
religious holidays 11
reproduction 30, 113
retribution 24
Roman tradition 22–7

S
Sagittarius, Moon in 74–7, 94, 105, 106, 110
Scandinavian tradition 24
Scorpio, Moon in 70–3, 94, 105, 107, 110
sea, and sex 28
seasons 111
seed collection 108
seismic activity 16
semi-barren signs 108
semi-fertile signs 108
sensitivity 113
sex 28–33
sexing 30, 32
sexual peak 28
shopping tips 106
Signs of the Times 90, 93–4
soil cultivation 108
solar eclipses 18, 19
sowing 109
spells 113
sports penalties 34
spring-cleaning 104
spring tides 16
Sumerian tradition 27
Sun God 22
Sun sign dates 39
Sun signs 18

Moon signs vs 38
superstition 112–14
surgery 98

T
talismans 113
Taurus, Moon in 46–9, 93, 105, 106, 110
three faces 24
tides, Moon's effects on 16, 34
timing, golden rules of 90
total eclipse 18, 19
    14 December 2020 chart 21
transplanting 108, 109
triggering 101
12 houses 20

U
Underworld 27

V
Virgo, Moon in 62–5, 93, 105, 106, 110
visualization 113

W
waning Moon 8, 10
    recommended activities 100–3
Water signs 40, 99
waxing Moon 8, 10
    recommended activities 100–3
weather 16
Weird Sisters 22
wellbeing 96–111
White Goddess 111
William, Duke of Cambridge 41
wishing on the Moon 113

Y
Yin and Yang 22

Z
Zodiac 20, 38, 127
    choosing the correct signs 110
    four elements of 40
    nature of 12 signs of 108
    see also individual star signs

PICTURE CREDITS

ALAMY: /Antiqua Print Gallery: 20, 113; /Patrick Guenette: 15; /Interfoto: 29; /Prisma Archivo: 18; /Charles Walker Collection: 32B
BRIDGEMAN IMAGES: /Musee Conde: 39
GETTY IMAGES: /Florilegius/SSPL: 111; /Hulton Archive: 25; /Vera Petruk/iStock: 35; /SSPL: 104
PEXELS: /Eberhard Grossgasteiger: 114
SHUTTERSTOCK: /Denis Andricic: 36–37; /Castleski: 7, 8, 10; /Alfredo Dagli Orti/REX: 23; /Gianni Dagli Orti/REX: 97, 109; /Claudio Devizia & Kovalto1: 1, 3; /Azarii Gorchakov: 100, 102; /Ieronim777: 32T, 108; /Intueri: 4; /Peratek: 19B, 105; /Vera Petruk: 42, 46, 50, 54, 58, 62, 66, 70, 74, 78, 82, 86, 99; /Siloto: 91; /Universal History Archive/Universal Images/REX: 95
UNSPLASH: /Ganapathy Kumar: 31; /Ryan Loughlin: 17; /Ian Parker: 9
WELLCOME IMAGES: 26

Front cover images: Shutterstock (Claudio Divizia/Kovalto1 & Intueri). Spine image: Unsplash (Ian Parker). Back cover images: Shutterstock (Foto2rich & Peratek)
Front and back endpapers: Wellcome Images